# Southwestern Landscaping with Native Plants

# Southwestern Landscaping
## with Native Plants

# By Judith Phillips

Museum of New Mexico Press

To Wildwood and the pleasures of childhood that become the preoccupations of adulthood. A list of sources of Southwest native plants and seeds is available from Source List, Native Plant Society of New Mexico, P. O. Box 934, Los Lunas, NM 87031. Please enclose a self-addressed stamped envelope.

Further information on Xeriscape is available from: National Xeriscape Council, Inc., 8080 South Holly, Littleton, Colo. 80122.

Copyright © 1987 the Museum of New Mexico Press
10 9 8 7 6 5

All photographs © Judith Phillips except p. 38, 58 © Ken Ball (Arvada, Colo.); p. 36 © Dan Scurlock; p. 40 © Marie Torrens; p. 60 © Ellen Wilde.

Printed in the United States of America.

Library of Congress Cataloging-in-Publication Data

Phillips, Judith, 1949–
    Southwestern landscaping with native plants.

    Bibliography: p.
    Includes index.
    1. Wild flower gardening—Southwest, New.
2. Landscape gardening—Southwest, New.
3. Plants, Ornamental—Southwest, New.
4. Botany—Southwest, New.   I. Title.
SB439.2.S68P48  1987    635.9'51'78    86-12675

ISBN: 0-89013-165-1 (cloth)
ISBN: 0-89013-166-X (paper)

Designed by Daniel Martinez.
Plant profile drawings by Phyllis Hughes.
Diagrams by Jeffrey Horton, Daniel Martinez, and Judith Phillips.

Museum of New Mexico Press
P.O. Box 2087
Santa Fe, New Mexico 87503

# CONTENTS

# FOREWORD

Until relatively recently, the use of native plants in the home landscape was generally frowned upon. Wild plants were usually placed in the category of "weeds" or "undesirables," because they tend to be less spectacular and more difficult to control than the artificially selected cultivars typically found in the home garden.

Judith Phillips has been concerned, as have many others, with why gardeners and landscape professionals spend so much time and so many resources trying to grow introduced cultivars in often unsuitable habitats, when there is such an abundance of native plants of pleasing and desirable texture, color, and form existing in the wild landscape. These plants have a special advantage in being adapted, through many millenia of natural selection, to our own Southwestern climate. New Mexico, with its approximately 4,000 species of flowering plants and ferns, is well supplied with hundreds of species of plants suitable for use in nearly every kind of Southwestern landscape, from mountains to deserts, and fitted for various gardening tastes.

Gradually, increasing numbers of gardeners are beginning to adopt an acceptable compromise between the more traditional lush but time-consuming and expensive garden of introduced cultivars and the also somewhat traditional Southwestern landscape composed of a monotonous expanse of gravel, accented at intervals by a few specimen plants such as yucca, juniper, or piñon. There is no question about the utility or practicality of the latter landscape, but it leaves much to be desired aesthetically.

Although there are many publications dealing with general cultural practices or instructions for plants recommended for gardens in less rigorous climates than ours, few books have been produced which address the needs of those hardy souls who are taking a new, fresh approach to gardening in their use of plants already adapted to the arid Southwest. Fortunately, during the past twenty years or so, more and more individuals and organizations, including certain botanical gardens and garden clubs, have directed their talents toward solving the problems of development of landscapes under xeric conditions.

Recognizing the need, Judith Phillips, in this book, has endeavored to bring to the arid-land gardener the techniques and cultural instructions so necessary for successful development of landscape designs, using plants adapted to growth in New Mexico as well as the rest of the Southwest. The author has presented a practical guide to Southwestern gardening, utilizing plants much more fitted to the rigors of our particular climate, plants requiring less care and less water than

Limiting high water-use plants to high traffic areas and landscaping the balance with adapted arid-land natives is an acceptable compromise between lush and desolate.

do the majority of the artificially selected cultivars. In addition to the usual widely accepted techniques for growing plants in arid environments, Phillips has presented data derived from her own notes and practical experiments to produce, as she puts it, "a very basic cookbook for native-plant growers."

The author includes a discussion of the climate of the New Mexico area and of how plants of arid climates have evolved a host of interesting, often unique specializations which aid in their adaptation to our more than sufficient sunlight, excessive heat, strong winds, low humidity, and relatively poor soil. These specializations are even found in the seeds in the form of built-in chemical or physical features which may delay germination until conditions are favorable for germination. There is also an extensive discussion of how certain plants of arid environments tend to develop defenses against the perennial Southwestern drought, particularly in the specialized conditions found in the succulent tissues, and especially in those tissues found in the leaves and stems. These kinds of information are rarely encountered in books of this type.

There is much technical data in Phillips' book, sufficient to provide everyone—amateur and professional alike—with much valuable information. The author offers an extensive discussion of principles of landscape design for arid environments, pointing out that design tends to be a personal thing and that informal gardens are better adapted to arid environments, in addition to being easier to develop and maintain. Obviously, there are no completely maintenance-free gardens, but some Southwestern gardens may approach that condition and at the same time retain their charm and utility.

She points out how important it is to become familiar with plants in their native habitat and how they operate in their own ecosystem in harmony with associated organisms. This is proposed in order that one might gain a better idea of how each plant would develop and interact with other plants in the garden landscape. Simplicity is the key to a native-plant garden, involving relatively few, tastefully selected species rather than a hodgepodge of many diverse ones. There is a certain appropriateness to a well-designed, nicely balanced garden which reflects the inherent charm, tenacity, and natural beauty of the Southwestern flora.

Of considerable interest are her site analyses of hypothetical existing landscapes associated with certain types of architecture. These analyses indicate the presence of a number of existing problems or conditions

High desert natives must be as well adapted to cold as they are to heat, and the natives selected for landscape use must remain attractive despite the extremes.

often seen in long-established gardens. The weaknesses of each situation are pointed out, and a number of practical solutions are proposed for each of these special cases.

A discussion of "wild-flower meadows" and their establishment provides the reader with the pros and cons of development of such a garden. Exposure, grade, soil type, potential seasonal fluctuations, and size of the area are all considered. One should keep in mind that mixed seed batches may produce a wide variety of species at first, but competition will ultimately determine what will remain after conditions have stabilized.

For those hardy gardeners who prefer to start new plants from scratch—and this is far preferable to transplanting from the wild, there are sections on growing from seed or by propagation from cuttings, layering, or division. These sections are especially useful, particularly because much of the information has been obtained by experimental work in the author's own test garden.

The balance of the book is devoted primarily to lists of plants adapted to certain uses or habitats; all plants listed are native to the Southwest. There is also an extensive treatment of some major plants useful in the Southwestern landscape. These individual treatments are extensive and include information on habitat, elevation, description, usage, propagation, and maintenance. This information, as well as the index of key terms and concepts used in the text, should be extremely interesting to any gardener.

An especially attractive feature of the book is the section on design plans based on moisture requirements

Soil, rock, water, and plants are major elements in the landscape. Exposure, grade, and elevation are the variables that create ecosystems.

and color, form, and textural features. This and all other treatments are well done and very useful to any gardener. I like this book very much and believe it should be very well received by gardeners of the arid Southwest. It will be a fine adjunct to other publications dealing with gardening in desert and semi-desert environments.

*William C. Martin*
*Department of Biology*
*University of New Mexico*

# PREFACE

As anyone who has done any gardening knows, there is very little that is absolute about working with plants. To survive a harsh climate, plants native to arid lands are erratic by nature. In the wild, diversity assures that there will be a few plants especially well suited to the habitat, and seeds in reserve as a hedge against extinction. The very unpredictability required for success in the wild causes some problems in adapting arid-land natives to ornamental landscape use. Seeds that won't sprout, plants that, whether carefully tended or ignored, never seem to take hold in the garden, and those that, sometimes uninvited, move in and refuse to leave—it's enough to make a gardener want to head for the hills! And that's exactly what we have to do. Examine the plants where they grow wild. Do they grow along road cuts where the soil is routinely disturbed? Do they cling to rocky slopes, grow in arroyos that flood seasonally, or are they tucked into protected niches out of harm's way? Does a plant dominate an area, or does it occur infrequently in isolated groups? Do birds eat the seeds and soften otherwise impermeable seed coats?

As a transplant to New Mexico with eastern roots, I realized early on that I had a few things to learn about gardening in the desert. I tried to surround myself with familiar foliage, and it looked more homesick than I was. As a landscape designer and contractor, I was soon disillusioned with Yuccas and gravel as an alternative to the high cost in time and water of a traditional, lawn-focused landscape. I wondered why the wild flowers carpeting the roadsides, and the trees and shrubs scattered across the floodplains and mesas, so successful in the natural landscape, weren't being used in man-made gardens. As a nursery grower, I was bored with the annual routine of mass-producing hybrid flowers, every year more brassy and artificial, fabulous fakes so easy to start in the controlled environment of the greenhouse and so costly to maintain in the hot, dusty real world. Licensed by the New Mexico Department of Agriculture as a plant collector, I soon abandoned that idea as a source of landscape stock. Plants collected from the wild often transplanted poorly, and it was difficult to find "digable" plants where removal on a commercial scale wouldn't alter the ecology of the area.

A few of my colleagues questioned my sanity when I retired from traditional horticulture to explore the cultivation of "weeds," but I found that I was in good company. Throughout the Southwest, there are surprising numbers of native-plant growers. Some are professional horticulturists looking for more appropriate landscape options. Others are ecologists and conservationists looking for native solutions to environmental problems, or for a way to preserve rare and endangered plants. But the majority are curious amateurs who pursue native-plant growing for personal satisfaction. Together we are well on the way toward solving the basic problems of taming many wild plants. We have reached a point where there is a broad enough selection of nursery-grown arid-land natives available to enable us to design and build ecologically sound landscapes that are aesthetically equal to exotic gardens.

Interest begets interest. Public gardens such as the Sonoran Desert Museum near Tucson and Superior, Arizona's Boyce Thompson Arboretum inspire visitors with the beauty and regional integrity of the wild garden. The ecosystem samplers, the alpine garden and prairie garden at the Denver Botanic Gardens, refine wild gardens in a metropolitan setting. Xeriscape, a program that encourages the use of drought-tolerant ornamentals in Western communities, also began in the Denver area, as a cooperative response to water conservation needs. Urban Forest Park in Albuquerque is a city park that solves the problems of noise, dust, and storm drainage using arid-land native plants. Soil contouring and massed plantings of deciduous and evergreen trees and shrubs act as sound barriers, insulating a residential area from the Interstate highway. Storm runoff is channeled through the park to supplement the thirstier plants with waste water, and wild flowers and native grasses prevent erosion. In this working landscape, drifts of seasonal flower and foliage color are a bonus. The National Wildflower Research Center (NWRC) near Austin, Texas, is exploring the potential of wild flowers for conservation and beautification. Field research is backed by a computerized nationwide clearinghouse for related information. Because the most effective native plantings are local in nature and yet many plants are regional in distribution, it is impossible to include all the possibilities in any one publication. The NWRC computer network will provide a vital data search link, accelerating research by making information available on a national level. (A regional shout of "Eureka!" is easier to hear than a thousand muffled "Eurekas!" uttered in Alpine, Texas; Veguita, New Mexico; Brighton, Colorado; Logan, Utah . . .) Still, a national data base is only as valuable as the input it receives, so local research, such as the testing of wild-flower meadow mixes at the Agricultural Science Center of New Mexico State University at Los Lunas (photo opposite page), provides specific recommendations that are the basis for more general guidelines for native plant use.

Native plant societies, dedicated to promoting the

appreciation of wild plants, offer varied programs of interest to both the novice and the veteran native plant enthusiast. With strong emphasis on civic beautification as well as private garden use, the National Council of State Garden Clubs' "Operation Wildflower" workshops have introduced thousands of experienced gardeners, the semi-pros, to native plants. The more you learn, the more there is to learn.

Hardly anyone asks, "Why native?" anymore. Now the questions are more specific: "How?" "Where?" and "Which ones?" Here in the Southwest, the ambiguous concepts of native, drought tolerant, and low maintenance are sometimes used interchangeably with varying degrees of inaccuracy. I prefer to define native broadly, as native of arid lands, rather than to limit the selection to those plants originally found on a site, or within a few miles of it, since a few miles can encompass many different ecosystems. Basing selection on the suitability of plants to a particular site and style of garden, a gardener can decide how naturalized, how self-sustaining, the landscape will be, and choose plants accordingly. The better adapted the plants are to the site and to each other, the less maintenance there will be.

Of the hundreds of plants available for landscape use, I have chosen to describe a sampling in detail. That decision was probably the most difficult one to make in writing this book. At the risk of snubbing old friends (my apologies to Indian Paintbrush [*Castilleja* species]—as popular as it is erratic; Palo Verde [*Cercidium* species]—beautiful but limited by its sensitivity to cold; and the Columbines [*Aquilegia* species]—well-known but not drought tolerant), I have focused on plants that are adaptable and either serve a multitude of landscape functions or fill a unique niche in the arid garden. I have tried to include a taste of mountains, mesas, prairies, river valleys, and desert grasslands. Most of these plants are available (sometimes with a bit of a search) in the nursery trade. The cultivation of rare and endangered plants requires very limiting environmental conditions. Indeed, most threatened species are confined to ecosystems that are themselves endangered. Preservation of these rare endemics is a complex issue. It is related to native landscaping only as an example of how plantings can be native yet *not* represent a low-maintenance approach to gardening.

This book began as my crop notes and grew into a very basic cookbook for native-plant growers, no matter where their specific interests lie. Gardening is an inexact science, and gardening with natives is a balance of local considerations and universal methods. Acacias, for example, not listed because of their limited range, are legumes, the seeds of which respond well to a hot-water soak before sowing—if you can't find the exact information you need, you may find a clue in a close relative.

Many people have generously provided their time and expertise to this work. I'd particularly like to thank all my good friends in the Native Plant Society of New Mexico for their ongoing support. Phyllis Hughes not only provided the wonderful Plant Profile illustrations and landscape elevation drawings, but also made the vital publisher connection. As publishers go, the people at the Museum of New Mexico Press have been this native gardener's daydream, attuned to the spirit of the work and skilled in the art of keeping all the hard facts "user friendly."

Finding model landscapes to photograph proved to be both a frustration and an education. The owner-designed gardens are the epitome of both, dynamic native-plant communities as ornamental as they are experimental. As art in progress, what some of these gardens lack in maturity they more than compensate for in the promises they offer. Even the established landscapes are undergoing constant refinement under the careful guidance of gardeners caught up in the challenge of new ideas. Ken Ball, Lorena and Fred Bear, Charlotte Blackmer, Jim and Dorothy Borland, Catherine Bunker, Jean Heflin, Margrit and Horst Kuenzler, Zern and Margot Phillips, Ellen Reed, Robert Squires, Frances Szeman, Susan Wachter, Ellen Wilde, Lucille Wilson, and Dale Zimmerman are among these pioneers.

Finally, there are two people who provided both the tangible help (research with pen and shovel, thoughtful feedback, typing) and the indispensible element of humor that has kept this project more or less on center throughout. They are Lisa Johnston, whom I'd rather be mistaken for than anyone else alive, and Roland Phillips, my personal underwriter, coach, and critic. Thank you all very much.

# THE PROCESS

It's hard to improve on the plant communities that are the result of centuries of evolution as role models for low-maintenance plantings. Threadleaf Sage, Broom Dalea, and Bush Penstemon thrive in the sun-and-sand conditions typical of high-desert ecosystems.

# 1 🐝 LIVING WELL ON LESS—THE GROUND RULES

The idea of using native plants in naturalized landscapes is not new. In 1870 *The Wild Garden* was published in England. The author, William Robinson, found the trend toward replacing perennial borders in Victorian gardens with introduced tropical annuals "monotonously gaudy." His aim was to restore subtlety and add variety to English landscapes, using nature as a design guide.

It wasn't a bad idea then. In the American Southwest today it is essential. The Southwestern "Sunbelt" is faced with the necessity of accommodating a booming population on a limited water budget. Our sunny, dry climate is encouraging development in the Southwest. The climate is also a major consideration, sometimes a drawback, to gardening here.

## CLIMATE

Climate consists of available sunlight, the resulting air and soil temperatures, and available moisture and wind. The elevations of the site itself and of the surrounding area greatly influence climate. The Chaco Basin, Rio Grande Valley, and Tularosa Valley are cut off from moisture-laden clouds by neighboring mountains and mesas, leaving them among the driest areas in New Mexico, with eight to ten inches average annual precipitation. The adjacent San Juan, Sangre de Cristo, Jemez, Sandia, and Sacramento mountains may catch twenty to forty inches of precipitation on their exposed slopes. Temperatures decrease an average of 2 F for every degree of latitude northward and 5 F for every 1,000-foot rise in elevation. Still, low, sheltered spots where air stagnates may regularly record temperatures lower than the surrounding highlands. Corrales, New Mexico, often records temperatures as low or lower than Santa Fe, fifty miles to the north and 2,000 feet higher. The effects of climate are much broader than average temperatures and precipitation.

Because limited rainfall doesn't allow the leaching of mineral salts and hot, dry winds blow off leaf litter before it can decompose into humus, Western desert soils are generally alkaline, sometimes saline. A gardener then has three options: to create and maintain soil that will support exotic vegetation, to landscape with plants adapted to the existing soil, or to compromise— create a pocket of humus for a few exotics and go native for the balance.

Iben Browning, an Albuquerque climatologist, describes another wrinkle in the ecological canvas: "Climate is what you expect. Weather is what you get." One year in ten, winter lows might drop to − 20 F in an area where 6 F is the expected bottom line. So we can add inconsistency to the list of the Southwestern gardener's demons, along with too much sun, heat, and wind, not enough water, and poor soil. Besides low moisture to begin with, bright sunlight and high temperatures stimulate the evaporation of moisture from leaf surfaces. Wind accelerates moisture loss. Soil alkalinity and salinity reduce the absorption of water and nutrients.

## SURVIVAL OF SEEDS

Adaptability is the plants' salvation. As a group, plants native to arid lands have evolved means of coping with, even capitalizing on, the extremes of climate. Survival begins with seeds. Seeds of many arid-land natives are equipped with chemical or physical mechanisms that delay germination until conditions for the survival of seedlings are, if not optimum, at least more favorable.

The papery husks that enclose seeds of Fourwing Saltbush contain chemical inhibitors. Rains heavy enough to soak the soil and provide a temporary reservoir of moisture will also wash away the inhibitor. Seeds can then germinate while the soil retains enough moisture to support the initial growth of new seedlings. The chemical concentration and permeability of the seed coats vary. Some seeds require several successive launderings, in effect keeping a reserve of seeds "in the wings," waiting for still another downpour.

Chemical inhibitors present in many Penstemons prevent germination during hot, dry weather. On the average, Penstemon seeds mature within two months of flowering. Spring blooming species disperse seeds during the intense heat of summer, but the percentage of germination on newly ripened seeds is low, saving the seedlings from a baptism by fire. Viability improves with time when seeds are stored under cool, dry conditions. Many Penstemons are cold-hardy when they are juvenile; seedlings germinated in early September survive near 0°F winter temperatures unprotected. Germination improves with seeds at least a year old, and cold-moist stratification improves the germination of fresh seeds dramatically.

Giant Four O'Clock, Bush Morningglory, Sumac, and

Giant Four O'Clock (*Mirabilis multiflora*): woody seed coat is impervious to moisture.

Indian Ricegrass (*Oryzopsis hymenoides*): hairs covering hard seed coat improve seed-soil contact.

Paperflower (*Psilostrophe bakerii*): composite flower, disk with seeds, seeds with pappus.

Screwbean Mesquite (*Prosopis pubescens*): bean seedpod and cleaned seeds.

Fourwing Saltbush (*Atriplex canescens*): tough, fibery seed coat is impervious to moisture.

Sand Verbena (*Tripterocalyx species*): papery "wings" and woody seed coat are impervious to moisture.

Littleleaf Sumac (*Rhus microphylla*): fruit and cleaned seeds.

Palmer Penstemon: seeds and seed capsule.

Creosotebush exhibit seed protection of another type. Their seeds possess extremely tough seed coats that restrict the penetration of water and the exchange of gases necessary for germination.

Nature's seed pretreatment techniques include a trip through the digestive tracts of birds and animals, a battering wash down gravel-strewn arroyos, tannic-acid baths through the digestive systems of hoarding ants, freezing, thawing, rain, snow, and the passage of time. The average gardener, more kind than the Southwestern climate, resists inflicting the apparent abuse sometimes necessary to induce the germination of well-protected native seeds. While these defenses against a harsh climate can make propagation difficult, in a landscape the problem can be a blessing.

If even *half* the seeds produced by the plants in a landscape germinated, it would be a jungle out there! Some seed coats are so impermeable and some germination inhibitors so concentrated that, for practical purposes, the seeds will never sprout—Nature's equivalent of hiding something so well that even she can't find it. Insects and wildlife carry off and consume a portion of every seed crop. In a naturalized landscape, leaving the soil undisturbed and limiting available moisture reduces the likelihood that "volunteers" will gain a foothold. Using a thick, dry-surfaced mulch such as bark makes germination even less likely. The plants described as "self-sowing readily" are good candidates for mixed meadows, where competition for space, nutrients, and water will help control invasiveness. All in all, a well-designed and naturalized arid-land landscape reaches a balance, thanks to the same difficulties that frustrate the propagator. A dense stand of Desert Marigold two years in a row is an accomplishment. The Siberian Elm should be so difficult!

Like the Elm, some arid-land natives rely on sheer volume in seed production to assure future generations. Evolution and the survival of a species seem to be a high-stakes game of chance. A mature Rabbitbrush/Chamisa produces millions of light, chaffy seeds annually. Many are sterile. Inhibitors prevent otherwise viable seeds from sprouting. Unseasonably early cold weather may freeze moisture-laden seed embryos before they harden. Thirty to thirty-five percent germination is an accomplishment even under optimum conditions. Forestiera, Russian Olive, and Golden Currant produce succulent fruit, sweet fleshy delicacies that attract foragers to consume, scarify, and distribute seeds. The process is more costly in terms of the per seed moisture requirement and so fewer seeds are produced, but less is left to chance. One approach leaves the answer "blowin' in the wind," while the other involves "a wing and a prayer"; Mother Nature plays the odds. Without human interference she has seemed to be winning—definitely breaking even.

1

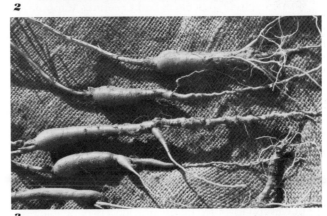

2

3

4

**DROUGHT-RESISTING ROOT SYSTEMS:** Rose Locusts form nitrogen-fixing nodules on their roots (**1**). Most Artemisias produce a mass of fiberous roots. Mature plants often have deep, woody taproot as well (**2**).
Gayfeather roots are pithy conical tubers similar to carrots (**3**). Yuccas have a deep taproot and few fiberous laterals (**4**).

# DEFENSES AGAINST DROUGHT

In the intense competition for water among desert plants, a new seedling must rapidly establish itself or give way to the more robust. Survival of the fittest is a fact of life and many adaptations in form, foliage, and root system yield a competitive edge. The most obvious to the casual observer is the ability to store moisture in succulent tissues. As a group, cacti are masters of defense. Their moisture-filled tissues are their security in times of drought, but there are more subtle adaptations. Picklebush (*Allenrolfea occidentalis*) is a medium-sized shrub akin to the Saltbushes, with blue green fleshy stems lacking recognizable leaves. Usually found in saline soils where water may be readily available, but due to its high salt content not readily absorbable by the plant, Picklebush overcomes both problems. The plant cells maintain high osmotic pressure with a reservoir of moisture within the plant tissues, a key to both drought and salt tolerance.

Many Yuccas, as well as Bush Morningglory, Gayfeather, and Four O'Clock, produce fleshy or pithy roots capable of supplying stored moisture during intermittent drought. Plants with less succulent root tissues are often capable of rapid regeneration of roots, or like some cacti, Fringe Sage, and Creeping Mahonia, produce extensive lateral roots fairly close to the soil surface. Such fibrous root systems are capable of rapidly absorbing a large percentage of the sporadic rainfall that arid climates offer.

Many natives, including Mesquite, Soaptree Yucca, Desert Olive, Chamisa, and Desert Willow, have deep, rarely branched roots designed to tap underground water strata. The most active portion of taproots is far from the crown of these plants. Such a root system makes transplanting difficult unless the plants are very young, have been grown in containers, or have been root-pruned regularly. Once established in a landscape, however, taprooted plants provide a dependable framework upon which a drought-enduring environment can be built. Regardless of root-system type, arid-land natives possess a large ratio of root mass to top growth. What you see above ground is a small percentage of what you get in the way of drought resistance. Bush Morningglory displays an airy, mounding head, rarely greater than three feet in height and diameter, yet its root system may weigh a hundred pounds. Mesquite is used as firewood in many desert areas, the wood cut not from the shrubby top growth but from the seemingly endless root system. Many Yuccas employ a backup system. In addition to extensive lateral rooting, as in *Yucca rostrata,* or deep, starchy taproots, as in *Y. elata,* adventitious roots form under the layers of dead leaves that insulate the trunks of mature plants. Any moisture absorbed by the fibrous mat of bygone foliage is made available to the entire plant. Little is wasted in the desert. Survival may hang in the balance.

Rooting adaptations contribute to survival by maximizing the availability of water. Once absorbed, the emphasis shifts to conserving precious fluids. Winterfat, Desert Marigold, Chamisa, and the Sages have leaves covered with downy hairs that shade the leaf surface. Creosotebush and many Poplars have a resinous or waxy coating that reduces transpiration. Broom Baccharis and Fourwing Saltbush have scurfy leaf surfaces (botanic dandruff, if you will) that reflect intense sunlight.

Stomates—the pores on leaf surfaces—open and close, allowing for the exchange of gases and resulting in significant moisture loss. Stomates of some drought-tolerant plants remain closed during the heat of the

**DROUGHT-RESISTING LEAF TEXTURES:** Narrow, woolly foliage of Threadleaf Sage reflects light.

Resinous leaf surface of Creosotebush.

Scurfy leaf texture of Fourwing Saltbush.

day or when soil moisture is low. Ordinarily this would interfere with photosynthesis, since carbon dioxide ($CO_2$), water ($H_2O$), and light are all necessary for the reaction to occur. Some arid-land natives, particularly cacti, contain crassulacean acid, a substance that absorbs $CO_2$ when temperatures are cool and releases it as temperatures rise. $CO_2$ is absorbed while stomates are open in the cool night hours. As daytime temperatures rise and the stomates close, water vaporizes within the plant body and the acid releases $CO_2$ while light is available for photosynthesis. Some plants revert to typical stomate behavior when heat and moisture stress decrease. Crassulacean acid metabolism (CAM) is quite a neat solution to a thorny problem.

The quantity as well as the quality of the evaporative surface determines moisture retention or loss. While moisture-conserving leaves are good, no leaves at all may be better. Some plants are drought deciduous. During dry periods, leaves drop to reduce the evaporative surface of the plant. Broom Dalea leafs out briefly in response to summer rain, but usually relies on the chlorophyll in the stems to maintain photosynthesis. New Mexico Privet may defoliate and releaf two or more times a season. The scaly, resinous foliage of the evergreen Junipers and Arizona Cypress more closely resemble stems than leaves. Leaf texture yields the competitive edge in year-round food production, but these evergreens are not typical in the driest of desert microclimates. Creosotebush, also evergreen, retains small leaves that give off less moisture to hot, dry winds. During monsoon rainy seasons, Creosotebush also produces larger leaves to increase the photosynthesizing surface. Thus, the plant can take advantage of heavy rains and still maintain its status among the most drought-tolerant of arid-land natives. Flexibility is a definite advantage when dealing with a climate so apt to defy the norm.

Akin to the tactic of reducing leaf surface is the more extreme ability to cut short the entire life cycle in times of moisture stress. Annuals generally bloom all summer if spent blooms are removed and water is available. Without the necessary moisture, seasonal annuals like early spring Nama are as short-lived as the showers that trigger their growth. At one time, when plant inventorying coincided with periods of drought, Nama was believed to be an endangered species. Perennials like Four O'Clock and Bush Morningglory cut short their growing season when moisture is not forthcoming, yet will bloom for extended periods when rainfall is ample or irrigation is possible.

The compact, rounded form of many arid-land natives is a further drought response, minimizing overall evaporative surface. Blackfoot Daisy is so regularly mounded it looks carefully manicured, when in fact it owes its compact habit to its conservative nature.

The globular shape of some cacti is another example of conservation by virtue of form; the additional ability to orient the growing tips toward the sun increases the capacity for evaporation control. The plant creates its own shade! Prickly pears not only temper their microclimate by "self-shading," but an established plant actually increases the moisture available to it by trapping leaves and litter around itself, gradually building up a pocket of mulch and humus. Agaves and some Yucca species combine the advantage of a rosette form above a dense mat of fibrous roots, to funnel rainwater directly to the absorbing surface. This rosette "funnel form" is also the efficient manner in which many annuals, biennials, and herbaceous perennials (Nama, Baileya, Paperflower, some Penstemon, and Gilia) begin their growth cycles.

Some natives are in a fluid state of rapid genetic change. Fourwing Saltbush and its subspecies hybridize readily, producing an infinite variation in leaf shape, plant size, and chemistry uniquely adapted to the specific site a plant occupies. Such diversity is natural selection in progress.

A single plant is usually a composite of several defensive characteristics. Forestiera combines an extensive taprooted absorption system, small leaf size, ability to defoliate in times of drought and releaf rapidly when moisture becomes available, compact growth habit, and succulent berries which are relished and disseminated by many songbirds. An impressive résumé! Fourwing Saltbush combines a taproot with leaf and plant size specifically adapted to on-site conditions, silver-blue green reflective foliage color, mounding growth habit, and extremely palatable seeds with concentrated germination inhibitors. Fringe sage combines an extensive, fibrous root system, small stature, finely cut silver gray reflective foliage, and prolific wind-dispersed seeds. It is only coincidental, albeit happily so, that some of these adaptations for drought tolerance—mounding compact growth habit, interesting leaf color and texture, ornamental fruit and flowers that attract an entertaining assortment of pollinators such as butterflies and hummingbirds—give arid-land natives high marks as landscape plants.

# A PROCESS OF SELECTION

Yet simple solutions are rare. It seems a perverse quirk of nature that a naturalized low-maintenance landscape takes more effort to plan and establish than a standard formula "Southwestern" gravel bed studded with exotic landscape ornamentals. The evolution of an ultimately easy-care native garden takes either careful planning and work or a few centuries of natural succession. Few of us have that kind of time, so a little mental and physical exercise seems a reasonable alternative.

"Naturalized" means able to survive on a site unassisted. There is a large gap between surviving and thriv-

**EROSION:** Threadleaf Sage holds soil (**l**). Apache Plume stands high and dry—two feet above water- and wind-eroded soil surface (**r**). Unstable soil washes out where no plant roots act as anchor (**below**).

Agave foliage rosette illustrates funnel-form, alternately whorled-leaf arrangement that directs water to roots.

most tolerant of extremes, most uniform in performance, and most able to be reproduced reliably by seeds or cuttings. Through cultivation on a trial-and-error basis, the grower learns the limitations of the subject: the conditions that produce the best plant performance, how adaptable the plant is to variables, under what conditions it will not survive, and under what conditions it will become invasive, a "weed" in the negative sense.

To the landscaper, designer, and contractor, selection means translating the grower's cultural (cultivating) information into viable living space—using selected natives on appropriate sites to establish functional, attractive, low-maintenance environments. The success of native plantings lies in this suitability of plant materials to site. To the homeowner, selection implies an intelligent balance of investment and expectations. No plants will tolerate the extremes of our climate unassisted until they have become established. Once established, a well-designed native landscape is an extremely safe investment—one that will survive, even thrive, unattended while you're on vacation or occupied with family and career responsibilities.

In this book, selection has an even more limited meaning. The plants I describe and recommend for landscape use are those currently or soon to be available in nurseries. There's no point in encouraging the use of plants that are not readily obtainable, since most arid-land natives don't transplant easily from the wild. Besides, they are often needed in their habitat as forage and cover for local wildlife or as critical erosion control. Living in a flash (and I do mean flash) flood area has given me a very intimate and immediate awareness of erosion and a keen appreciation of native soil binders.

I am a commercial grower of native plants today largely because ten years ago, as a nursery manager and landscaper interested in developing low-maintenance naturalized landscapes, I found that the availability of native plants was a "collect-and-hope-for-the-best" situation. This was limiting and definitely frustrating. Not unlike the Victorian author of *The Wild Garden,* I found the trend toward "Southwestern" gravel landscapes monotonous and a short-term easy answer that rarely improves with age.

Native landscaping has matured in the last ten years. Extensive research is yielding a better understanding of the native plant's physiology and drought tolerance. Greater availability of nursery-grown natives is both broadening and refining their landscape potential. These are exciting times. The more we learn, the more we see there is to learn.

ing, though, so other compromises may be in order. Low maintenance is relative, and although it may be easier to naturalize a landscape using arid-land native plants, "native" does not guarantee easy care. Some native plants are extremely specific in their ecological requirements. Others are broadly adaptable. The materials discussed in this book fall within the broadest definitions of native, "native of arid lands." Emphasis is given to the landscape potential of local plant material, but plants native to similarly arid climates, especially those that fill local gaps in adaptability or appearance, are also recommended. Because we are dealing with high desert climates, cold hardiness is as important as heat and drought tolerance.

"Selection" is a key word. We are in search of "well-behaved weeds," the best plants that arid lands have to offer. To the grower this means tapping a vast arid landscape for natives that meet high horticultural standards for attractive form, foliage, color, and texture. Selection is based upon how well these "weeds" respond to cultivation. We are interested in the biotypes

Developing a "sense of place" is especially appropriate in southwestern landscapes. The lure of an oasis lies in its contrast to the desert surrounding it.

Be honest. Do you want a showplace landscape? Masses of seasonal color: pastels in spring, russet and gold in autumn? A summertime oasis and a winter shelter? And do you want it all with no effort on your part? Native or not, keep dreaming.

Water is a scarce commodity in the Southwest. In June there are 101 F days; clouds trail streams of rain that evaporate a thousand feet above the ground, and the soil crunches dry underfoot. Desert Willows are just beginning their burst of color. Apache Plume's filmy elegance is at its early-season peak. Buffalograss steadily inches its way across baked soil. It's finally warm enough to suit these arid-land natives, and you're pumping water to a gasping bluegrass lawn or avoiding the glare from that convection oven—gravel mulch substitute. Conservation aside, consider your utility bills.

There are many beautiful and drought-tolerant alternatives to the bluegrass-gravel "Southwestern" syndrome. Arid-land native plants, placed with intelligence and established properly, can substantially minimize the cost in time, water, and fertilizer involved in maintaining a handsome landscape. You eventually can even have a totally maintenance-free landscape, but there are trade-offs, concessions to be made. Native landscaping is more attractive to the avid gardener than to the reluctant one. There is a lot of satisfaction in orchestrating a blend of climate, caliche, form, and flower. It offers immediate gratification, and it ages well.

Observing established landscapes, both commercial and residential, helps in visualizing potential landscapes. Notice which are appealing and which are not. Analyze how and why the plantings relate to the structures and to each other in proportion, color, and texture, as well as in the mood created. Such thoughtful observation will put you in touch with your preferences. Do flowing lines, dramatic splashes of color, a casual attitude suit your life-style, or are you more comfortable in a symmetrical, "ducks in a row" orderly landscape? Informal landscapes are usually easier and less costly to maintain. Symmetry and geometrical patterns are attractive only as long as they remain perfect. Plants, like people, are rarely that.

The more self-sustaining you want your landscape to be, the more important it is to select plants that require soil and exposures similar to those on your site. Studying plants as they occur in their native habitats and the roles they play within local ecosystems will give you a better idea of how to use them appropriately in your landscape. Go to the source. It's hard to improve on the plant communities that are the result of centuries of evolution as role models for low-maintenance

plantings. Just as observing man-made landscapes can help clarify your stylistic preferences, observing the dominant plant associations in natural landscapes can give you a basic framework of plant preferences on which to build. The "Origin and Adaptations" data in the Plant Profiles section of this book is the next best thing to firsthand observation and serves the same purpose—to familiarize you with how individual plants fit into plant communities and how these communities fit into the larger landscape.

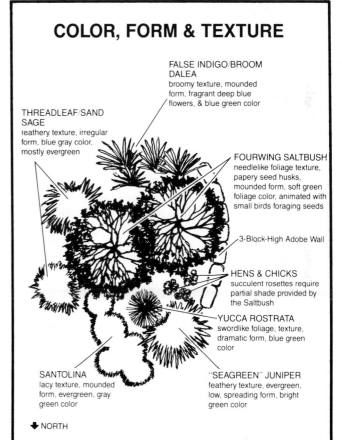

## COLOR, FORM & TEXTURE

**FALSE INDIGO/BROOM DALEA**
broomy texture, mounded form, fragrant deep blue flowers, & blue green color

**THREADLEAF/SAND SAGE**
feathery texture, irregular form, blue gray color, mostly evergreen

**FOURWING SALTBUSH**
needlelike foliage texture, papery seed husks, mounded form, soft green foliage color, animated with small birds foraging seeds

3-Block-High Adobe Wall

**HENS & CHICKS**
succulent rosettes require partial shade provided by the Saltbush

**YUCCA ROSTRATA**
swordlike foliage, texture, dramatic form, blue green color

**SANTOLINA**
lacy texture, mounded form, evergreen, gray green color

**"SEAGREEN" JUNIPER**
feathery texture, evergreen, low, spreading form, bright green color

↓ NORTH

*Color, form, and texture are the landscape designer's means of creating impact. Color is the most obvious. Contrasting and complementing colors, especially in mass plantings, make a strong visual statement. Texture has more subtle visual impact. In this accent grouping, the similarity and contrast in textures provide the interest and focus amid shades of green. Form provides continuity and refers to both the shape of individual plants and the spatial relationships created by their placement in the landscape.*

# DESIGN PRINCIPLES

Although most of the man-made landscapes you observe will not be native and will require more care than a low-maintenance design should, the principles of design, of form and line, color and texture, are universal. In some cases, it is possible to mentally substitute more conservative alternates: replace a bluegrass lawn with buffalograss; expand paved areas and substitute Coyotebush or Desert Zinnia for the remaining lawn; replace a Weeping Willow with a clump of Desert Willow; substitute Golden Currant for Forsythia, Littleleaf Sumac for Pyracantha, or Forestiera for Privet hedge. Simple substitution of drought-tolerant plants, one on one, for their more thirsty counterparts establishes a more drought-tolerant landscape and nets a relative decrease in water consumption. This is only the first timid step toward a really low-maintenance naturalized landscape.

Simplicity itself is a giant step forward. You may have a list a mile long of likely candidates for your native garden, but your selection of plants is limited by the ecology of the site you are landscaping. Selection must be tempered by adaptability as well as appearance. If red fall color is your objective, consider Golden Currant; but if water will be very limited, Threeleaf Sumac is a better option.

A selection of a few plant species compatible with the site and with each other can achieve the desired impact better than the confusion of a one-of-a-kind botanical gallery. Massed plantings of a few species can effectively cover much ground without creating the need to maintain twenty types of ecosystems within the same 5,000-square-foot plot. Through repetition, such plantings establish a sense of unity that is basic to good design.

Each site is unique. The landscape layouts that are included in this chapter are graphic examples of design concepts applied to site limitations and native or naturalized plantings—natural solutions to local landscape problems. They are accompanied by commentary explaining the reasons why certain choices were made, the interplay of conditions, the relative drought and maintenance levels in balance, the concessions and trade offs in process. Plant selection is based upon size and shape, leaf color and texture, flower color and season, adaptability to on-site conditions, and compatability with other plantings. The indoor space adjacent to the landscape is noted, and windows and doors are indicated. That these spaces merge with and extend each other is especially important when space is limited or traffic flow is heavy.

# ECOSYSTEMS

Plants can create ecosystems. Quaking Aspen, native to high elevations and cool summer temperatures, will adapt well even on unshaded southern exposures if a compatible shrub or vine like Juniper, Coralberry, or Clematis is massed at the base of the trees, shading and cooling the root zone. Grading to control and utilize runoff can create interesting ecological niches and reduce the need for supplemental watering. Unmowed ground covers and meadows can be "tamed" by bordering them with neat edges—paving or compact shrub islands. Combining elements harmoniously, we take a further step in the design process.

Developing a "sense of place" is especially appropriate in the Southwest. We have mountains that literally leave the viewer breathless; mesas alive with the presence of "the old ones"; river valleys unwinding like green ribbons in the sand; dunes whose faces change with every breeze; and prairies that roll on, the same forever. Why then should our cities resemble the suburbs of Chicago or St. Louis? We do need lush green pockets to soothe urban tensions, but much of the lure of an oasis lies in its contrast to the desert around it. Green on green on green assumes the ambience of a cornfield, very appropriate blanketing the countryside of Iowa, but out of context in the sun-baked, arid Southwest. Landscaping our outdoor living spaces as shady refuges buffered by more drought-tolerant arid-land natives, we can enjoy our oases *and* our deserts. Effectively designing for minimal care means understanding the preferences of the plants and the limitations of the site.

Plant material enhances the quality of life on a site, expands or encloses space, and sets traffic patterns. Hedges, screens, windbreaks, shade trees, and ground covers afford privacy, humidify the air, filter dust, moderate temperatures, and muffle noise as they define space. Deciduous plants, those that lose their leaves during winter or extreme drought, provide seasonal interest, are often fast growing, and provide either a thorny physical barrier or a twiggy visual barrier. They also have the advantage of allowing solar penetration during the winter. Evergreens are generally slower growing and provide a dense screen year round, sometimes with the added advantage of a subtle seasonal color change. A combination of both, with a 3:1 or 4:1 ratio of deciduous to evergreen, is effective both in design and cost.

# USE AREAS

Typical use areas in a residential landscape include the public approach—driveway, front entrance, and total area open to public view; the leisure or personal use area—outdoor living space, including patios and adjacent areas; the service area—parking other than the driveway, storage and access to equipment, vegetable garden, and active play areas; and the transitional areas that tie together, lead into, or separate the

# DESIGNING FOR USE AREAS

Use of the public area is predetermined—to enhance and complement the structure. The entryway should be inviting. Emphasis is given to the entrance by using an accent grouping to lead up to and focus on the doorway. The mixture of low evergreens and flowering perennials provides an attractive approach to the front entrance as well as a picturesque setting viewed from the living room.

The dense semi-evergreen Apache Plume screen sep-

arates the kitchen patio from the more private bedroom patio. Another dense screen camouflages the dog run and reduces the late afternoon glare of a hot western exposure. The plant material enhances the quality of life on this site, enclosing space and setting traffic patterns. Plants are grouped for visual impact as well as functional screening. There is a seasonal progression of flower and leaf color.

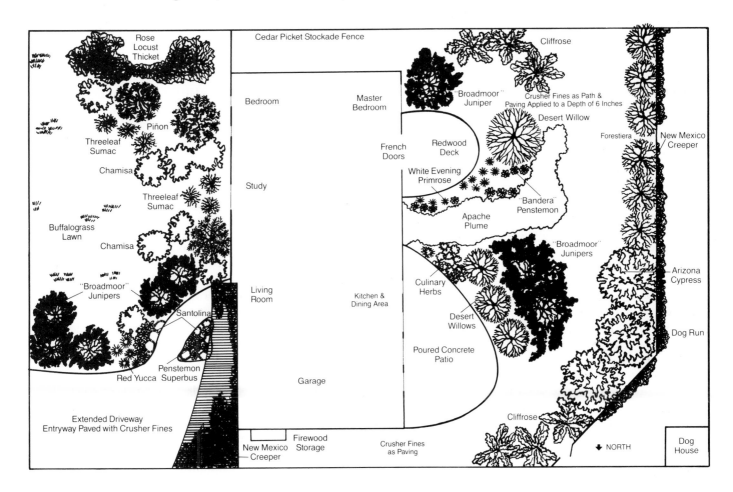

other areas.

The public area is often developed first, as its use is predetermined and less likely to change. The style of architecture on the site and the quality of neighboring landscapes suggest the approach. Pueblo-style adobe, cottage, bungalow, or ranch-style homes are complemented by an informal approach, while territorial-style adobe, Victorian, or modern stylized construction may suggest a more formal attitude. An unmowed, random-height mixed meadow will look out of place among well-kept bluegrass lawns, but a mass planting of ground cover that borders expanded walkways is in keeping with a manicured neighborhood. Walkways should be comfortable—a width of four feet is adequate. Often, the access provided by the contractor will need to be altered or expanded. Paving material can be either an extension of existing material or an alternate that complements the structure.

Emphasis can be given to the entrance by using an accent planting as a living punctuation mark. The entryway should be inviting: cool in summer, protected from wind, and attractive throughout the year. Foundation plantings—low- to medium-height shrubs along exterior walls—are commonly used to tie the structure into the landscape. Vestiges of Eastern and Midwestern landscape design that have migrated west, foundation plantings originally served to hide the high foundations on homes with basements. There are pros and cons to such plantings. Where the structural surface is maintenance free, evergreens have some insulating value when they are used as foundation plantings. Since many homes require periodic restuccoing, repainting, etc., plantings are damaged during routine maintenance if there is no walk space around exterior walls. Bush Morningglory or Giant Four O'Clock as ground cover allows seasonal access to areas. These plants provide cover six months of the year and can be removed at ground level when they are dormant. On the one hand, window cleaning can be difficult if access is blocked by plantings. Thorny plantings at the base of windows where security is a problem can be an effective deterrent, however.

Small specimen trees like Desert Willow, Desert Olive, Shrub Oak, and Russian Olive, set out twelve to fifteen feet from a corner or wall, frame the structure, while a blank wall forms a backdrop, silhouetting interesting forms and picking up the shadows of these arid-land natives as focal points in the design.

## SEASONAL CHANGES

Taking advantage of the seasonal changes in plant growth adds much to the appeal of the landscape. As the seasons change, so can the focus and impact of the plant groupings. Complementary textures, forms, and colors catch the eye and lead it through the landscape from street to entryway, from interior living

rooms through windows and doors to outdoor living spaces. If the public area is very large, space is otherwise at a premium, or individual needs dictate, a portion of the public area may be screened off, either structurally or with plants, to expand outdoor living space.

Increasing the proportion of hard-paved areas such as patios, decks, and walkways reduces the surface area requiring irrigation and increases living space. Shade is also an important consideration in this climate, creating cooler microclimates indoors as well as out. Evergreens insulate a northwest wall in summer as well as winter. Deciduous shade trees and vines can cool south and west rooms in summer and allow solar heat penetration in winter. Outdoor living spaces, especially with reflective pavement "floors," are much more inviting when they are shaded by tree or vine canopies that defoliate in season to provide a summertime oasis and, as needed, a "heat sink" of winter sunshine. Patio areas are often host to more active pursuits than corresponding indoor spaces. Allow plenty of leg room—wide walkways, expansive seating areas.

## PRACTICAL HINTS

Avoid "make-work" situations. Misplaced sprinklers will leave unsightly alkali stains on walls and windows. Any meadows or lawn/ground covers that will receive intermittent sprinkling to establish and will require more sprinkling during prolonged drought should be located away from such surfaces. A border of evergreen ground covers like Fringed Sage, Juniper, or Santolina can effect the transition from wall to meadow or lawn and can create a feeling of depth even in small areas.

References in Further Reading, pages 135–136, deal with the mechanics of landscape design. A working layout drawn to scale, with the plantings indicated at their mature dimensions, transfers to the actual plot and eliminates costly overplanting. Although you are dealing with juveniles at planting time, place them as adults. Mature size, as indicated in the Profiles section of this book, is the ultimate size of the plant, provided that it is given a good start and maintained as recommended.

Most natives establish themselves and grow rapidly while they are young. Inducing growth increases the initial water and nutrient requirements, but this early investment reduces the initial cash outlay for larger plant material and ultimately results in healthier and better adapted transplants. Large-sized natives frequently are collected from the wild, but the older a plant is, the less adaptable it is to environmental changes. The collected specimen, if it survives, is likely to put most of its energy into replacing lost roots, while a nursery-grown plant often doubles in size the first year after transplanting. Even nursery-grown natives seem to become less adaptable as they mature. Fewest transplanting losses, fastest establishment, and most rapid growth result when transplants are one to three years old.

Every good rule deserves at least one exception, however. When the scale of the building is large, especially if the site is also expansive, selecting healthy, large stock of slower-growing species and filling in the gaps with smaller transplants of faster-growing plants will reduce the dwarfing effect of grand scale in a new landscape. Cost-effective planning involves another compromise—using the best of what is available and affordable.

## STEPS IN DESIGNING

Begin with a plot plan—a scale drawing of the site to be landscaped which locates all structures, paving, and existing plant materials that will remain. Consider exposure and topography. List plants you like. Use the Profiles to determine which of your favorites are compatible with each other, the site, and your projected maintenance schedule. Now you have the blank canvas before you.

The next step is the design process—the strenuous mental exercise of seeing what isn't there. An effective design creates a mood. What is suggested is as important as what is visible. Design boldly. Naturalized landscapes soften with age as the mounding growth habit of many arid-land natives conceals the hard lines of the drawn design. One advantage of designing on paper is the bird's-eye-view perspective that makes it easier to establish strong, flowing lines.

Begin at the beginning, with the surface of the site. A flat expanse can be made more interesting by varying the grade. Low spots then accommodate thirstier plants by creating reservoirs that can also trap runoff, "free water." When harvesting runoff, be sure the basin can handle the flow and that the soil drains fairly rapidly, or your desert may resemble Okefenokee Swamp during monsoon season. Be gentle with your grade changes. Recreating the Alps on the typical city lot is not only out of scale but also creates watering and erosion problems. Steep slopes are best terraced, but terracing requires horizontal space or high retaining walls. When a site is naturally sloped and terrac-

ing is not an option, drip-irrigated drought-tolerant plants as soil binders are the best alternative.

Once you have molded the surface, define the walkways and other paved areas and establish the "floor" of the landscape. If some of the function of "walls" and "ceilings" will be fulfilled by structural materials—adobe or block walls, fences, patio covers, arbors, etc., place those next. In both planning and construction phases, most of the inert materials are considered and installed before the live materials. Plant material then can be used to soften hard surfaces and enhance the built environment. Next, place the largest of the live materials—shade trees, tall pines, tree-type Yuccas. Follow up with windbreaks, screens, and mass plantings that delineate space and outline form, giving shape to the landscape. The carpeting is last—mid-height to low ground covers, lawns, meadows, and inert mulches. Layers of detail overlap and color each other until the final image comes together.

There is a lot to consider here. Even so, many of the most beautiful and functional native gardens that I have visited have been owner designed and built. If your project will involve major site alterations, if you aren't sure which end of the shovel goes into the ground (and are in no hurry to find out), if you don't trust your aesthetic instincts, or most likely, if you just don't have the time, you may decide to consult a landscape architect or designer and/or hire a landscape contractor to do the work. No matter who does the design and construction, only you know how the site will be used, the style/mood with which you will be comfortable, your budget, and how much maintenance you have the time or inclination to do. Take the time to determine your needs, and shop around for professionals who will satisfy them.

Local native plant societies and wild-flower and garden clubs host slide programs illustrating the plants and discussing their landscape use. Such programs are announced in the weekly calendar section of the newspaper and are open to the public. These organizations also sponsor field trips to areas of botanical interest—guided tours of local plant communities that offer insight and inspiration to budding native landscapers. Take advantage of this valuable resource in your community.

# LOW MOISTURE REQUIREMENT

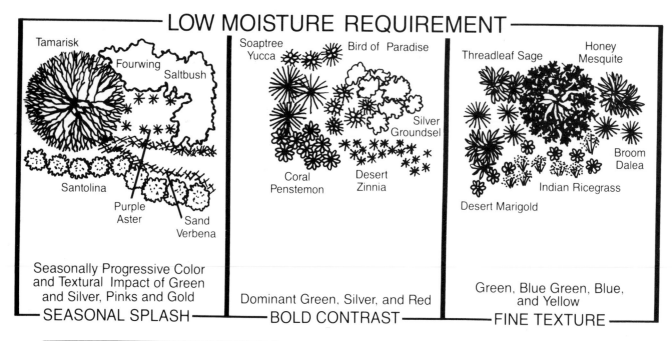

Tamarisk
Fourwing
Saltbush
Santolina
Purple Aster
Sand Verbena

Seasonally Progressive Color
and Textural Impact of Green
and Silver, Pinks and Gold

**SEASONAL SPLASH**

Soaptree Yucca
Bird of Paradise
Silver Groundsel
Coral Penstemon
Desert Zinnia

Dominant Green, Silver, and Red

**BOLD CONTRAST**

Threadleaf Sage
Honey Mesquite
Broom Dalea
Indian Ricegrass
Desert Marigold

Green, Blue Green, Blue,
and Yellow

**FINE TEXTURE**

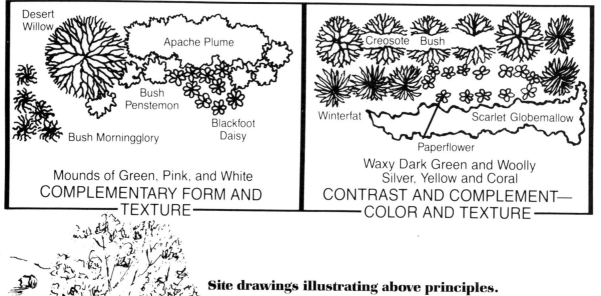

Desert Willow
Apache Plume
Bush Penstemon
Blackfoot Daisy
Bush Morningglory

Mounds of Green, Pink, and White

**COMPLEMENTARY FORM AND TEXTURE**

Creosote Bush
Winterfat
Scarlet Globemallow
Paperflower

Waxy Dark Green and Woolly
Silver, Yellow and Coral

**CONTRAST AND COMPLEMENT— COLOR AND TEXTURE**

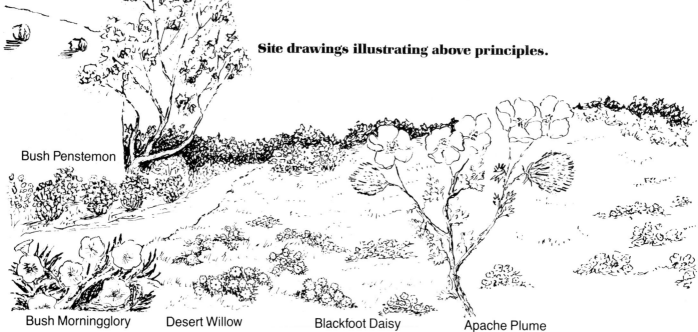

**Site drawings illustrating above principles.**

Bush Penstemon

Bush Morningglory    Desert Willow    Blackfoot Daisy    Apache Plume

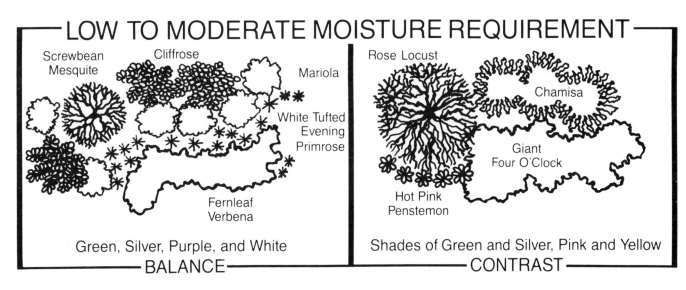

# LOW TO MODERATE MOISTURE REQUIREMENT

Screwbean Mesquite

Cliffrose

Mariola

White Tufted Evening Primrose

Fernleaf Verbena

Green, Silver, Purple, and White
## BALANCE

Rose Locust

Chamisa

Giant Four O'Clock

Hot Pink Penstemon

Shades of Green and Silver, Pink and Yellow
## CONTRAST

Locust

Penstemon          Giant Four O'Clock          Chamisa

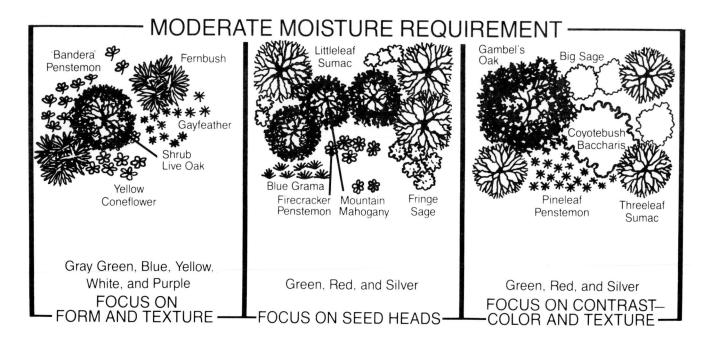

## MODERATE MOISTURE REQUIREMENT

'Bandera' Penstemon
Fernbush
Gayfeather
Shrub Live Oak
Yellow Coneflower

Gray Green, Blue, Yellow, White, and Purple
**FOCUS ON FORM AND TEXTURE**

Littleleaf Sumac
Blue Grama
Firecracker Penstemon
Mountain Mahogany
Fringe Sage

Green, Red, and Silver
**FOCUS ON SEED HEADS**

Gambel's Oak
Big Sage
Coyotebush Baccharis
Pineleaf Penstemon
Threeleaf Sumac

Green, Red, and Silver
**FOCUS ON CONTRAST— COLOR AND TEXTURE**

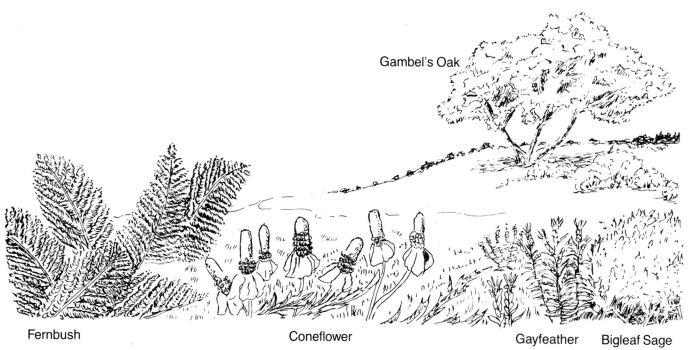

Gambel's Oak

Fernbush          Coneflower          Gayfeather     Bigleaf Sage

# MODERATE TO AMPLE MOISTURE REQUIREMENT

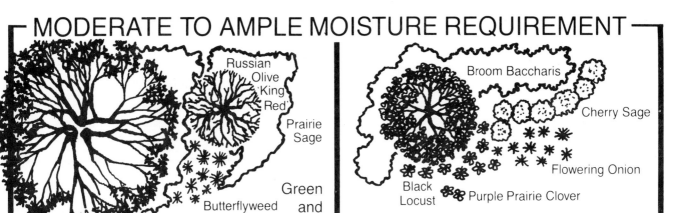

Russian Olive 'King Red'

Prairie Sage

Green and Silver, Red and Yellow

Butterflyweed

Woodbine as Ground Cover

Cottonwood

**BOLD COLOR CONTRAST**

Broom Baccharis

Cherry Sage

Flowering Onion

Black Locust

Purple Prairie Clover

Shades of Green, Pink, and White

**SOFT COLOR CONTRAST**

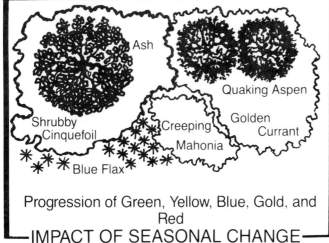

Ash

Quaking Aspen

Shrubby Cinquefoil

Creeping Mahonia

Golden Currant

Blue Flax

Progression of Green, Yellow, Blue, Gold, and Red

**IMPACT OF SEASONAL CHANGE**

Desert Olive

Blanketflower

Buffalo Grass Lawn

Arizona Sycamore (Multiple Trunk)

Western Virgins-bower on Wire & Post Fencing

Green, Red, Yellow, and White

**DEFINITION OF SPACE**

Aspen

Multi-trunk Cottonwood

Ash

Shrubby Cinquefoil    Blue Flax    Creeping Mahonia    Golden Currant    Blanketflower

# THREE-STEP SITE DEVELOPMENT

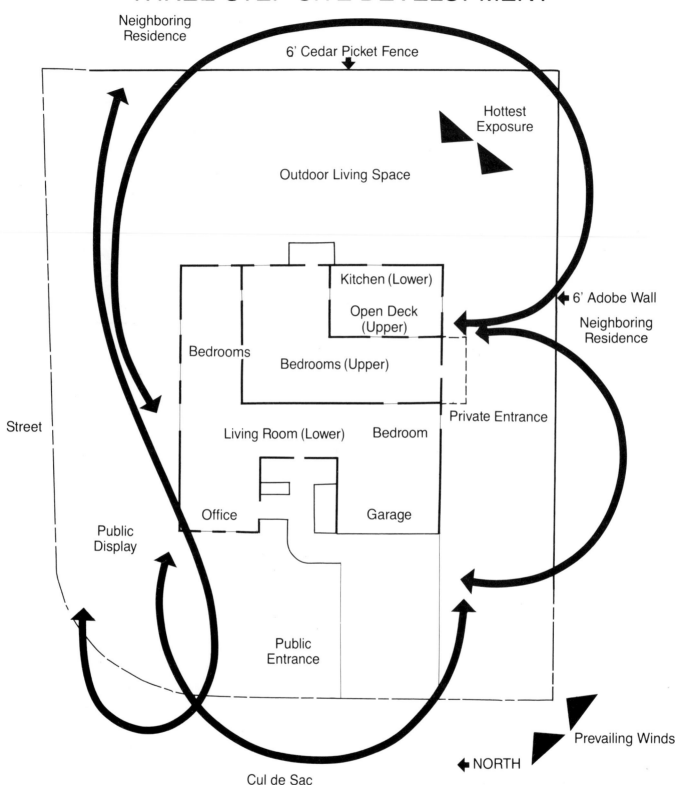

Neighboring
Residence

6' Cedar Picket Fence

Hottest
Exposure

Outdoor Living Space

6' Adobe Wall

Neighboring
Residence

Kitchen (Lower)

Open Deck
(Upper)

Bedrooms

Bedrooms (Upper)

Private Entrance

Street

Living Room (Lower)      Bedroom

Public
Display

Office      Garage

Public
Entrance

Prevailing Winds

NORTH

Cul de Sac

## STEP 1. SITE ANALYSIS:

*SITE LIMITATIONS.* The imposing adobe is stuccoed an earth brown color; wood trim is natural cedar. The corner lot exposes the entire site to public view. Partially two-story, the upper deck looks into neighbor-ing yards as well as out over the bosque and bluffs. Vehicles on the site include three cars, a motorcycle, a vintage pickup truck, and five bicycles. In addition to living space, the structure also houses a computer pro-gram design and consulting business. Although busi-ness services are usually handled by telephone and at

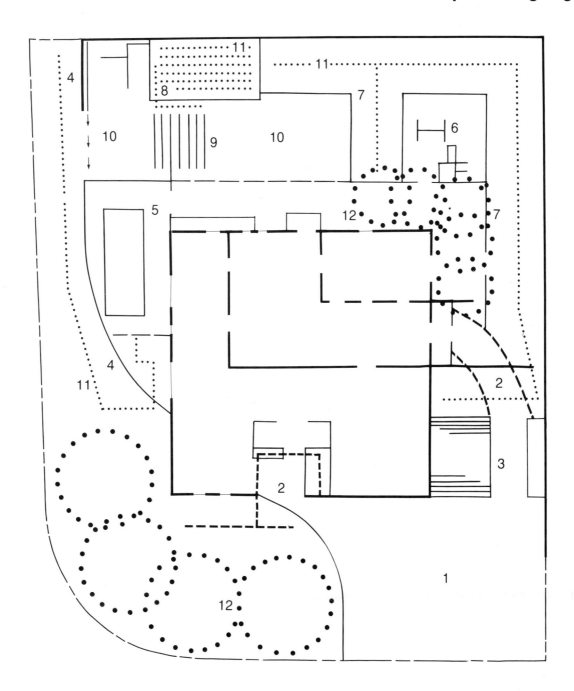

the clients' offices, limited parking for visitors is a consideration. The site is flat, and soil is clay loam over sandy subsoil. One of the last lots to be developed in a relatively new subdivision, it is surrounded by manicured landscapes that are bluegrass, gravel, or a composite of the two.

*HUMAN CONSIDERATIONS.* The site serves an extended family of seven. The adults are in their mid thirties, career and family oriented, and self-employed. Swimming, bicycling, and gardening are preferred leisure activities. The children include two teenagers and preschool-age twins. A college student is employed as a live-in family helper. A rapidly expanding business limits leisure time. The landscape must be low maintenance yet appear cultivated.

## STEP 2. PAVING, STRUCTURAL ADDITIONS, AND IRRIGATION SYSTEM:

*1.* The concrete driveway is extended to accommodate family vehicles, provide off-street parking, and eliminate a difficult-to-maintain planting area.

*2.* Poured concrete walkways with brick-in-concrete edging extend existing paving. The brick accents soften the hard line of the concrete.

*3.* A lath-covered carport of rough cedar extends garage space and encloses the private entrance. A combination tool and bicycle cabinet further extends storage space.

4.   An adobe wall, 6' high and stuccoed to match the house, screens the outdoor living space from the street and encloses the lap pool. A sliding cedar gate completes the enclosure.

5.   The lap pool, isolated from the mainstream of outdoor activity, provides a quiet oasis and recreation for the family and is completely enclosed to protect the young twins. The pool is edged with sealed clay tiles that complement the brick border on the extended concrete walkways and patio.

6.   The play area, a 20' × 20' sand bed as a soft base for swings, slide, and a post and platform construction, is bordered with 8" × 8" cedar beams, sanded smooth and oiled to prevent splintering. The area is visible from the house, patio, and deck without dominating the outdoor living space.

7.   Large planters are defined with 8" × 8" rough cedar beams.

8.   A small, heavily mulched and drip-irrigated vegetable garden provides fresh produce with a minimum of work. The garden is also bordered by 8" × 8" rough cedar beams, with an adjacent compost bin and screen for trash cans.

9.   A rough cedar-post-and-beam grape arbor partially screens the patio from the gate/parking lot and emphasizes the sheltered feeling of the private area.

10.   Decomposed granite porous paving allows access to the rear door and extends the patio. The neutral tan color complements the adobe and wood architecture.

11.   Drip lines, individually set on an automatic timer, irrigate major plantings without water waste due to evaporation and forgetfulness.

12.   Sprinkler areas, individually set on an automatic timer and using low angle droplet (rather than mist) spray heads, reduce water use and maintenance chores. Although the irrigation systems will be used less than half as much as they would on a conventional landscape, the savings in water and time will compensate for the initial cost.

## STEP 3. PLANNING THE LANDSCAPE:

*SITE MODIFICATIONS.* Although the grade was not altered, the varied height and density of the plantings provide several distinct outdoor "rooms." No soil amendments were used except in the play area, where the surface clay was removed and replaced with sand. The lawn and meadow areas were tilled, irrigated to encourage weed seeds to germinate, sprayed with herbicide to kill noxious perennial bindweed, and retilled before grading and seeding.

The lawn was seeded at a rate of 2 pounds per 1,000 square feet, the meadow at 1 pound per 1,000 square feet. The seed was scratch-raked into the surface to increase soil contact, and the areas were rolled with a half full roller. Once the meadow stand was established, wild-flower transplants were placed to fill in open spaces. Because of the growth habits of the grasses and flowers, the plants will rapidly knit together and reduce weed problems. During the first growing season, periodic weeding will be necessary. (Weed control = gas money for the family teenagers.)

*MOOD CHANGES.* The emphasis in the private area is on enclosure. The evergreen screening materials were chosen for their rapid growth. Reduced watering as the desired height is reached will limit the ultimate height so that distant views will be framed and immediate privacy maintained. The desert willow encloses the play area without reducing visibility and adds summer flower color. Four O'Clocks counterbalance the willow flowers and also attract hummingbirds to the patio area. Russian Olives act as color foil, spring flowers perfume the private entrance, and red fruit adds color in autumn. In the pool area, evergreens visually create a cool spot, while the mahonia adds color in season.

The emphasis in the public area is on color. Mixed wild flowers and flowering trees and shrubs provide a succession of brilliant color displays. Fall foliage, evergreens, and dormant tree silhouettes extend the visual impact throughout the year. Densely planted shrub and tree borders and paving tame the meadow/lawn. The low growth habit of the plants used also keeps the meadow neat with only two mowings, in late June and November.

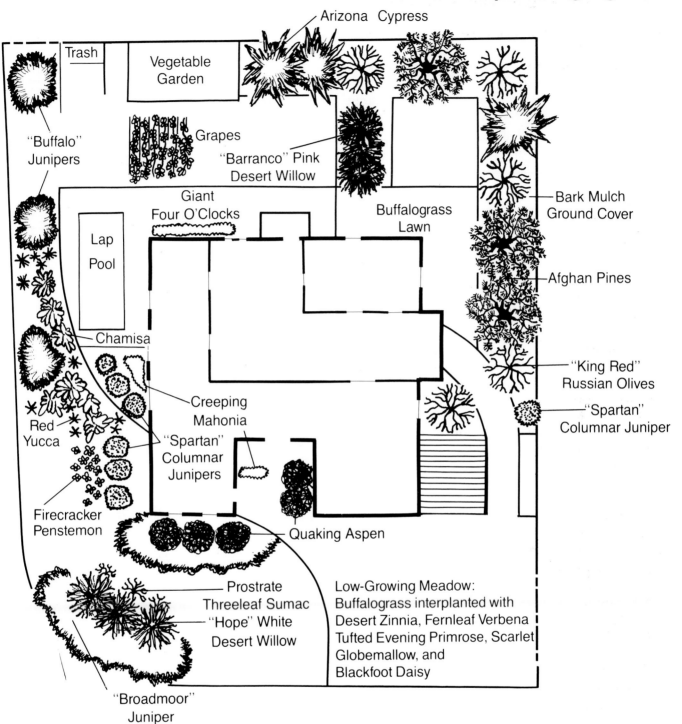

Arizona Cypress

Trash

Vegetable Garden

"Buffalo" Junipers

Grapes

"Barranco" Pink Desert Willow

Giant Four O'Clocks

Buffalograss Lawn

Bark Mulch Ground Cover

Lap Pool

Afghan Pines

Chamisa

Creeping Mahonia

"King Red" Russian Olives

"Spartan" Columnar Juniper

Red Yucca

"Spartan" Columnar Junipers

Firecracker Penstemon

Quaking Aspen

Prostrate Threeleaf Sumac

"Hope" White Desert Willow

Low-Growing Meadow: Buffalograss interplanted with Desert Zinnia, Fernleaf Verbena Tufted Evening Primrose, Scarlet Globemallow, and Blackfoot Daisy

"Broadmoor" Juniper

CARRICO
SOUTHWESTERN
WOOD DESIGNS

# LANDSCAPING SMALL SPACES

*Simplicity is paramount. Small spaces clutter easily.*

*Select plant material that matures to a size proportionate to the space available. The small stature of many native trees is a distinct advantage here.*

*Avoid plants that self-sow readily. A weed is often a good plant in the wrong place.*

*Expand the actual area by borrowing from the surrounding landscape. Whether foothills, open desert, or cultivated landscape borders an intimate garden spot, that expanse of space can be drawn into the smaller area by using dense plantings to frame views, airy plantings to filter views, and well-defined lines to direct the eye.*

*Dense vertical screens using little horizontal space are created by vines on a structural support (fencing or trellises). When neighborhood eyesores or heavy traffic preclude the use of "borrowed" space, vines can provide privacy and an attractive backdrop using a minimum of the available space. Draping foliage softens the hard lines of walls and fences.*

*Aside from considerations of scale, the east-facing exposure of this site requires selection of plant material that will thrive in a shady microclimate. The owners of this wood shop desire a landscape that demands little care (watering can be done with soaker hoses, lit-tle or no pruning will be needed as plants mature), yet acts as an advertisement for their quality craftsmanship. Many of the plants used here are native to higher elevations, where they are found growing as the semi-shaded understory of tall trees. There is a balance of deciduous and evergreen. Seasonal color changes create visual impact. Located near downtown Albuquerque, screen-covered windows are a security measure. The plant material frames the business sign, the focal point of this landscape. The landscape acts as a 400-square-foot billboard facing a major artery in the business district, changing seasonally and renewing its impact with no expense to the advertiser.*

*By tying a small garden into the larger landscape (see next page)—in this case an eighteen-hole golf course, a functional living area, with a feeling of both privacy and spaciousness, is created. The Desert Willows provide light shade from afternoon sun and the illusion of enclosure without creating a total visual barrier. The Chamisa outside the wall makes the transition from garden to golf course. The balance of the plantings creates seasonal interest yet maintains controlled, compact forms. Crusher fines are a paved surface easy to walk on but refined in texture, in keeping with the casual but controlled feel of this garden.*

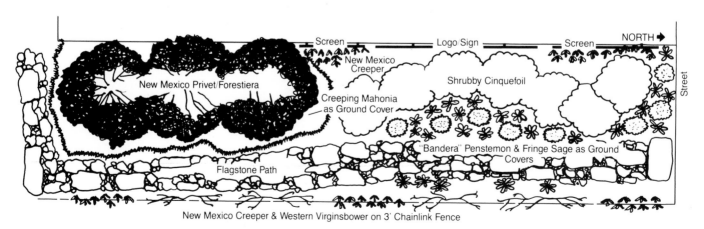

Screen
Logo/Sign
Screen
NORTH ➡
New Mexico Creeper
New Mexico Privet/Forestiera
Shrubby Cinquefoil
Creeping Mahonia as Ground Cover
"Bandera" Penstemon & Fringe Sage as Ground Covers
Flagstone Path
Street

New Mexico Creeper & Western Virginsbower on 3' Chainlink Fence

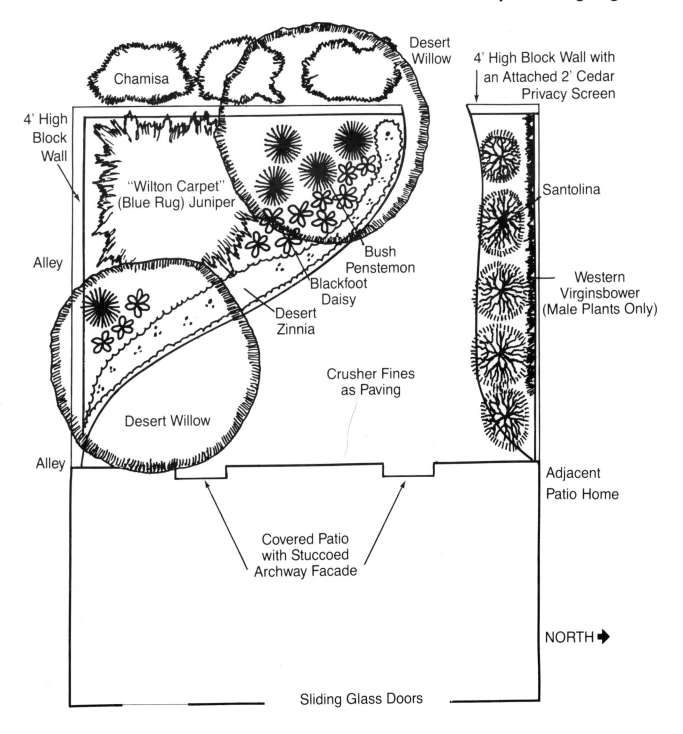

Desert
Willow

4' High Block Wall with
an Attached 2' Cedar
Privacy Screen

Chamisa

4' High
Block
Wall

"Wilton Carpet"
(Blue Rug) Juniper

Santolina

Alley

Bush
Penstemon

Blackfoot
Daisy

Western
Virginsbower
(Male Plants Only)

Desert
Zinnia

Crusher Fines
as Paving

Desert Willow

Alley

Adjacent
Patio Home

Covered Patio
with Stuccoed
Archway Facade

NORTH ➡

Sliding Glass Doors

PATIO HOME

# MISSION-STYLE TOWNHOUSE

## SITE ANALYSIS:

*SITE LIMITATIONS.* Space is at a premium in and around this Mission-style townhouse. The building and front wall are stuccoed light sand and have red tile trim. The wall enclosing the backyard and the side retaining wall are raw cinder block. The soil is decomposed granite underlain in places with caliche. The present grade was established to facilitate runoff during heavy rains and cannot be altered. (Altering established drainage is illegal in some communities.) Rain, draining off the roof through the canales, washes soil away from the house, across the sidewalk, and over the retaining wall. The sunken area along the adjacent townhouse acts as a runoff channel. In the front yard, the northwest corner slopes 4 feet in 3 feet. Water draining out of the side yard runs along the base of the slope and into the street.

*HUMAN CONSIDERATIONS.* This site serves a retired couple who enjoy both gardening and traveling. As gardeners, they want space for intensive vegetable and fruit growing. Avid bird watchers, they favor plantings that will attract wildlife. As travelers, they require a landscape that can survive unattended at least a month at a time from September to May and that will pose no heavy maintenance problems. Still, they would like color and fragrance throughout the year.

## LANDSCAPE SOLUTIONS:

The runoff problem is top priority. The railroad-tie-bordered planter and raised beds channel runoff from the patio and along the stepping-stone pathway. The stones break up the flow and control erosion in the back yard.

The roof runoff into the side yard can be controlled by installing an updated version of the traditional Mexican watering jug. Using 14" × 18" × 24" clay fireplace flue liners set into the soil under the canales, 5"-diameter ABS drainpipe with elbows on each end opening in the opposite directions, and cement and gravel, a functional gutter system that complements the architecture can be constructed.

Remove the top blocks in the retaining wall opposite the flue liners and canales. Using water pressure to displace the soil, run the 5" pipe under the sidewalk to the flue liner. Glue the elbows in place and cement in the base of the flue liner, leaving the elbow open. Place hardware cloth (1/8" mesh screen) over the elbow and put a thin layer (3 or 4") of coarse gravel in the bottom of the flue tile. Replace the double blocks removed from the wall with single blocks and a cement cap, or chisel out an opening in the blocks removed and reset them. Plantings in the runoff channel will break up the current and will benefit from the "free water." The slope in the front yard can be retained with sandstone boulders that complement the structure and can be interplanted with flowering perennials.

The raised beds in the backyard provide the space for dwarf fruit trees, grapes, and compact varieties of vegetables without interfering with the drainage pattern. Since intensive gardening requires both rich soil and ample moisture in this climate, compost, drip irrigation, and mulches compensate for close planting and the limited root system of dwarf trees. Desert Willow, Penstemon, Evening Primrose, tall Juniper, Desert Olive, Currant, and Saltbush are inviting bird forage.

Flowering trees, shrubs, and perennial wild flowers provide seasonal bursts of color, while evergreen Juniper, Mountain Mahogany, Santolina, Cliffrose, and Saltbush provide dormant season interest. The Primrose, Cliffrose, Currant, Juniper, Sage, and Blackfoot Daisy provide the fragrance.

Once established, the native portion of the landscape can survive extended periods of drought. Periodic deep watering during the summer will promote flowering. Light pruning, shaping the trees and shrubs, and dead-heading the wild flowers is the only other maintenance required.

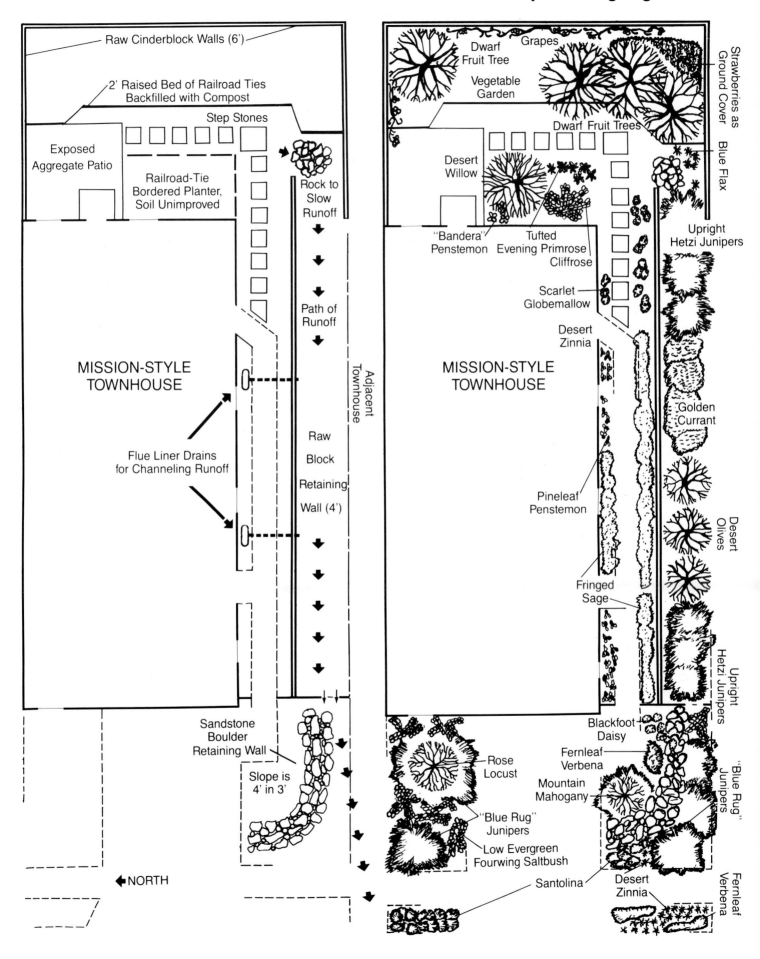

Raw Cinderblock Walls (6')

2' Raised Bed of Railroad Ties
Backfilled with Compost

Step Stones

Exposed
Aggregate Patio

Railroad-Tie
Bordered Planter,
Soil Unimproved

Rock to
Slow
Runoff

Path of
Runoff

MISSION-STYLE
TOWNHOUSE

Adjacent
Townhouse

Raw
Block
Retaining
Wall (4')

Flue Liner Drains
for Channeling Runoff

Sandstone
Boulder
Retaining Wall

Slope is
4' in 3'

◀NORTH

Dwarf
Fruit Tree

Grapes

Vegetable
Garden

Strawberries as
Ground Cover

Dwarf Fruit Trees

Blue Flax

Desert
Willow

"Bandera"
Penstemon

Tufted
Evening Primrose
Cliffrose

Upright
Hetzi Junipers

Scarlet
Globemallow

Desert
Zinnia

Golden
Currant

MISSION-STYLE
TOWNHOUSE

Pineleaf
Penstemon

Desert
Olives

Fringed
Sage

Upright Hetzi Junipers

Blackfoot
Daisy

Rose
Locust

Fernleaf
Verbena

Mountain
Mahogany

"Blue Rug"
Junipers

"Blue Rug"
Junipers

Low Evergreen
Fourwing Saltbush

Santolina

Desert
Zinnia

Fernleaf
Verbena

# 1920s BUNGALOW

## SITE ANALYSIS:

*SITE LIMITATIONS.* The 1920s bungalow is stuccoed a cream color with dark green trim and features many long, narrow, wood-framed windows. It is located in an old neighborhood that is gradually undergoing a revival. North and west neighboring homes are two-story buildings in need of renovation. The soil on site is sandy, grade is level. Ailanthus seedlings have colonized the backyard. The front yard is randomly planted with declining exotic shrubs and a well-shaped specimen apricot tree. A 2' × 4' field-stone wall runs the length of the front yard along the sidewalk. Neighboring north and west properties are marked with sagging vine-covered fences and decaying stone walls. The driveway is narrow and the adjacent house abuts the property line. A small efficiency apartment on the northeast corner will be used as a workshop/guest house.

*HUMAN CONSIDERATIONS.* The new owner is an energy conservation specialist for a state university. A transplant from the Midwest, she prefers a "green" landscape, but would rather devote time and water to food gardening, and maintain the balance of the landscape as naturalized plantings. The entire landscape will be irrigated with various types of drip equipment, a personal research project that will eventually determine irrigation renovations on campus.

## LANDSCAPE SOLUTIONS:

Of the existing plantings only the apricot was worth salvaging. The once ornamental exotics could be re-

moved by simply digging them out, but the Ailanthus were cut off at ground level, drilled, and packed with copper sulfate to kill off the aggressive root systems.

The north and west property lines are screened with tall, fast-growing evergreens. Most of the backyard is given over to vegetable garden and orchard. Mostly evergreen Mountain Mahogany screens the patio from the apartment/guesthouse. A small mowed blue grama lawn extends patio space. The crushed stone driveway and paths unite the various garden areas. A dismantled flagstone patio extension provided the stone for the east patio and north paths.

Although the landscape is mostly native and relatively drought tolerant, plantings are grouped by moisture demand to facilitate drip system evaluations. Plant groupings are also "generic" in nature; the plants are mostly native in origin but their informal placement and lush growth habits complement the house and create cool green microclimates that are physically and aesthetically comfortable. The layouts of garden/orchard and front tree, shrub, and flower borders extend to meet each other. The grama/clover area, Baccharis hedge, and path tie the area together and eliminate the side yard "wasteland," too isolated to use effectively and too large to leave unlandscaped.

The driveway is bordered with vines to screen the east windows and entrances. A small east patio expands the living space of both study and dining room without significantly reducing the already narrow driveway. The open construction of upright timbers complements the bungalow's long narrow windows and gives the 100-square-foot area the illusion of spaciousness.

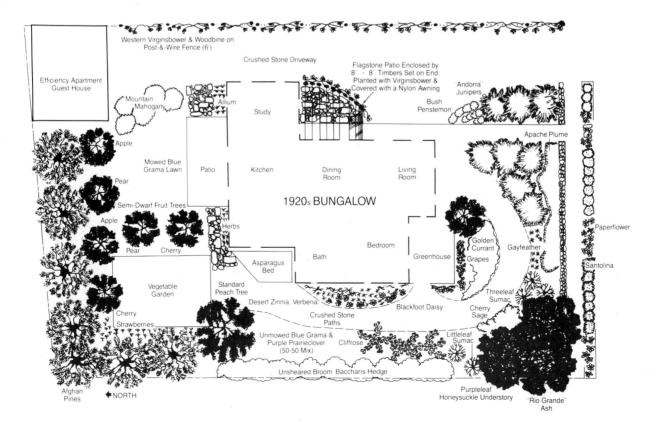

# LANDSCAPING LARGE SPACES

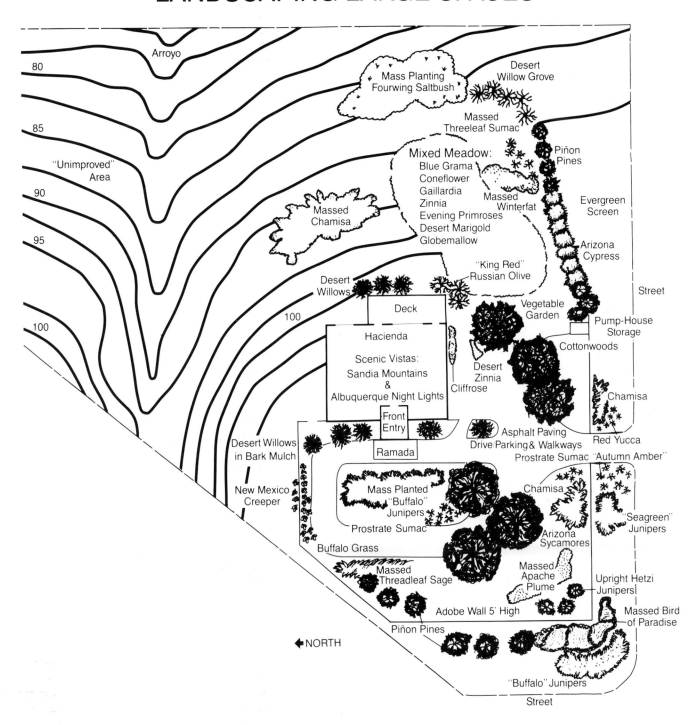

**LARGE SPACES: ZONING/MASS PLANTING.** *This home is located on the West Mesa above Albuquerque. The soil is mostly sandy with a few large clay pockets underlaid with volcanic rock, providing moderate to rapid drainage. Except for the walled entry and driveway which are fairly level, the land slopes eastward one vertical foot for every ten horizontal feet. The expansive hacienda-style adobe is owned by a real-estate developer and an artist, and serves as office and studio space for the couple. The structure and landscape ac-* *commodate frequent business and social gatherings.*

*The typical use areas are modified somewhat on this site. The walled entry and driveway enclose what is usually a public area, providing sheltered access and off-street parking for guests. The southwest-facing drive is shaded by Cottonwoods and Arizona Sycamores, used both to temper the hot exposure and to provide large-scale plant material in keeping with the proportions of the site.*

# GRADING FOR WATER EFFICIENCY

## LEGEND AND KEY

| Plant Name | Size | Quantity | Use |
|---|---|---|---|
| Apache Plume | 3 Gal. | 5 | Flowers & Seed Heads, Mostly Evergreen |
| "Bandera" Penstemon | 1 Gal. | 7 | Blue Flowers, Crisp Green Foliage as Ground Cover |
| Blackfoot Daisy | 1 Gal. | 9 | Form, Flower, & Adaptability to Well-Drained Site |
| Blue Flax | 1 Gal. | 6 | Blue Flowers & Fine-Textured Foliage |
| "Blue Rug" Juniper | 5 Gal. | 5 | Evergreen/Blue Green Color & Low Growth Habit |
| Butterfly Weed | 1 Gal. | 9 | Red Orange Flowers & Adaptability to "Water Trap" Site |
| Dalea | 3 Gal. | 3 | Broomy Texture, Flower Color & Fragrance |
| Fringe Sage | 1 Gal. | 9 | Color Foil—Ground Cover |
| "Hope" Desert Willow | 3 Gal. | 3 | Light Shade, White Flower, Textural Contrast, & Dormant Silhouette |
| "King Red" Russian Olive | 15 Gal. | 1 | Shade, Red Fruit, Foliage Contrast |
| "Tam" Juniper | 5 Gal. | 3 | Evergreen, Extension of Neighboring Landscape Adding Continuity |
| Threeleaf Sumac | 3 Gal. | 3 | Red Fall Color |

---

Shredded bark mulch applied at a 6" depth over approximately 1,250 square feet: 18–20 cubic yards.

Crusher fines as paving applied at a 6" depth over approximately 700 square feet: 12 cubic yards.

Landscape timber or railroad-tie retaining wall and curb uprights set 12" or more into ground and lined with black poly film to retain soil:

| | |
|---|---|
| 1–6' section (curb) | 12–3' sections |
| 30–4' sections | 12–2' sections |

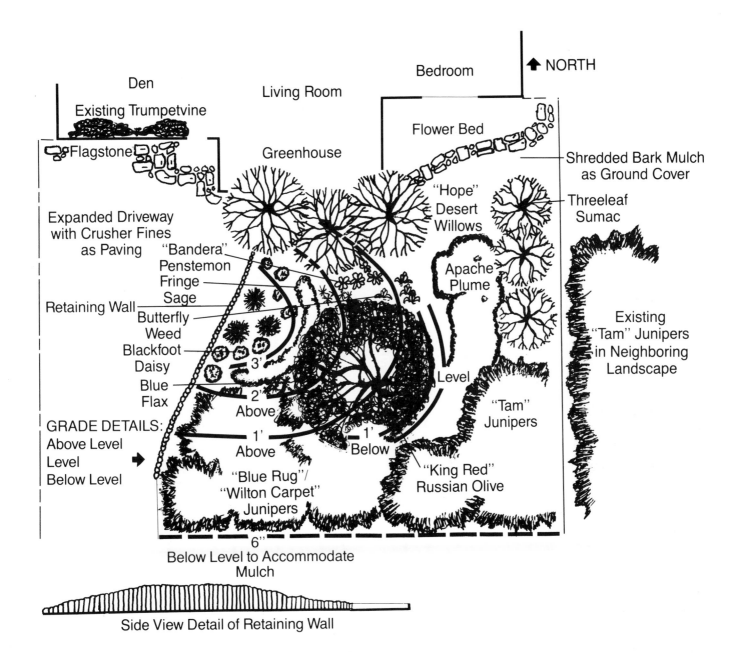

Den

Existing Trumpetvine

Living Room

Bedroom

↑ NORTH

Flagstone

Flower Bed

Greenhouse

Shredded Bark Mulch
as Ground Cover

Expanded Driveway
with Crusher Fines
as Paving

"Hope"
Desert
Willows

Threeleaf
Sumac

"Bandera"
Penstemon
Fringe
Sage

Apache
Plume

Retaining Wall

Butterfly
Weed

Existing
"Tam" Junipers
in Neighboring
Landscape

Blackfoot
Daisy

Blue
Flax

3'

Level

GRADE DETAILS:
Above Level
Level
Below Level

2'
Above

1'
Above

1'
Below

"Tam"
Junipers

"Blue Rug"/
"Wilton Carpet"
Junipers

"King Red"
Russian Olive

6'

Below Level to Accommodate
Mulch

Side View Detail of Retaining Wall

GRADING FOR EFFICIENT WATER USE. *This remodeled residence is surrounded by anonymous bluegrass or bermudagrass lawns interrupted by an occasional "Southwestern" rockscape. The present owners converted the single-car garage into a den-workroom and added a solar greenhouse to the living room. The driveway was expanded to provide off-street parking for their two small cars. The original bermudagrass lawn, weakened by lack of water and foot traffic during remodeling, was killed off with glyphosate, a potent systemic herbicide that leaves no residue in the soil. The lawn was watered several times to stimulate growth, then sprayed while it was actively growing to maximize the uptake of the herbicide. To add interest and partially screen the parking area, a retaining wall was built. A berm was constructed by pushing soil up toward the retaining wall as per the grading detail. Soil along the sidewalk was also removed to allow for the heavy bark mulch. The new grade utilizes runoff to supplement watering of the larger trees. The Desert Willows will provide light summer shade for the greenhouse without reducing solar absorption in the winter. The white variety of Desert Willow, "Hope," was used as a color foil in the predominantly red orange and blue color scheme. The berm was planted with a compatible combination of the most drought-tolerant plants at the top and those that require more moisture at the base.*

# SEASONAL COLOR FOR LANDSCAPE INTEREST

Use this chart to plan progressive color interest in your landscape. While flowers are the primary source of color, foliage and fruit often contribute to ornamental value. Combining color and texture values gives greater interest and depth to a design.

| Plant Name | Seasonal Interest (Mar → Feb) |
|---|---|
| **TREES** | |
| 3 **Desert Olive** — *Forestiera neomexicana* | Cream Flowers (Mar–Apr); Blue Black Fruit (Jul–Aug); Yellow Gold Foliage (Sep–Oct) |
| 2 **\*Desert Willow** — *Chilopsis linearis* | White, Pink, or Purple Flowers (May–Jul); Dormant Silhouette (Oct–Nov) |
| 5 **Gambel's Oak** — *Quercus gambelii* | Russet to Red Foliage (Oct–Nov) |
| 4 **"King Red" Russian Olive** — *Elaeagnus angustifolia* "King Red" | Gray Green Foliage—Cream Flowers (Apr–May); Russet to Red Fruit (Sep–Nov); Dormant Silhouette (Nov–Dec) |
| 3 **\*Rose Locust** — *Robinia neomexicana* | Pendulous Rose Pink Flower Clusters (Jun–Jul) |
| 4 **Shrub Live Oak** — *Quercus turbinella* | Evergreen (Mar–Aug); Red Bark on New Growth (Dec–Jan) |
| 3 **Tamarisk** — *Tamarix pentandra* | Feathery Pink Flowers (Apr–May and Aug–Sep); Yellow-Gold Foliage (Oct–Nov) |
| **SHRUBS** | |
| 2 **\*Apache Plume** — *Fallugia paradoxa* | Semi-Evergreen; White Flowers Followed by Pink Plumes Most Prolific May & September; Reddish Cast to Foliage (Dec–Jan) |
| 2 **Bigleaf Sage** — *Artemisia tridentata* | Ever-Gray to Ever-Green Foliage (all year) |
| 2 **Bird of Paradise** — *Caesalpinia gilliesii* | Large Yellow Flowers with Red Stamens (May–Jul) |
| 3 **Broom Baccharis** — *Baccharis emoryi* | Bright Green Foliage/Evergreen; White Seed Pappus/Female Plants Only (Sep–Oct); Bronze Winter Color (Dec–Jan) |
| 1 **Broom Dalea** — *Dalea scoparia* | Bright Blue Green Foliage; Light Bloom (Jun); Deep Blue Flowers (Aug) |
| 2 **Chamisa** — *Chrysothamnus nauseosus* | Evergreen; Yellow Gold Flowers (Sep–Oct); Downy White Twig (Dec–Jan) |
| 2 **Cliffrose** — *Cowania neomexicana* | Evergreen Foliage; Fragrant Creamy White Flowers; Intermittent Yellow Flowers Through Summer; Evergreen Foliage (Oct–Nov) |
| 1 **Creosote Bush** — *Larrea tridentata* | Finely Cut Evergreen Foliage; Profuse White Flower Clusters; Finely Cut Evergreen Foliage (Nov–Dec) |
| 3 **Fernbush** — *Chamaebatiaria millefolium* | Semi-Evergreen Foliage; Large Winged Seed Clusters, Green, Curing to Tan Opalescent Blush on Foliage on Some Varieties (Sep–Nov) |
| 1 **Fourwing Saltbush** — *Atriplex canescens* | Yellow Spicy Flowers; Brilliant Scarlet Foliage (Oct–Nov) |
| 3 **Golden Currant** — *Ribes aureum* | Yellow White Flowers (Mar–Apr); Red Fruit (Jun–Jul); Scarlet to Burgundy Leaf Color (Oct–Nov) |
| 2 **Littleleaf Sumac** — *Rhus microphylla* | Evergreen; Creamy White Flowers (May–Jun); Red Fruit (Jul); Scarlet to Burgundy Leaf Color (Oct) |
| 1 **Soaptree Yucca** — *Yucca elata* | Yellow Flowers (Apr); Evergreen with Dramatic Form & Textural Interest (all year) |
| 5 **Threeleaf Sumac** — *Rhus trilobata* | Red Fruit (Aug); Scarlet to Burgundy Leaf Color (Oct–Nov) |
| 1 **Winterfat** — *Ceratoides lanata* | Persistent Wooly White Foliage (Mar–Apr); White Seed Plumes are Long Lasting (Sep–Nov) |

# GROUND COVERS

| # | Common Name | Scientific Name | Description |
|---|---|---|---|
| 3 | "Bandera" Penstemon | *Penstemon strictus* | Shades of Blue |
| 2 | *Blackfoot Daisy | *Melampodium leucanthum* | White Daisies with Yellow Centers, Most Profuse After Summer Rains |
| 3 | *Blanketflower | *Gaillardia species* | Showy Red, Yellow & Bicolor Daisy-like Flowers with Dark Red Centers |
| 5 | *Blue Flax | *Linum lewisii* | Profuse Blue Flowers |
| 1 | *Bush Morningglory | *Ipomoea leptophylla* | Large Magenta Trumpet-Shaped Flowers |
| 3 | Coneflower | *Ratibida columnaris* | Yellow or Mahogany Ray Petals Ring Brown Conical Center |
| 2 | Coral Penstemon | *Penstemon superbus* | Coral |
| 2 | Coyotebush (Dwarf) | *Baccharis pilularis* | Dense Bright Evergreen Foliage / Dense, Bright Evergreen Foliage |
| 4 | Creeping Mahonia | *Berberis repens* | Yellow Flower Clusters / Evergreen Foliage / Evergreen—Red to Plum Winter Color |
| 1 | *Desert Marigold | *Baileya multiradiata* | Large Yellow Gold Flowers with Wooly White Foliage |
| 1 | Desert Zinnia | *Zinnia grandiflora* | Yellow Gold Flowers Fade to Papery Everlastings |
| 3 | *Fern Verbena | *Verbena bipinnatifida* | Umbels of Lavender-Purple Flowers / Ferny Foliage |
| 3 | Firecracker Penstemon | *Penstemon eatonii* | Scarlet |
| 2 | Fringed Sage | *Artemisia frigida* | Matlike Evergreen Silver Foliage / Evergreen Matlike Foliage |
| 2 | Gayfeather | *Liatris punctata* | Nodding Rayless Flowers / Magenta Spikes Then Purplish Plumes |
| 3 | *Giant Four O'Clock | *Mirabilis multiflora* | Tubular Magenta Flowers All Summer, Given Adequate Moisture |
| 2 | Hot Pink Penstemon | *Penstemon pseudospectabilis* | Magenta |
| 2 | Lavender Cotton | *Santolina chamaecyparissus* | Ever-Gray to Ever-Green Foliage / Ever-Gray to Ever-Green Foliage |
| 2 | *Paperflower | *Psilostrophe tagetina* | A Profusion of Yellow Papery Flowers, If Dried Flowers Are Removed Periodically |
| 1 | *Pink Bush Penstemon | *Penstemon ambiguus* | Loose Flower Spikes in Shades of Pink—Loves Heat |
| 3 | Pink Prairieclover | *Petalostemon purpureum* | Rose Pink "Cones" |
| 2 | Purple Aster | *Machaeranthera bigelovii* | Lavender Daisies |
| 2 | *Sand Verbena | *Tripterocalyx (Abronia) species* | Hot Pink Flowers with Cream to Pink Seed Clusters |
| 2 | Scarlet Globemallow | *Sphaeralcea coccinea* | Coral Red Flowers on Semi-Procumbent Stems |
| 2 | Silver Groundsel | *Senecio longilobus* | Yellow Daisies Especially Profuse After Late Summer Rains |
| 4 | Western Virginsbower | *Clematis ligusticifolia* | White Flower Clusters / Feathery Seed Heads/Female |
| 2 | *White Evening Primrose | *Oenothera caespitosa* | Large White Flowers Fade to Salmon Pink in Heat Given Summer Water |
| 4 | Woodbine or Creeper | *Parthenocissus inserta* | Scarlet Fall Color |

Additional foliage notes:
Foliage Rosettes Blue, Flush Red in Frost — Coral

*To aid in planning compatible plantings, moisture requirements are keyed on a scale of 1 to 5, 1 being most drought tolerant and 5 requiring consistent supplemental watering when grown on sites warmer, drier, at lower elevations or watertables, or in different soil types than the natural habitat (see origin section of Profiles).*

*\* Indicates plants that will flower continuously and more profusely over a given period if not subjected to extreme moisture stress.*

# 3 🐝 MEADOW MALAISE

The concept of a "mixed wild-flower meadow" is one of the most confused in native-plant landscaping. Mother Nature has had ten thousand years and billions of seeds at her disposal to develop her colorful, seasonal wild-flower displays. Naive gardeners, lacking those resources but full of good intentions, spend $40 for a "meadow-in-a-tin" and are soon disenchanted with this approach to a low-maintenance ground cover. Presently, there are more questions than answers with regard to mixed meadows. Still, there are some generalizations that can be made.

Whether approached as a low-maintenance lawn substitute or an ongoing nature study, the meadow is a place of change. A meadow is not a lawn substitute in any sense other than that it occupies as much space as a lawn does. In fact, a meadow is the antithesis of a lawn. A lawn is a monoculture: seeds are broadcast, they germinate relatively quickly and uniformly, and plants of similar appearance knit together in a homogeneous sod carpet. In contrast, the most interesting meadows are those that entertain the observer with their diversity. Meadows offer an interplay of textures and seasonal color that acts as a magnet for hummingbirds and butterflies, quail and doves that are drawn by mature plants dispersing seeds. An understory of newly emerging seedlings provides meadows with continuity in transition.

## THE VARIABLES

To plan and plant a meadow is to create and maintain a balance, producing in a year or two what evolves over a millenium in the wild. Consider the variables.

First, the exposure and grade of the site create microclimates that limit or enhance the variety of plants that will grow well there. When a seed mix is broadcast, natural selection determines what will grow where. The actual percentage of plants that survive compared with the quantity of seeds broadcast may seem quite low, but that cost must be balanced with the alternative of increased man power.

Second, the soil type further determines selection of material. The more self-sustaining an area is to be, the more important it is to select species that prefer the on-site soil type. The larger the area, the less advisable it is to amend the soil, unless salinity or compaction severely limit the options.

Third, seasonal temperature fluctuations influence germination. Artemisias and Penstemons prefer cool

soil for germination. Zinnias, Blackfoot Daisies, and Blue Grama require warmer soils. Many natives will not germinate without a cold, moist stratification period and/or scarification to break down the seed coat. It is not unusual for untreated seeds to lie dormant in the soil for a year or two, taxing the faith of seasoned gardeners and demoralizing the novice. Still, establishing large areas from seed is more economical, as direct seeding produces a population of naturally selected survivors with the advantage of uninterrupted root development.

Fourth, the size of the area influences the planting method. Small areas, less than an acre, can be treated as extended perennial beds, massing transplants or preparing seedbeds based on individual plant needs. Cultivating and broadcasting premixed seeds is more economical for large areas. When the area is so large that seed cost becomes prohibitive, areas can be selected within the site to act as "nursery plots" from which seeds will disperse and eventually cover the site at random. Whether to clear the site or work around existing vegetation is a further consideration. Incorporating desirable existing plant material with the "nursery plot" approach is most cost effective for larger areas, where clearing can contribute to erosion and reduced germination.

And fifth, available moisture is generally the bottom line in our arid climate. Most flowering meadows will require a minimum of fifteen to twenty-five inches of annual precipitation or supplemental watering. Although the plants will survive with less moisture, regular (at least twice a month when temperatures are 90 F or above) deep waterings bring on the drifts of flowers that are the hallmark of a meadow planting.

## MAKING A MIX

A meadow seed mix is best tailor-made for a given site. A few suppliers offer "ready mixes." If the price is right and the mix contains seed suited to your purpose (either a list of contents or a type-location description is given—a mix formulated for "the Southwest" is a greater gamble than one formulated for "sandy soils in the warm desert Southwest" or "rocky soils in cooler mountain foothills"), then by all means save yourself the time involved in preparing the mix. If you are a confirmed do-it-yourselfer, formulating a seed mix is great gardening exercise, especially during seasons too cold or too hot to otherwise flex a green thumb.

Information in the Plant Profiles section of this book will give you the data you need: soil preferences, seeds per pound or per ounce, appearance, habit, etc., to select possible mix components. Seed catalogs will offer other possibilities.

The greater the variety of plants in the mix, the more complex the interplay of variables becomes. Maintenance is increased as competition for moisture and space increases. When low maintenance is a priority, visual impact may rely on masses of a few compatible species of wild flowers and grasses, rather than on a "crazy quilt" of color and texture.

Forty-five to sixty percent of the mix should have a predictable and fairly rapid germination rate to provide immediate soil stabilization. Twenty-five to thirty percent of the mix may be grasses. Select grasses carefully, as many germinate rapidly and are valuable as fast cover but become invasive, choking out the choicer, slower, flowering plants. Blue grama and Indian Ricegrass are two well-behaved meadow grasses. Twenty-five to thirty percent of the mix may be annuals or biennials, especially those that self-sow readily and compete well with grasses. Annuals provide color the first year and bloom throughout the growing season if moisture is available. Forty to sixty percent of the mix may be perennial wild flowers, at least thirty percent of which are predictable and rapid germinators. Perennials are the mainstay of the meadow, providing one or two prolonged periods of heavy bloom every growing season and increasing in mass every year.

A simple formula for determining seed quantities based on the number of plants desired per square foot of the site area is:

$$\frac{cd}{ab}$$

where $a$ = number of seeds per pound

$b$ = percentage of pure live seed (PLS) per pound and/or the germination percentage to be expected under field conditions (including season, soil type, available moisture, and dumb luck)

$c$ = number of plants desired per square foot within the first growing season (as the meadow develops, natural selection will determine plant population)

$d$ = area of the site in square feet

For example, if the site is a sandy, windswept, 30,000-square-foot area that is relatively level, seeding will be done in early September. Sprinkler irrigation is available at a rate of up to one hour per week once the meadow is established. Unlimited water is available for the first growing season. Other allowed maintenance is one selective weeding in late August the first year and an annual mid-December mowing thereafter. The following mix fulfills site requirements, produces interesting seasonal color and textural effects, and appears somewhat subdued owing to the uniform height of the components.

Blue Grama at 2 plants/square foot
Desert Marigold at 2 plants/square foot
Blue Flax at 2 plants/square foot
Gaillardia at 2 plants/square foot
Coneflower at 1 plant/square foot
Gayfeather at 1 plant/square foot

To determine the quantity of Blue Grama seed required·

$a$ = 725,000 seeds per pound

$b$ = thirty percent PLS and forty percent germination (Germination may approach seventy percent, but the late sow date, optimal for wild flowers, may reduce the surviving grama seedlings to the forty percent rate.)

$c$ = 2 plants/square foot

$d$ = 30,000 square feet

Approximately twelve ounces of Blue Grama seeds are required. The procedure is repeated for each of the components: Desert Marigold/8 ounces, Blue Flax/6 ounces, Gaillardia/8 ounces, Coneflower/4 ounces, and Gayfeather/14 ounces. The more harsh the on-site conditions, the more seeds per square foot may be necessary. If Robert's Rules are etched in stone, the meadow's rules are etched in sand.

## PLANTING THE MEADOW

Unfortunately it is one of life's injustices that weed seeds respond to the same growing conditions that the more attractive wild flowers do, only faster—they do indeed "grow like weeds." A well-adapted seed mix and soil preparation are the basis for successful meadow making. Tilling the soil and watering induce the germination of undesirable annuals such as Kochia and Tumbleweeds. Tilling again kills the emerging weed seedlings and eliminates their potential competition once the wild-flower seeds are sown. If noxious perennials such as Bindweed or Bermuda grass are the problem, one or more applications of a nonselective, contact, systemic herbicide (glyphosate) may be necessary. In any case, it is easier and less expensive to limit weed competition *before* planting than to try to control it within a newly seeded meadow. The tilling-watering and herbicide cycles may be repeated as many times as needed or convenient, depending upon the size of the plot, the potential weed problem, and how weed-free a seed bed you desire.

Since the best time for seeding is August through

**SOUTHWESTERN ECOSYSTEMS** suggest approaches to gardening with native plants. The success of native landscapes lies in the suitability of the plant materials to the site and to one another.

The Spruce-Aspen high mountain ecosystem: relatively cool, moist summers and snow-insulated, cold winters. Plants native to this ecosystem generally require irrigation and light shade to survive at low elevations.

High mesa and canyon ecosystem: hot, dry summers; cold, dry winters; and wind, wind, wind. Plants native to this ecosystem include some of the most adaptable survivors.

Riparian habitats: high water tables, seasonal flooding, and potentially high salinity. Many of the plants native to this ecosystem require consistent irrigation during hot, dry seasons.

High desert grasslands: extreme climatic condition, as with mesa/canyon ecosystems and second only to true deserts (**see photo pg. 2**) in heat and drought.

**LANDSCAPE DESIGN** is an ornamental approach to dealing with the harsh realities of climate. These landscapes, all very different in mood, are similar in their climatic adaptability and regional character. This Colorado landscape utilizes masses of Sumac and Sage to contrast needled evergreens in a water-conservative, seasonally focused design that is particularly appropriate in its foothills setting.

The water economy of the Bird of Paradise, cactus, yucca, and Mexican Evening Primrose balances the lavish "Blaze" rose arbor in this inviting hacienda courtyard.

Call it a mini-meadow or an extended perennial bed, the effect is the same: a crazy quilt of color with a relatively low moisture requirement. Combining plants of similar height but varied color and texture yields a casual yet controlled feeling appropriate in this urban setting.

This Arizona landscape combines the elements of sand and stone with the stark forms of Ocotillo, cactus ,and yucca balanced by the airy grace of Palo Verde. The same effect is possible in the high desert using cold, hardy species of cactus and yucca and substituting Desert Willow, Mesquite, or Creosotebush for the Palo Verde.

The contrast of stone and wildflowers is functional as well as visually appealing. The boulders stabilize the soil on the slope, trap moisture, and provide a foothold for the wildflowers that in turn soften the stonework and add seasonal color.

Mountain Mahogany, pruned as a small specimen tree and off-set by Apache Plume and Mexican Evening Primrose, is an effective focal point silhouetted against a stuccoed wall.

1

2

3

4

The most interesting meadows are those that entertain the observer with their diversity (**1**). At Urban Forest Park (**see pg. xi**) a wildflower meadow serves as groundcover and shredded bark is used as paving material for the meandering foot trails (**2**). Meadows offer an interplay of textures and seasonal color that acts as a magnet for birds and butterflies (**3**). A wildflower meadow is the carpet, Aspens and Chamisa are the walls that screen the buildings, providing privacy and serenity at a popular retreat and spa (**4**).

March depending upon the location (high elevation, cold winter sites: August/September or February/March; low elevation, mild winter sites: late August through February), soil preparation may begin anytime after spring winds diminish. Clay soils need to dry longer between tilling-watering cycles to avoid clodding and compacting.

If soil amendments such as compost, peat moss, scoria, or sand are needed to improve the aeration or water-holding capacity of the soil, they should be worked into the native soil thoroughly to avoid layering of soil textures. Pockets of soils of different textures accept water at different rates and result in spotty coverage when the meadow is seeded.

Once the soil is prepared and potential weeds are under control, the surface should be raked smooth or dragged smooth with a tractor on large sites. The seeds can then be broadcast by hand over small plots, with a seeder/spreader on medium-sized areas, or drilled in (¼-inch maximum depth) by tractor on large sites. Broadcast seedbeds should be scratch-raked to increase seed-soil contact. A light mulch will help retain moisture and improve germination. Hydromulch, a wet fiber material blown on after seeding, is helpful on large meadows, especially where slopes create potential erosion problems. Seeds should *not* be mixed with the mulch and blown on in a one-step operation, because as the mulch dries it shrinks away from the soil surface, leaving emerging seedlings high and dry. Binders or tackifiers can be mixed with the seeds and/or the mulch. When watered, these products actually glue the seeds and mulch in place, and because they are vegetable products, they are biodegradable.

The first two months after seeding are the most critical for maintaining adequate soil moisture. In our arid climate, seeding before or during normal rainy seasons can provide much of the necessary moisture. If *no* supplemental water will be available, sowing during periods of natural rainfall is absolutely vital. Rainy seasons also coincide with cooler air and soil temperatures. New seedlings develop deep root systems during cool weather, and dormant seeds receive a cold-moist stratification period that induces germination.

As the meadow becomes established some bare spots may become obvious: low spots where moisture collects, high spots that are drier than the rest, or eroded areas on slopes. Spot seeding with selected species best adapted to the problem areas is one solution. Gaps can also be filled in with container-grown transplants or divisions of established plants. Like any new planting, they will require watering until they are well rooted. If your plant selections for the meadow include species that are not available as seeds (Desert Zinnia is difficult and expensive to clean, White Tufted Evening Primrose and Giant Four O'Clock seeds are rarely available in quantity), container-grown plants can be transplanted into the meadow at seeding time to take advantage of the initial watering necessary to sprout the seeded area.

## MAINTENANCE

Aside from the modest water requirement, maintenance can include the periodic removal of spent and undesirable plants, thinning of aggressive species, and an annual winter mowing (4" to 12" blade height). Jim Lewis, University of New Mexico Continuing Education professor (Gardening Without Work), recommends weeding with pruners rather than a hoe. Repeatedly disturbing the soil surface while you are weeding provides a medium for the germination of still more weed seed. Cutting annuals off at ground level after they complete their growth cycle but before they go to seed immediately improves appearances and reduces potential weed problems. Allowing desirable annuals to mature and reseed, later mowing and leaving the clippings as mulch, completes the maintenance cycle. Mowing can be done as an annual cleanup anytime after the first hard freezes of autumn. Many wild flowers and grasses have seed heads and seed capsules that provide landscape interest long after the last flowers have faded. A meadow gone to seed is more attractive than the stubble left after mowing, so cleanup can be delayed even until very early spring as long as the dry meadow poses no fire hazard. Once it is well established and you are satisfied with the balance of plants in your meadow, a light application of fertilizer (see p. 54) as the plants begin actively growing in the spring will help maintain a dense stand and heavy flowering.

## LAWNS

Buffalograss and Blue Grama are the two native grasses most suitable for lawn use. Buffalograss spreads by stolons, or surface runners, to form a dense, fine-textured sod. Unmowed, it averages about four inches in height and has a wavy, soft look. For a more traditional lawn, Buffalograss can be mowed monthly, June through August, to a height of two to three inches. Blue Grama is a fine-textured bunch grass that forms a dense sod if seeded heavily and mowed periodically. Unmowed, it will grow to eighteen inches tall with curved, brushy seed heads.

Since they are both warm-season grasses, they green up late in spring and turn a soft russet tan after the first hard freezes in autumn. Both are very drought tolerant, require much less mowing and feeding than commonly used turf grasses, and tolerate a fair amount of foot traffic. They do not have the dark green color of typical lawn grasses and take longer to develop a dense sod. If you want a Bluegrass lawn, plant Bluegrass and resign yourself to its benign slavery. If you want an attractive lawn and the freedom to enjoy it, plant Buffalograss or Blue Grama.

The steps to establishing a native lawn are similar to those for sowing a mixed meadow. Soil preparation is equally important in reducing competition from faster growing weeds. If you are replacing a traditional lawn with native grasses, the quickest and easiest approach is to kill off the existing lawn with glyphosate, a non-selective systemic herbicide that leaves no residue in the soil. The dead thatch can then be raked off and the soil tilled. A sod cutter (available as rental equipment) can be used to salvage vigorous Bluegrass sod for use elsewhere but will not remove enough of the root system to eliminate Bermuda grass. Two or more herbicide applications while the grass is actively growing may be necessary to eradicate it entirely. No matter what the turf being replaced is, tilling it into the soil and waiting for it to compost is not recommended. Besides having a long wait, the resulting seedbed is uneven in texture and consequently will absorb moisture unevenly. Uniform soil texture is very important in establishing a dense sod carpet. Soil amendments are not usually needed, except to break up very heavy clay. Again, sand or scoria should be tilled in thoroughly to avoid inconsistent soil textures.

After the seedbed is tilled and reasonably weed free, it should be raked level. Seeds can be broadcast by hand or with a spreader and scratch-raked into the surface. Firming the soil with a lawn roller (also available to rent) increases seed-soil contact, especially where wind is a problem. The seedbed should be kept moist until germination is complete—ten days to two weeks depending on soil and air temperatures, available moisture, and seed quality. Since native-lawn grasses germinate best during hot weather—late May through August, it may take two or three light sprinklings a day for fast and complete sprouting. Once the grass is up and growing, waterings should be deep and less frequent to encourage deep rooting.

How much and how often to water varies with the site, soil, slope, and season. Sandy soils require less water per application to penetrate deeply, but also dry out faster. Water penetrates clay soils more slowly, but clay remains wet longer. The type of sprinkler used on impermeable soils and slopes is important. Water must be applied slowly, at a rate the soil can absorb,

or much of the water is wasted as runoff. Impact sprinklers that cycle over an area and low-precipitation-rate sprinklers that produce a low volume spray are designed to reduce runoff. Decomposed granite and loamy soils fall somewhere between sand and clay in absorption and evaporation rates. Evaporation rates are highest during hot, windy weather. An average sprinkler delivers between ½ and 1 gallon of water per minute. A newly sprouted native lawn on decomposed granite may require an hour of sprinkling at five-day intervals during June and July (forty-five minutes twice a week on sand and an hour once a week on clay). In August and September (into October in warm-winter areas), frequency of watering can be reduced by half, including rainfall. Late fall through early spring, monthly soaking is adequate.

The first season it is planted, a native-grass lawn should not be mowed or fertilized, especially if weed competition was not eliminated before seeding. If annual weeds are a problem, they should be weeded out by hand before they go to seed. Cutting them off at ground level with shears is better than pulling them, because cutting doesn't disturb new grass roots. To help thicken the sod, 20–10–10 fertilizer can be applied at a rate of two pounds per thousand square feet in late May or early June the year after planting. Fertilizing an established native lawn is optional, as is watering.

Once the lawn is well established, it is very drought tolerant. Periodic deep watering during hot, dry weather will keep it green and growing actively. Mowed lawns should be watered regularly, at least every two weeks May through September. Mowing encourages growth and reduces the self-shading of taller grasses, and so increases the moisture needed to sustain the lawn.

Lawns provide a uniform, neutral foil for the trees and shrubs in a landscape. They offer a playing surface for backyard games and give fast erosion control on harsh sites. Meadows are, by nature, the opposite of uniform and neutral. Their seasonal drifts of color are framed by tree and shrub borders. They provide a play area for the game of natural history. Once established, meadows are the lawn's equal in erosion control, but because they are an ecosystem in transition, it takes longer to establish an effective balance.

Both Buffalograss lawn and wild-flower meadow are problem-solvers in the following layout (**see pg. 45**).

# WORKSHEET – HORTON DAIRY FARM

*Landscaping is problem solving. Prepare a fact base—the site analysis. Then set objectives: site modifications and a working materials list.*

## SITE ANALYSIS

### I Site Limitations

Style of architecture _FARMHOUSE, 2 STOREY, PITCHED ROOF, SAGE GREEN STUCCO_

Placement of structures on site _DEVELOP AREAS WEST, SOUTH & EAST OF HOUSE ONLY_

Solar orientation _LARGE SOUTH FACING WINDOWS_
Exposures _SOUTHWEST SPRING WINDS - PATIO_

Grade _LEVEL NORTH, EAST & WEST ; 1' IN 2½' SLOPE TO SOUTH_

Soil type _SAND WITH CLAY POCKETS ON EAST & WEST_

Traffic patterns _REDIRECT TRAFFIC TO NORTH ENTRANCE; BARRIER AT SOUTHEAST CORNER_
Access (Driveway & paths) _STONE & PLANK PATH; DRIVE & PARKING EAST TO NORTH ENTRY_
Patios _NORTH PORCH / MASSED LOW JUNIPERS; SOUTH PATIO / FAMILY USE & FOCAL POINT_

Surrounding landscapes _RURAL SETTING: DAIRY/NORTH; ORCHARD/EAST; OPEN FIELDS/SOUTH & WEST_
Complement/incorporate _SOUTH MEADOW SLOPES TOWARD OPEN FIELDS_
Frame views _SOUTHWEST SCREEN & SOUTHEAST BARRIER FOCUS ON OPEN FIELDS_
Screen eyesores _SOUTHWEST WINDSCREEN ALSO EXCLUDES INTERSTATE HWY. TO WEST_
Provide privacy _ENCLOSE PATIO WITHOUT OBSTRUCTING VIEW SOUTH_

### II Human Considerations

Lifestyle of inhabitants _WORKING DAIRY / HOME & BUSINESS - EMPHASIS IS ON FUNCTION_
Visitors _FREQUENT, SOMETIMES LARGE GROUPS_
Pets _2 DOGS, 5 CATS, 200 COWS_
Budget _COST SPREAD OVER 12 MOS.; LABOR BY DAIRY HANDS; ALLOW FOR LARGE SPECIMEN PLANTS_
Level of maintenance desired _LOW TO MODERATE : WATERING, PRUNING, MOWING_

### II Aesthetic Considerations

Symmetrical/formal vs. asymmetrical/casual _EMPHASIZE RUSTIC INFORMALITY - CONTRAST & MASS_
Focal points _SOUTH PATIO_
Seasonal interest _SUMMER / COLOR     —     WINTER / TREE FORMS & EVERGREENS_
Color preferences (intensity; hue) _BRIGHT, HIGH CONTRAST ~ NO COLOR THEME_
Fragrance _SAGE AROMA - PATIO_

## SITE MODIFICATIONS

### IV Organize Space

Expand or enclose _PATIO AREA_

Create outdoor "rooms"/ecosystems _ENCLOSURE FUNCTIONAL: WINDBREAK & SHADE_
Shade _SOUTH & WEST SIDES_
Windbreaks, screens, barriers _TALL & DENSE TO SOUTHWEST; THORNY PHYSICAL BARRIER TO SOUTHEAST_
Paving _SOUTH & EAST PATH ; DRIVEWAY & PARKING CRUSHED STONE_
Groundcovers _INERT: BARK MULCH TREE & SHRUB MASSES; NO HARD BORDERS BTWN. MATERIALS_
Lawns _BUFFALOGRASS NORTHEAST, EAST & WEST_
Meadows _1000 SQ. FT. SLOPE TO SOUTH_

### V Develop a Plant List

Function (Shade, screen, carpet) _DENSE SHADE : COTTONWOODS, AZ. SYCAMORES ; SCREEN &/OR LIGHT SHADE : JUNIPERS, ROSE LOCUST, MESQUITE, DESERT WILLOWS; CARPET: BARK, TURF, MEADOW_
Appearance (Shape, color, texture) _30% EVERGREEN ; COLOR: MEADOW, DESERT WILLOW; ROSE LOCUST, DALEA ; TEXTURE: DALEA, MARIOLA, JUNIPERS, MESQUITE, SYCAMORE BARK_
Adaptability (Soil, exposure, scale & size at maturity) _LARGE SCALE COTTONWOODS, JUNIPERS, AZ. SYCAMORE TO BALANCE PROPORTIONS OF THE HOUSE & SITE_

# FARMHOUSE LAYOUT

*SITE LIMITATIONS.* This large country home is the hub of activity on a dairy farm. Stuccoed sage green, it has a series of south-facing windows and a massive gold sandstone chimney as focal points. The main entrance faces north, but the private entrance is more visible on approaching the site and traffic needs to be directed away from this south entrance. The south patio is open to prevailing spring winds. Eight feet from the patio the land slopes 1 foot in 2.5 feet toward the road, creating a potential erosion problem. The soil is sandy with heavier clay pockets around the sides of the building. The dairy is at the end of a country road, surrounded by pasture and orchards. Privacy is not a consideration.

*LANDSCAPE SOLUTIONS.* Sandstone slabs left over from chimney construction, combined with pressure-treated wood planks, form a patterned walkway that limits access to the private entrance and complements the house. Dense plantings of evergreen and thorny deciduous thickets act as windbreaks and traffic barriers. Large-scale trees tie the two-story house to the site and provide welcome shade. Desert Willows enclose the patio without obstructing the view from the south windows. A mixed wild-flower and grass meadow covers the slope with a crazy quilt of color.

*LANDSCAPE CONSTRUCTION.* The paving, tree, and shrub borders and lawn were developed in the spring into summer. Before any planting was done, the entire area was irrigated and cultivated repeatedly to eliminate weeds. The path, trees, and shrubs were then installed and heavily mulched with bark. After a final grading, the Buffalograss was seeded at a rate of two pounds per 1,000 square feet. The seeds were scratch-raked in and the surface was rolled to increase seed/soil contact.

## CONSTRUCTING THE MEADOW:

The meadow area was cultivated again after late summer rains. Final grade was established and seeding was done in September to take advantage of natural rainfall and limit the development of the grass until the wild flowers are well established.

The seed mix, consisting of

8 oz. Blue grama (33% live seed)
1/2 oz. Coneflower
1/2 oz. Penstemon (mixed species, two-year-old seed)
1/2 oz. Coreopsis
1/2 oz. Prairie Clover
1/2 oz. Blue Flax
1/8 oz. Purple Aster
2 oz. Sand Verbena (scarified)

was broadcast by hand, scratch-raked into the surface to insure good seed/soil contact, and sprinkled. Transplants of Gayfeather, Zinnia, Globemallow, Paperflower, and Primrose were massed wherever washouts occurred or seed coverage was poor.

The entire meadow was lightly mulched with shredded bark and sprinkled every two weeks in September/October, monthly in November through January, every two weeks in February through April, and weekly through the first summer. Two mowings a year, one in July after the Prairie Clover sets seed and another in November, are all that will be needed. Selective hand-weeding the first year to fine tune the mixture, eliminating annual weeds before they set seed and reducing populations of "booming" species to encourage the less aggressive ones, is advisable.

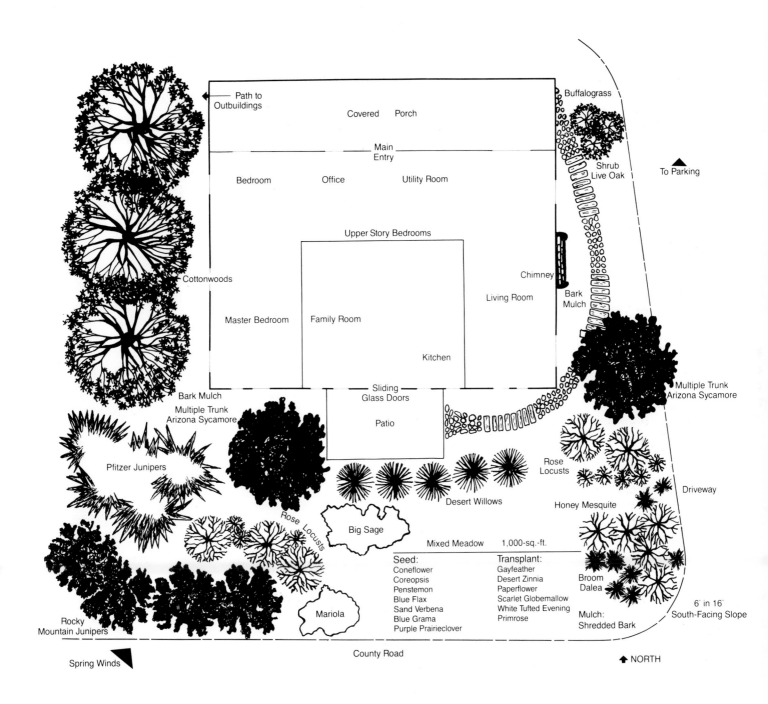

Path to Outbuildings

Covered    Porch

Main Entry

Bedroom        Office        Utility Room

Upper Story Bedrooms

Chimney

Cottonwoods

Living Room

Bark Mulch

Master Bedroom    Family Room

Kitchen

Sliding Glass Doors

Patio

Bark Mulch

Multiple Trunk Arizona Sycamore

Pfitzer Junipers

Rose Locusts

Big Sage

Desert Willows

Rose Locusts

Honey Mesquite

Driveway

Mariola

Rocky Mountain Junipers

Buffalograss

Shrub Live Oak

To Parking

Multiple Trunk Arizona Sycamore

Broom Dalea

6' in 16' South-Facing Slope

Mixed Meadow    1,000-sq.-ft.

| Seed: | Transplant: |
|---|---|
| Coneflower | Gayfeather |
| Coreopsis | Desert Zinnia |
| Penstemon | Paperflower |
| Blue Flax | Scarlet Globemallow |
| Sand Verbena | White Tufted Evening |
| Blue Grama | Primrose |
| Purple Prairieclover | |

Mulch: Shredded Bark

Spring Winds

County Road

NORTH

When you view your landscape as the stage upon which the drama of natural history unfolds, recognizing the cast members becomes part of the maintenance regime. To spray or not to spray — in this case Monarch Butterfly larva feasting on the Butterflyweed — is the question. A few leaves seems a small price to pay for the miracle of a Monarch drifting on a breeze.

# 4 🐝 GETTING IT GOING—PLANTING AND MAINTAINING THE LANDSCAPE

## TRANSPLANTING

With a design on paper and a shovel in hand, we come to the business of translating an idea into a thriving landscape. Transplanting native plants into a landscape is similar to establishing exotic ornamentals when you use container-grown nursery stock. The most effective transplanting technique is the one that keeps root loss to a minimum. Allowing the root ball to dry out, or cutting off a large portion of the root mass, as is often unavoidable when transplanting from the wild, reduces the plant's capacity to absorb moisture and nutrients. Transplanting during cool weather, while the plants are dormant, is the least stressful. As temperatures increase, especially when wind is a factor, moisture loss from plant tissues accelerates and more water is needed to replace the moisture lost to evaporation.

If the root mass cannot support the moisture demands of the top growth, no amount of moisture will replace the lost absorbing surface. Fall–winter is the ideal time to transplant arid-land natives a year or more old, as long as the plants have been hardened off. Taking a greenhouse/shade house-grown plant and transplanting it on an exposed site is cruel and unusual punishment no matter what the time of year. The shock can be fatal. All plants should be acclimated, given a transitional period outdoors in a relatively sheltered spot so that soft growth can adjust to higher evaporation rates, light intensity, and heat or cold. Transplanting while it is dormant gives the plant a low-stress period for extending its root system, but circumstance dictates. Dormant season planting is not always an option, and acclimated, container-grown arid-land natives make a ready transition any time of year if they are given adequate care. Keeping the root ball intact is a must, and the hotter, windier, and/or drier it is, the more moisture will be needed. Make sure the root ball is moist before transplanting, and water the plant well immediately after planting. During the 100 F days of midsummer it may be necessary to water daily for at least a week. In any case, avoid drying to the point of wilting. Removing some top growth to compensate for lost root surface helps maintain a moisture balance. Thinning entire branches rather than shearing, crew-cut fashion, reduces moisture stress, makes the plant more wind resilient, and allows the life processes to continue, including the production of new roots. Shearing temporarily halts root initiation and is not advisable until plants are well established.

Some arid-land natives can be successfully transplanted from the wild when they are dormant. Plants with fibrous rather than taproot-type root systems make the transition more successfully. Taprooted plants move best when they are young. Often, young plants are difficult to identify—*Penstemon ambiguus* and Snakeweed look very much alike until they reach blooming size, too late to transplant the Penstemon easily. Cactus should be marked on the south side and reoriented south on the new site to avoid sunburning. Providing temporary shade for newly transplanted wildlings can ease the stress of an abrupt move. Be kind. Success depends on it.

## SITE AND SOIL

Climate and soil are two factors you purchased with your site, and while tempering the climate may be one of your landscape goals, modifying the soil is a constant and thankless task. Selecting plant material suited to your soil type eliminates the need for "improving" the soil. You can generally assume that you will be dealing with a mineral soil. "Topsoil" in the desert Southwest indicates location rather than quality. The rich organic matter that blankets the earth in wetter climates is a Western gardener's daydream. To make it represents a major undertaking—the manufacture of compost. I don't intend to limit your fantasies, but determining your soil type and comparing it with the soil preferences of the plants in the Profiles section can reduce or eliminate the need to labor over a compost pile or import a Canadian peat bog bale by bale.

Drainage is a key consideration in determining soil type. Ideally, soil should allow water to penetrate and drain yet retain enough moisture, nutrients, and oxygen to sustain plant growth. Most arid-land natives require well-drained soil. While those plants native to stream banks and floodplains—Cottonwoods, Saltcedars, Clematis, and Baccharis—can tolerate waterlogged soil intermittently, the roots of most arid-land natives require plenty of oxygen for proper growth. Your soil is clay if it sticks to you when it's wet and water penetrates it slowly. When planting deeply rooted trees and shrubs, it is best to dig through the clay to sandier subsoil and incorporate pumice, sand, or fine

# TRANSPLANTING

*v i p*

*Thoroughly moisten the rootball of the transplant and allow the excess water to drain.*

*Dig a hole two to three times larger than the rootball of the transplant, both in diameter and depth.*

*Backfill with loose soil removed from the hole so that the rootball will sit either at grade, if the plant will be drip irrigated, or 4 to 6 inches below grade to provide generous watering basins and/or collect runoff.*

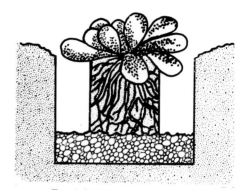

Backfill With Loose Soil

*Disturb the rootball as little as possible. If the plant is rootbound, gently loosen any circled or matted roots. Shorten very long, entwined roots so they will not be coiled up in the planting hole.*

*Place the transplant on the loosened backfill in the hole and fill in around the rootball with the same soil removed from the hole. Gently tamp the soil around the roots to increase soil contact and eliminate air pockets. Unless the soil is heavy clay, do not alter the backfill in any way except to break up large clods.*

*Radically altering the backfill when transplanting arid-land natives is not "improving" the soil. Backfill enriched with compost or peat moss creates pockets, in-ground containers, that limit root growth. Moisture does not move readily between soil strata. Root development remains massed within the "improved" soil.*

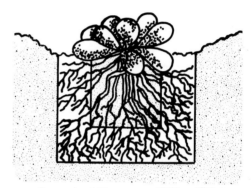

Compost "Improved" Backfill

*In heavy clay or where subsurface caliche is a problem, dig through the clay or caliche to more permeable soil. Use a power auger if necessary. Mix sand or scoria fines into clay backfill to increase drainage.*

*Using the native soil as backfill reduces layering of soil strata. Moisture and roots move freely into the surrounding soil. Plants establish faster, root more extensively, and are more drought tolerant. This is one of the few times when the easiest and least expensive technique is also the most effective. Enjoy it.*

*Immediately after transplanting, water well to improve soil-root contact and replace moisture lost during transplanting.*

Original Soil Backfill

gravel into the backfill. If caliche—impermeable layers of calcium carbonate—prevents drainage, it is necessary to perforate the hardpan to open the soil. There is no easy way of penetrating caliche. Softening the hardpan with water and attacking it head on with a pick or auger are accepted methods. The neighbors will object to dynamite, no matter how reasonable it

seems after an afternoon of caliche combat.

Extremely sandy soils pose other problems. Moisture moves rapidly through the soil, washing precious nutrients beyond the root zone. Addition of organic matter is temporary, a teardrop in the ocean, and can be expensive. Manures are of questionable value. They are often high in undesirable salts, sometimes consist

## HOW SOIL TYPE INFLUENCES WATER ABSORPTION

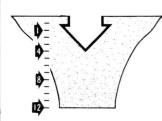

*CLAY SOILS, characterized by very fine particles, are impermeable and easily compacted.*

*One inch of water penetrates four inches of soil.*

*Two or more inches of water may be stored per foot of depth.*

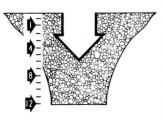

*DECOMPOSED GRANITE or SANDY LOAM ALLUVIAL SOILS, characterized by a mixed texture, are moderately permeable aggregate soils.*

*One inch of water penetrates six inches of soil.*

*One to two inches of water may be stored per foot of depth.*

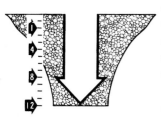

*SANDY SOILS, characterized by coarse particles, are highly permeable, loose, and granular.*

*One inch of water penetrates twelve inches of soil.*

*Up to one inch of water may be stored per foot of depth.*

If you are unsure about "reading" your soil, invest in an inexpensive moisture meter and use it until you become familiar with the look and feel of your soil at various moisture levels. All types of soil will stick together in a ball when they are at moisture levels optimum for absorption by plant roots. In the coarsest soils, the ball will be loose and tend to crumble. In the heaviest clays, the clay, when squeezed, will ooze out in ribbons between your fingers.

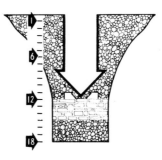

*As water penetrates the permeable layer of soil, it pools up on the surface of the caliche layer below. Caliche is almost completely impermeable and acts as a barrier to moisture absorption.*

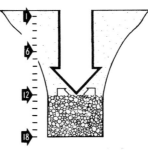

*Water penetrates impermeable clay very slowly. When it reaches the highly permeable sand layer it pools up on the sand, spreading horizontally between strata, and very slowly begins to move into the sand.*

In both instances water moves vertically through the soil and spreads horizontally when it reaches a soil layer of different texture, regardless of the permeability of the soil.

of raw sawdust that requires nitrogen for decomposition, and rarely provide beneficial nutrients. Peat moss is expensive and tends to be difficult to rewet once it dries. Studies on commercial cultivars of landscape exotics have shown that plants transplanted into radically altered soil tend to root only into the amended soil, but not beyond it. In effect, you would be growing plants in containers and they would be considerably less drought-tolerant than a plant encouraged to root extensively. True of exotics, this is amplified for arid-land natives that originate in soils naturally devoid of humus. Use of time-release fertilizers and heavy mulching are practical alternatives to soil amendments on sandy sites.

For ground-cover areas where many small transplants are set out or cover will be established from seed,

the addition of sand or pumice in clay—or compost or peat in sand—can be helpful, since root coverage will be dense and relatively shallow. Any amendments should be thoroughly tilled into the existing soil. Avoid layering of soil textures, as water will not move readily between strata.

For container-growing natives, a well-drained, easy-to-wet soil mix is best. Varying ratios of sand, bark, peat, pumice, and native soil can be used. A comparatively large percentage of sand makes the mix heavy and the nutrients leach rapidly, but it is inexpensive, readily available, and drains well. Bark can produce variable results depending upon the source. Locally available shredded bark is inexpensive and helps hold moisture but creates a mucky-textured mix. Bark, like sawdust, requires nitrogen to decompose and may rob the nutrients from plants. Aged/composted bark is preferable and is best kept as a minor element in native mixes. Peat is expensive and difficult to rewet, but makes a light, relatively weed- and disease-free mix. Pumice or scoria—volcanic ash—is a good soil-mix component because it is relatively inexpensive, available in bulk, and drains well yet retains nutrients. Pumice, however, should be used with another medium that holds together, so that the root ball remains intact when the plant is unpotted. Native soils as a container-mix component determine the percentages of the other amendments. Clay soils are good complements to sand and pumice, while sandy soils require a higher ratio of peat or compost as a binder.

# WATER

Water and nutrients are the variables that, with climate and soil, determine survival. Consider this. A plant may be up to forty percent water while dormant, up to ninety percent water while actively growing. Water pressure within cell walls is what gives them their shape and rigidity. Water acts as a solvent for nutrients and other essential auxins or hormones. (Auxins are growth-regulating chemicals synthesized in the buds and young leaves that influence cell growth, root and fruit development, and lateral branching. Hormones are auxins synthesized more generally throughout the plant.) Then consider that our climate may provide less than ten inches of this precious stuff annually. The better we use what is given, the less we need to add.

Efficient use of water assumes a knowledge of the nature of the soil—how quickly it accepts water, its total water-holding capacity, how much water is applied, and how frequently application is needed. This understanding of the interaction of soil and water, coupled with a knowledge of the plants selected for landscaping an area, is essential in establishing a low-maintenance environment. Water use is not consistent. The potential evapotranspiration rate, as determined by temperature and wind, affects moisture loss from leaf surfaces. The gas exchange during photosynthesis and respiration, two fundamental plant processes, consumes moisture. The development of the plant affects water use. Root depth and root-to-shoot ratio influence the amounts of moisture absorbed and returned to the air. The drought-resisting characteristics of deeply rooted natives, with foliage modified to reduce transpiration, maximize absorption and minimize water loss. Finally, the maturity of the plant—the initiation of flowers and development of fruit—temporarily increases moisture demands.

Gardening techniques greatly influence water use. While weeds compete with ornamentals for moisture, cultivation to eliminate weeds exposes more soil surface area to evaporation. Where soil tends to crust over, tilling opens up the surface to increase penetration of moisture and air. This provides an excellent medium for the germination of seeds, both desirable and not.

# Mulching

Mulching reduces weed growth, moderates soil temperature, and eliminates soil crusting, effectively conserving moisture overall. Mulches, to be really effective, should be applied lavishly—four-inch depth is adequate, six-inch depth better. There are many sources of mulching material. Decomposed sawdust, shredded or chipped tree bark, grass clippings, straw, and gravels are readily available. Sawdust should be aged or treated with nitrogen to avoid robbing nearby plants of their nutrient supply. Bark is an attractive mulch that can be used as a top dressing for a less expensive, less ornamental material. Shredded, fibery types knit together and withstand high winds best. Bark mulch does not favor the condensation of moisture within the medium. It remains dry at the surface, the moisture concentrated in the soil beneath it, and therefore wind-blown weed seed finds it a less attractive germinating medium. Grass clippings and straw are variable in quality. Know the source. Materials high in weed or grass seed (and in a native ground cover, bluegrass is a weed!) will aggrevate rather than control weed problems.

Gravel is a popular material for mulching, but is often poorly used. Applied as a thin layer topping black poly film, gravel is touted as low-maintenance Southwestern landscaping. Gravel mulch, like all mulches, needs renewing periodically; the thinner the cover, the more often renovation is necessary. Because one windstorm deposits enough sand and weed seed to give a gravel bed a loathsome green glow, annual herbicide treatments or marathons of hand-weeding are necessary. Actually, the expense of poly under gravel is justifiable only when the removal of the gravel within one or two years is foreseen. Otherwise, covering to a six-inch depth on raw earth is more economical and long-lived. When poly film is used, leave an area equal to the mature driplines of any plants growing within the gravel-on-plastic mulch open (graveled without plastic) to allow ample watering and oxygen exchange around the plants. Light-colored gravels are highly reflective and radiate heat, increasing potential evapotranspiration. Dark-colored gravels show litter and dirt all too well, and are best used as accents in small areas.

Decomposed granite, arroyo gravel, or crusher fines are mulches well suited for use as paving. Relatively fine in texture, these gravel products tend to compact well and form a surface crust that is easy to walk on, uniform and neutral in appearance, and unfavorable to weed-seed germination. Rather than covering large expanses with gravel, use these aggregates or hard paving to expand walkways and outdoor living spaces. Drought-resistant plant borders, islands, and screens

1

2

3

4

5

**MULCHING MATERIALS:** Lavish applications—four to six inches deep—are most effective and require infrequent renewal. Decomposed granite or other stone aggregates can add interesting textural accent when used to simulate dry streambeds or as porous paving (**1**). Stone mulches—1 1/2" round gravel and cobblestone—should be used to complement native plantings, not replace them (**2,3**). Shredded bark mulches provide non-reflective, dry surfaces that discourage weed-seed germination, are comfortable to walk on and aesthetically pleasing (**4**). Straw mulches are inexpensive and effective for moisture conservation but may include unwanted seeds (**5**).

relieve the monotony, moderate temperatures within paved areas, and offer a practical alternative to rockscaping ad infinitum.

## Irrigation Methods

Whether the motive is conserving water, reducing maintenance time and cost, or promoting the best plant performance, infrequent but ample watering is most effective. Frequent light sprinkling promotes a superficial root system and reduces drought tolerance. Excessive heavy watering is also self-defeating, as it reduces soil oxygen and stimulates weak, lush growth that is more susceptible to insects and disease.

A newly planted native landscape will not tolerate drought conditions unirrigated. If it is given a vigorous start, though, it can be gradually weaned of regular care. Supplemental watering then becomes optional. Pat answers to "how much to water" and "when a planting is established enough to survive unattended" are not possible. The more adaptable the plants selected are to the soil and exposure of the site, the more quickly they will become established there. Young nursery-grown plants and plants grown from seeds on site (wildflower meadows and native-grass lawns) will become established more rapidly than more mature transplants or plants collected from the wild. Plants native to cooler, high elevation or northern ecosystems in most cases will require additional moisture when they are grown in hotter, drier lowland landscapes. Even well-adapted and well-established native plantings benefit from periodic deep watering during periods of extreme heat and drought. If I seem to be emphasizing this point, it is because one of the most popular misconceptions concerning arid-land natives is that they require no care. Such half-truths torture your wallet, your landscape, and your pleasant disposition.

Deep watering, most easily accomplished with drip-irrigation equipment, produces controlled growth that enhances the natural form of the planting. Nutrients can be applied through the system or top-dressed at the emitters. Periodic leaching of excess salts is simply a matter of occasionally lengthening the operating time of the system. Little water is lost to evaporation and none to surface runoff. Deep watering can be achieved with bubbler heads that flood small areas, and also with overhead sprinklers. Bubblers should be adjusted so that water flow does not exceed the soil's absorption capacity, to eliminate runoff and erosion. Overhead sprinklers are the most difficult method of water application to control; wind seriously impairs efficient operation and surface runoff is common, especially on slopes, yielding the greatest water use with the least benefit. Low precipitation-rate sprinkler heads that have a lower angle of spray and cycle over an area to allow time for penetration are preferable to constant heavy-spray types.

Irrigation methods should be keyed to soil type. Water should be applied at a rate that allows for rapid drainage. Since a native landscape requires less assistance as it matures, the use of soaker hoses may be more cost effective than in-ground systems. Drip or bubbler systems are great time- and water-savers for plantings that require relatively frequent watering, in soils that drain very rapidly, or where dense foliage is desirable regardless of seasonal moisture fluctuations (as in maintaining privacy screens). Portable soaker hoses suffice for establishing or supplementing minimal care areas of mass-planted Broom Dalea, Chamisa, etc.

Excessive watering accounts for many maintenance problems of arid-land natives. Rank growth not only distorts the naturally compact form, requiring more frequent and severe pruning, but it is often accompanied by increased insect activity. Fourwing Saltbush is host to gall midges, gnatlike insects that deposit their eggs in swollen stem sections called galls. While the infestations are seldom fatal, the galls are unsightly and the number of galls seems to increase in direct proportion to the amount of soft growth available. Most native pests have parasitic predators, a tiny wasp in the case of the gall midge, that help control pest populations. Upsetting the natural balance of plant-pest-predator can put the ball in the pests' court.

Reduced oxygen availability, common in waterlogged soils, results in a general loss of vigor in oxygen-loving arid-land natives. Excessive watering also results in poor seed quality and reduced yields in many native species. Seed production of Four O'Clock is normally poor. Profuse watering encourages lush vegetative growth, while seed production goes from bad to worse. Similar results are evident in Fourwing Saltbush and Desert Marigold.

In determining optimum water application for a given species, observation of its native type-location is helpful. Plants like Creosotebush and Dalea, found mainly on rocky or sandy sloping terrain, will perform well in minimal care locations, while natives of moist canyons in deep soils, like Sycamore, require similar landscape situations for best results. Many arid-land natives, the Sumacs, Chamisa, Saltbush, Bigleaf Sage, and Desert Willow, for example, have a broad range that extends from deep bottomland soil with ample groundwater to sandy or rocky slopes and mesa country. These plants can function as transition plantings in the landscape also, linking areas of relatively intensive water use to minimal-care borders. The sample design given for large spaces (Chapter 2) is an example of "zoning," creating an oasis as outdoor living space and gradually reducing maintenance requirements to near zero in outlying areas. Zoning is another time-tested idea (golf courses have their greens, fairways, and roughs) that is newly applied to Southwestern landscaping.

# NUTRITION

The final consideration is plant nutrition. It is essential to associate nutrition with soil and water in the establishment and maintenance of a landscape. Soil type influences nutrient availability; clay soils retain nutrients, while sandy soils allow easy leaching not only of excess salts but of desirable ones as well. High soil and water pH, alkalinity, and salinity inhibit the absorption of certain nutrients, especially iron, magnesium, and zinc, even when they are present in the soil. Leaf scorch, the browning and crisping of leaf margins, is a symptom of stress. While leaf scorch could indicate an iron, nitrogen, or potassium deficiency, it could also signal a simple lack of moisture or a lack of oxygen due to compacted soil. As air quality worsens, leaf scorch may also be a result of air pollutants. Relieving the symptoms depends upon identifying the causes. Fertilizing plants that are suffering from drought is not only a waste of time and money but may also eliminate the plants along with the problem.

Nutrient requirements vary with soil texture, content, and moisture level, as well as with season and the type and age of plants being grown. Dry soils limit growth and, therefore, nutrient use. Generally, longer day length and greater light intensity increase the demand. Young plants require a higher phosphorous ratio than older plants. While nutrient consumption seemingly would increase with the size of the plant, established native plants require less feeding, as the extensive root systems draw off more soil volume. Excess feeding shortens the life-span of Penstemons, Ricegrass, Coneflower, and many other arid-land natives.

The list of references for this section in Further Reading includes sources of information concerning general plant nutrition. While it is beneficial to understand the full range of nutrients used by plants and their effect on growth and development, for the sake of simplicity the discussion here is limited to those nutrients which are helpful in cultivating arid-land natives but may be lacking in the soil and water on disturbed sites.

Of the sixteen elements commonly acknowledged as necessary to plant growth, we will consider five: nitrogen, phosphorus, potassium, iron, and sulfur, the first four to be used with restraint, the fifth to be avoided (with one exception). The other nine elements are micro-nutrients, so called because they are needed in very small amounts even by exotic plants. Arid-land natives, especially those that enjoy a very broad range of distribution, are well suited to many native soils, and once established they often thrive on naturally available nutrients. The better adapted the plants are to the site, the less fertilizer they require. Plants that need regular deep watering—those native to moist canyons and stream banks—also require periodic feeding, as routine deep watering leaches nutrients, especially nitrogen, beyond the root zone.

*NITROGEN (N).* The first of the big three is the most elusive. Necessary for protein synthesis and, therefore, growth, nitrogen leaches readily and is lacking in soils low in organic matter. Somewhere, shrouded by the mists of time, possibly in seventh-grade science class, we all learned about the nitrogen cycle. Nitrates are the form of inorganic nitrogen most readily used by plants. Fertilizers supplying ammoniacal N are not immediately absorbable. Warm soil temperatures, favoring bacterial activity, are imperative. When bacteria are inactive, the ammonia ions are absorbed instead of potassium ions, which are similar in structure. The ammonium does not supply nitrogen to the plants, and a corresponding potassium deficit results. Nitrogen applied at budbreak in early spring should be in nitrate form (ammonium nitrate or potassium nitrate), and because of rapid absorption, not strongly concentrated. Ammoniacal N can be used as an early summer feed for summer blooming and fruiting plants.

*PHOSPHORUS (P).* The second of the big three is necessary for photosynthesis and the transfer of energy within the plant. It is concentrated in the meristematic tissue, those plant parts that are capable of rapid change, as from shoot to root initiation. Phosphorus, therefore, increases the plant's potential adapt-

ability. P is available in Western limey soils when soil bacteria are active and it does not leach readily. Applications dug into the soil are more available and long lasting. To maintain a balance of available nutrients, overuse of phosphates should be avoided.

*POTASSIUM (K).* The third of the big three is instrumental in the manufacture and movement of carbohydrates in the plant, and contributes to the overall vigor and disease resistance of the plant. K is made more soluble by carbonic acid, a weak acid formed in the soil by the combining of water and carbon dioxide. $CO_2$ is a by-product of microbal activity in the soil. Potassium, like phosphorus, is concentrated in meristematic tissue, and, therefore, contributes to adaptability.

*IRON (Fe).* This is often unavailable to plants in alkaline areas, although it is present, in quantity, in the soil. Generally, arid-land natives are tolerant of alkaline conditions and are not prone to iron deficiency. Sycamores and Aspen, however, benefit from an annual application of chelated iron, that is, Fe molecules surrounded by a chemical agent that prevents interaction with substances that would render the iron insoluble. Chelated iron is the most effective treatment for iron deficiencies.

*SULFUR (S).* Application is often recommended as a treatment for combating salinity and alkalinity. Accumulations of soluble salts interfere with water absorption by raising the osmotic tension of soil water above that of the plant cells, resulting in a movement of water out of the cells into the soil. Conversely, plant vigor and growth depend upon maintenance of high osmotic tension within plant cells through the uptake of water by the plant, replacing moisture that has been lost through transpiration. With respect to most natives, alkalinity is not detrimental unless it is extreme, while salinity can cause severe local problems. Where high sodium is a problem, the use of sulfur and sulfur compounds is recommended because sulfur hastens the leaching of sodium and temporarily reduces salinity. Sulfur reacts with water to produce sulfuric acid, which has a deleterious effect upon soil microorganisms, so general use of sulfur compounds is not beneficial.

## SALINITY

Soils become excessively saline in three ways: by an extremely high water table which causes soluble salts to rise to the surface through capillary action, by irrigation with saline water, or by overfertilizing. The buildup of salts due to poor water quality or overfertilizing can be remedied by leaching—periodic heavy watering to wash salt out of the root zone.

Salt buildup is common where soils are heavy clay and water does not penetrate rapidly or rises by capillary action from a shallow water table. Applications of gypsum (calcium sulfate) are of some value in this instance, as gypsum causes fine-textured clay particles to group into larger units, opening up the soil to air and water while the sulfur displaces sodium and allows it to be washed below the root zone. Strongly saline soils support a very limited plant community, so if you wish to establish a varied and interesting landscape, you have the options of periodically applying gypsum, amending the soil with a large volume of sand or pumice to mechanically open the soil, or limiting plant selection to salt-tolerant species. This is a localized problem in areas where irrigation water, poor management, or high water tables have created and sustain an imbalance.

## SYMBIOTIC RELATIONSHIPS

In recent years, research has begun to decipher the complex relationship among plants, soil, microorganisms, and nutrient availability. The value of nitrogen-fixing bacteria, present in the nodules on the roots of legumes and other plants, has long been recognized. Rose Locust, Broom Dalea, Bigleaf Sage, and Russian Olive all have symbiotic relationships with bacteria, e.g. *Rhizobia* and *Frankia*, that render the free nitrogen in air useful to their hosts. Generally, plants growing in close association with these bacteria-fed species also benefit from the available nitrogen. A group of fungi, collectively termed mycorrhizae, live in similar symbiosis with most native species, providing their hosts with hormones that result in greater nutrient mobility and increased mineral absorption. Mycorrhiza effects the conversion of organic nitrogen and phosphorus to usable form and stimulates growth, resulting in a more vigorous and adaptable plant.

The association of various mycorrhizae with host plants is almost universal, yet it is extremely specific. It is part of the interrelationship of climate, soil, and plant. Exotic plants have mycorrhizal associations also, but as the fungi thrive within a very limited range of pH, moisture, and heat and cold, they will not flourish in arid-land soils. In short, native soils harbor microorganisms beneficial to native plants. The association continues only as long as it remains mutually beneficial. Excess shade, water, or fertilizer reduces or eliminates mycorrhizal activity. Studies have suggested that nurturing the association can reduce fertilizer cost by thirty to seventy percent in commercial production, and in some cases can eliminate the need for nutrient applications.

Innoculation can be spontaneous by airborne spores. Mycorrhizae that are symbiotic with arid-land plants grow best in native, unimproved soils. Naturalizing landscape plantings by gradually weaning them of the nutrients and additional moisture that were needed for successful establishment allows for a gradual increase in beneficial microorganisms to take over a portion of

your landscape maintenance. Any chemical that acts as a fungicide, such as sulfur in calcium sulfate, ammonium sulfate, iron sulfate, and super-phosphate; chlorine in muriate of potash; or formaldehyde in urea formaldehyde, may destroy beneficial microorganisms. As with insect pests and predators, the balance is fragile. Healthy mycorrhizal populations effectively resist the invasion of harmful bacteria. Since the conditions optimum for native-plant growth are also best for the development of beneficial microorganisms, providing for one encourages the other. Use of fungicide is advisable for rooting of cuttings or for seedling production; use of fungicide, or nutrients with like reactions, on established plants should be limited or avoided, however, to encourage microorganism activity.

## FERTILIZERS

The most cost-effective fertilization programs key nutrient source to soil type and season. Potassium nitrate is an excellent cool-weather source of nitrogen and potassium, especially in sandy soils. Potassium nitrate tends to fragment soil particles. In clay soils this would further disperse fine clay particles, the net result being reduced permiability—no advantage in soil already poorly aerated. Reduced particle size in sand, however, would be beneficial, helping to limit too rapid drainage. Urea, not urea formaldehyde, is an excellent slow-release nitrogen source for warm-season use in any soil. Ammonium nitrate is a more fast-acting, warm-season nitrogen source, best used in clay soils where constant leaching is not a problem. Superphosphate, phosphate rock that has been leached with sulfuric acid, is a good source of phosphorus if it is used moderately and infrequently. Rock phosphate and bone meal are more alkaline in reaction and should not be used on extremely alkaline sites.

Blended or "balanced" fertilizers were created in response to a customer demand for convenience. They contain nitrogen, phosphorus, potassium, and sometimes one or more micro-nutrients in varying ratios. For general landscape use a 2–1–1 or 3–1–1/N–P–K ratio works well, with infrequent applications of micro-nutrients in very small amounts. Container-grown plants, especially plants grown in soilless mixes (peat moss, pumice, bark mixes containing no native soil or compost) need regular applications of complete fertilizer, including micro-nutrients, to compensate for the greater moisture demands and the absence of nutrients in the soil.

Consider a typical "general purpose" fertilizer. The label indicates that the blend is specially formulated for the Southwest. The N–P–K ratio is 16–8–8 plus 10% sulfur, 1% iron, and 1% zinc. A 50-pound bag then contains 16% (8 pounds) of nitrogen, 8% (4 pounds) each of phosphorus and potassium, 10% (5 pounds) of sulfur, and 1% (½ pound) each of iron and zinc. The 22 pounds of nutrients are bonded to 28 pounds of inert filler that helps to disperse the nutrients more evenly. In smaller print, the label informs that all the nitrogen is in the quick release form of ammonium nitrate, so it is best used when soil microorganisms are active. The phosphorus is available as phosphoric acid, so it temporarily lowers the soil pH. The sulfur also creates an acid reaction which lowers the pH still more and makes the iron and zinc more available to the plants. The recommended application rate is 50 pounds per 2,000 square feet, broadcast with a fertilizer spreader for more uniform coverage. This fertilizer is one of the best for growing exotic plants in what is for them an alien and hostile environment. Most arid-land plants, however, prefer alkaline soils. The sulfur is unnecessary at best, and destroys beneficial mycorrhizae. Although the N–P–K ratio is good, the suggested application rate is at least double the amount useful for establishing most native plantings. When you purchase such a fertilizer, you are paying not only for the elemental nutrients but also for the convenience of pouring them out of a single attractive package. In terms of native plants, you may be paying more for what you need less of for optimum growth.

The ideal nutrient formula is the one that maintains plant vitality. Well adapted arid-land plantings may require only one feeding, at bud break the first spring after transplanting. Plants transplanted in early spring benefit from a very dilute nutrient application (2–1–1 ratio) a month or two after transplanting, when the reserves of the new plants are depleted and before they have rooted deeply enough to draw on natural resources.

Fertilizers should not be mixed into the backfill at transplanting time. Aside from the danger of burning fragile root hairs, rapid absorption may force uneven growth, shoots and foliage at the expense of roots. This is another good rule that deserves an exception. Controlled-release, polymer-coated fertilizers usually require two to four weeks of soil/moisture contact before the nutrient becomes available through osmosis. The coating also buffers contact with tender new roots and prevents damage. Since the application rate is standardized for common landscape exotics, decreasing the amount by half better serves the light-diet life-style of arid-land natives.

Time-release fertilizers are useful in nutrient programs for containerized plants and for establishing landscapes in sandy or rocky soils, where irrigation will be relatively frequent, moderate to rapid growth is desirable, and leaching of costly nutrients is a consideration. Such fertilizers are usually temperature formulated—the polymer coating becomes permeable at temperatures consistent with plant growth. Nutrient programs recommended by organic gardening advocates are formulated to encourage microorganism activity and are useful in maintaining established native landscapes. Incorporation of organic matter into the soil at planting time is of questionable value, however, due to the containerizing effect on trees and shrubs.

As well as knowing what fertilizer to use, timely application is important in getting the most for your fertilizer dollar. Plants make their most efficient use of fertilizers at the time of shoot elongation and budbreak in spring. Absorption and synthesis are rapid if the right nutrient source is applied. On established plantings, one level tablespoon of potassium nitrate per inch of trunk diameter or two feet of shrubby growth is adequate to support a season's growth. Chelated iron should be applied to species that are subject to deficiency at this time also, at a rate of one to two ounces per inch of trunk diameter. Chelating agents are sometimes photosensitive—intense sunlight renders them inactive. It's best to dig chelated nutrients into the soil to reduce exposure to light. Since rainwater is a source of rapidly absorbable nitrogen, applications of fertilizer from midsummer on are unnecessary. Plants should not be stimulated to produce soft growth late in the season, as immature growth is less cold hardy. Besides losing any late-growth advantage to winter burning, you may jeopardize the overall vitality of the plant. Once winter dormancy of top growth is evident, superphosphate can be applied. As long as the soil is not frozen, phosphorus uptake will occur and will be stored in the plant until active growth resumes. Such late applications reduce interference of the sulfur in the superphosphate with soil microorganisms. Applications should be infrequent and conservative; usually one application the first autumn after transplanting, at a rate of one-fourth the label recommendations for exotic plants, is adequate.

## SOME SUGGESTED APPLICATION RATES FOR COMMON FERTILIZERS (based on 15 to 20% nitrogen content)

Ammonium nitrate or Urea
   1 cup per 100 square feet of flower bed, meadow, or native-grass lawn
   ½ cup per 100 square feet of shrub and tree border or 2 tablespoons per 3 gallon or larger transplant
Potassium nitrate
   2/3 cup per 100 square feet of flower bed, meadow, or native-grass lawn
   ¼ cup per 100 square feet of shrub and tree border or 1 tablespoon per 3 gallon or larger transplant

# MAINTENANCE CALENDAR

| Task | Active Months |
|---|---|
| Seed next year's wild-flower display & transplant cold-hardened plants. | September |
| Plant bare-root deciduous plants from sources at least as cold as your site. | October–December |
| The fall dormant season is the ideal time to establish all major landscape projects except warm-season grass lawns (Buffalograss & Blue grama). | October–November |
| Once plants have leafed out, transplant only container-grown stock. Wind & rising temperatures increase water requirements of new transplants. | April–August |
| Divide & reset perennials to increase stands (Fringe Sage, Blanketflower, Allium, Flax, etc.), especially of spring flowering species. | October |
| Divide & reset summer & fall blooming perennials. | March–April |
| Clean seeds that will be flat sown indoors or in cold frames. | November–December |
| Prepare soil for early spring seeding. | February–March |
| Plant lawns of warm-season grasses (Buffalo-grass & Blue grama). | May–July |
| Set out hardened off perennials. | January–April |
| Sow seeds indoors for transplanting when outdoor temperatures moderate. | December–March |
| Fertilize new lawns to promote denser coverage. | June–August |
| Take softwood cuttings. | July–August |
| Apply mulches lavishly after hard freezes. | October–January |
| Mow meadows (6" to 12" height), leaving the clippings as mulch to encourage reseeding & "tame" a wild garden. | November–January |
| Cold-moist stratify seeds for later sowing. | December–February |
| Fertilize new plantings & treat iron (Arizona Sycamore) or zinc (Ash) deficiencies. | March–April |
| Collect seeds of early flowering plants. | June |
| Sow perennials for flowering next year. | August |
| Sow seeds of perennials & annuals outdoors. | March–April |
| Sow seeds with a preference for cold-germinating temperatures outdoors under cover (Artemisias). | February–March |
| Cold temperature germinators (Penstemons & Scarlet Flax). | February–March |
| Mid-range temperature germinators (Butterflyweed & Calliopsis). | March–April |
| Apply mulches lavishly as days get hotter. | April–May |
| Sow seeds of heat-loving plants (Desert Willow) & Bird of Paradise). | June |
| Prune to remove winter damage (young Desert Willows). | May |
| Remove faded blooms to prolong flowering cycles. Summer prune plants that tend to sucker while young (New Mexico Privet & Desert Willow grown as trees). | June–August |
| Prune (thin) to enhance form & make plantings more wind resilient. | December–February |
| Mow early-flowering meadows as hot weather reduces flowering & seeds ripen. Cut at 6" to 12" height. Cut Purple Asters as above to maintain a 12" to 18" flowering height. | June–August |
| Early weeding of newly emerged "undesirables" eliminates heavy work & potential for reseeding. | January–April |
| Check for aphids on plants resuming active growth. Control by washing soft growth with a high-pressure hose nozzle (Pines, Penstemons, Sumac, & Butterflyweed). | February–April |
| Check for flea beetles on Evening Primroses. Control with carbaryl. | April–June |
| Remove annual weeds (Kochia & tumbleweeds) at ground level with shears after the growth cycle is complete but before seeds set. | August |
| Clean & repair drip-irrigation systems. | February–March |
| As temperatures rise, check for & control spider mites by washing dusty foliage. | May–June |
| Check for & remove caterpillars by hand or biologically with Bacillus thuringensis. | January–June |
| Watering, keyed to soil type & relative "thirst" of the plants in a landscape, should be managed to supplement available precipitation. | — |
| Increase volume & frequency as winds & warming temperatures increase water use. | March–June |
| Decrease the volume & frequency as rains & cooling temperatures reduce the need for water. | — |
| Water evergreens monthly, deciduous plants every 6 weeks. | December |
| Water biweekly, monthly. | October–November |
| Water monthly, biweekly. | March |
| Water biweekly. | April |
| Water biweekly/weekly. | August |

New plantings & relatively "thirsty" plants (native to cooler, moister habitats: higher elevations, riparian habitats) require watering at the more frequent rate. Established landscapes of arid-land natives remain ornamental at the above recommendations but survive on less in most cases.

*The seasonal planting & maintenance chores outlined above are based on average conditions in south central New Mexico at 4,500 to 5,000 feet elevation. The desert Southwest is characterized by extremely local microclimates. At higher elevations & northern latitudes, the calendar dates may be pushed back to reflect local conditions. (Because flea-beetle problems peak as Evening Primroses decline under heat stress, cooler microclimates suffer the plague later or not at all.) Lower elevations & southern sites warm sooner. (Ideal seeding dates, based on air & soil temperatures, occur a month or more earlier.) Some chores are loosely timed—anytime during winter or summer dormancies. Many maintenance tasks are outgrown as the landscape matures.*

**PLENTY OF IMPACT** with very little water. While formal landscapes require constant attention, the casual moods of naturalized landscapes may vary greatly without effecting the degree of maintenance required. This lush looking landscape leaves no room for weeds to gain a foothold. Plants, including Desert Willow, Threeleaf Sumac, Chamisa, Cherry Sage, Blanketflower, several Penstemon species, and Blue Grama, were selected for drought tolerance, seasonal color, texture, and ability to compete in close quarters.

The border of cut barrel staves and lid lends a rustic feeling to this very drought-tolerant grouping of Desert Willow, cactus, and Groundsel (**left**). A crisply casual feeling here is partly due to the color contrast between the light (*Artemisia frigida* and *tridentata*) and the darker stucco, and partly due to the unclipped but controlled growth habit of the plants (**top**).

**ZONING AND UTILIZING RUNOFF** are two common-sense ways to conserve water without compromising comfort and beauty in a southwestern landscape.

The selection and placement of plants along a meandering path is an inviting approach to this Colorado residence. Watered substantially by runoff, the landscape is attractive even while dormant, an important consideration where winters are long and severe (**top**).

An arid-land native border (Desert Willow, Chamisa, Apache Plume, Junipers, Blue Flax, Coneflower, and Evening Primrose) utilizes runoff from the small bluegrass lawn and roof. The contrast between lawn and border amplifies the fine points of both.

The bluegrass-sod bordered patio contrasts with the wildflower-dotted dry streambed that meanders below it. Several species of Penstemon, Sage, Verbena, Coneflower, and Piñon are an appropriate transition from turf to foothills chaparral. The sage-green stained fence encloses the area without intruding on it.

**SMALL SPACES** require plantings that are compact in form and controlled in feeling. In the sheltered microclimate of a courtyard, using wildflowers in an apparently random, meadow-like way, seems to expand the small space.

An entryway planter contrasts masses of cool flower colors for an inviting approach on a northeast exposure (**l** to **r**, Candytuft, Blue Flax, Creeping Mahonia).

Within the confines of this west-facing planter, "Hillspire" Junipers screen the patio from the hot afternoon sun. Giant Four O'Clock spills over the planter's edge, thriving in a location that would shrivel a less adaptable plant.

# PRUNING GUIDELINES

A l5-gallon container-grown Desert Olive, unpruned and shrubby.

After thinning, a multiple-trunked tree form emerges.

At the node where a branch is attached to the main stem a collar, a slightly raised ring of cells, has the potential to grow over a pruning cut.

Prune just outside the collar to preserve this biological barrier to pathogens.

# PRUNING "HOW TO'S" ARE   REALLY "WHY TO'S"

*Have a purpose in mind before you pick up the shears. (If you need exercise, take a walk—don't take it out on the shrubbery.)*

*What purpose does the plant serve in the landscape?*

*Thinning extraneous growth to enhance the natural shape of the plant is the purpose of pruning accent plants. Removing old wood also rejuvenates mature spec-*

*imens, and thinning reduces wind damage.*

*Shearing or tip pruning the entire shrub forces branching and increases the density of twigs and foliage when plants are used as screens or hedges. Note that the base of the shrub is broader than the top. If sunlight cannot reach the entire surface, lower limbs defoliate.*

Before:

After:

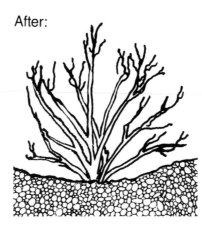

Thinning

Shearing

Before:

After:

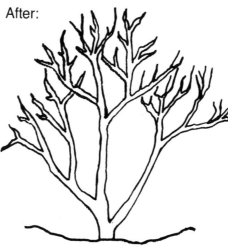

Multiple Trunk

Standard

*Many arid-land natives can be used as large shrubs or small trees depending upon how they are treated.*

*When the plant is used for its structural qualities in the landscape—foliage canopy and dormant silhouette—pruning involves lightly thinning the "head" of the tree and removing suckers and extraneous growth from the base of the plant. Note that wide-angle branch crotches are stronger and less likely to snap in high winds.*

*Pruning a plant to multiple-trunk tree form is thinning taken to the extreme, where only three to five main branches remain to develop as the plant matures.*

*Pruning to a multiple-trunked form forces the plant to share that energy among several terminal shoots. The*

*result is a dwarfing effect that brings extremely large trees such as Arizona Sycamore and Cottonwood into balance with small-scale structures and understory plantings.*

*A standard tree form is a single trunk with an open-branch scaffolding that creates an upward spiral of well-spaced lateral branches. Much of the plant's energy is focused on the terminal bud as it pushes skyward.*

*If plants are spaced with their mature size in mind when they are transplanted into the landscape and not over-watered or over-fertilized, they will not need to be pruned to limit their size. A plant in the wrong place is a problem forever.*

Limited use of carefully chosen nutrients has advantages beyond reducing fertilizer cost and encouraging mycorrhizal activity. Overfed arid-land natives that are forced to produce extremely lush and abundant growth are more attractive to insects and less drought tolerant. Resistance to attack by insects is often given as a plus in landscaping with natives. That is an oversimplification. Actually, insect activity on native plants is abundant but specific. The advantage gained when naturalizing a landscape is that along with native pests there are equally voracious native predators. The resultant balance reduces the potential for insect damage. Luxuriant growth upsets the balance, producing a booming pest population not immediately controllable by predators.

# PRUNING

When water and nutrient applications are managed intelligently, the need for pruning becomes negligible. For an outwardly natural appearance, as well as innate drought resistance, removal of dead wood and extraneous growth to display an attractive silhouette is all the pruning necessary. Forestiera or Desert Willow, used as a small specimen tree, may require annual removal of suckering growth while it is juvenile. This is best done in midsummer, after the spring flush of growth. Summer pruning is longer lasting than early spring pruning, because it does not stimulate further growth. Shearing of shrubs used as screens or hedges lends a formal feel to the landscape. To avoid an artificial "gumdrop" appearance, shearing is best done in early spring. Subsequent new growth will soften the severe lines of such pruning. Forestiera, Sumac, Chamisa, Winterfat, Golden Currant, and Saltbush all adapt well to shearing, while Desert Willow, Big-leaf Sage, and Cliffrose are enhanced by thinning, and Dalea is best left to its own devices.

After a long, cold high-desert winter (those of you transplanted from Maine or Wisconsin are entitled to a long, loud laugh), many people feel an irresistible urge to get out in their gardens and *do* something. The late summer rains and crisp autumn mornings have a similar effect after the dog days of a desert summer. Having a low-maintenance native landscape need not spoil your fun. The maintenance calendar (see p. 56) suggests a year full of chores—large and small—that satisfy the urge to participate in the life of your landscape. A new landscape, carefully directed to a state of dynamic equilibrium—eliminating weeds that colonize newly disturbed sites and shaping young trees and shrubs to accentuate their natural forms—outgrows the need for much human interference. At the same time, the landscape develops an animated population of foraging birds and insect predators to balance any pests the garden may attract. As the landscape matures, the major seasonal chore becomes "rake leaning," the art of enjoying the native community of which you have become a part. Your chores may become limited, but the rewards increase with age.

# 5 🌿 PROPAGATION—SEEDS AND CUTTINGS

The landscape ornamentals commonly available at nurseries today are the "discoveries" that resulted from a worldwide search for "useful" plants. The search began before recorded history, flourished in the late 1800s, and continues today. "Useful" covers a lot of territory, as did botanical explorers, and the interpretation of usefulness varied with the needs of the time. Prehistoric interests focused simply on the edible. As civilizations increased in complexity, medicinal and ornamental plants added texture to the botanic canvas. Ancient Persia may be the site of the first purely ornamental gardens. In a climate similar to the American Southwest, the Persians sought the refinement of oases. Where nature didn't provide them, the Persians built their own. The later Middle Ages saw a renewed interest in the art of cooking. Any plant that could spice up a dull medieval dinner was a welcome find. And so it went.

In the Southwestern United States today, horticultural introductions respond to the demands of a growing population and the maturing of the frontier towns that have become our metropolitan centers. The need is to temper our environment without creating an exotic anonymity that squanders our water, irritates our sinuses, and insults our sense of place.

Most landscape ornamentals originally were selected for ease of reproduction as well as for appearance and broad acceptability. Species requiring special pretreatments rarely enjoyed commercial interest. As metropolitan centers develop in arid lands and moisture demands soar, the benefits of drought-tolerant plant life assume an importance that challenges accepted ideas of commercial feasibility. The well-protected seeds of arid-land natives can be a challenge to growers accustomed to the easy predictability of many of the exotic plants used in landscapes. But while the natives outgrow these early demands, exotics continue to require pampering throughout their lives. Dormancies are drought defenses, and they must be dealt with if the conservation and beautification potential of arid-land plants is to be realized.

## PROPAGATION BY SEEDS

The characteristics that are the key to drought tolerance are often limiting factors in propagation. In the wild, seed germination is erratic by design, spanning the longest possible time in order to eventually strike upon a favorable set of conditions and thereby insure the continuation of the species. Given thousands of seeds and five years, two of which may provide adequate moisture, a plant may produce ten viable offspring, six of which are consumed by rodents. To Winterfat on rangeland, this is success. To nurserymen, it is bankruptcy.

A grower, by vocation or by hobby, tries to minimize this randomness of nature. The landscape ornamentals currently available are examples of such control. Less than seventy percent germination of petunia seed is disgraceful! With plants new to cultivation, the information needed to repeatedly produce uniform results is not readily available in "cookbook" format. The excitement of a mystery must balance the frustration of ten percent germination rates.

The basis for successful seedling production, on any scale, lies in good quality seed, properly treated. Seed quality in natives is extremely variable, however, especially when seed is collected from the wild. Growing conditions during flowering and embryo development determine seed quality. Lack or excess of moisture during and after flowering; frosts or excessive heat; absence of pollinators; or presence of insect pests—all contribute to poor seed yields and erratic germination rates. Availability of moisture, pollination, insect damage, and temperature can be controlled under cultivation. Seed produced under more favorable conditions is generally easier to germinate, having lower concentrations of germination inhibitors and a greater percentage of filled seed. As far as moisture is concerned, too little reduces yields, but too much can also be detrimental. Excess moisture and nutrients produce lush foliage at the expense of flowers, and such plants are more attractive to insects that can destroy the seed crop. As an example, Four O'Clocks grow a lot of foliage but flower very little if they are watered too much. Insects do eat flowers but generally if they eat flowers they eat leaves too and disfigure the whole plant. Arid-land natives that are overwatered are stressed, and stressed plants attract insects. A plant that is weakened, first by moisture (too much or too little) stress, then by insect attack, is physically unattractive and less able to produce flowers and seeds. There is sometimes a very broad range between too much and too little water (Apache Plume and Threeleaf Sumac are examples); sometimes the limits are very narrow (Bush Morningglory and some Penstemon species are very sensitive to overwatering).

## Collecting Seeds

Improper collection and storage will reduce seed viability. The methods I discuss here are limited to small seed lots, and seed cleaning and storage techniques are limited to simple, inexpensive operations. Collection techniques vary with the type and quantity of seed required. Seed collection should coincide with seed maturity. Generally, the greatest quantity of seeds ripen within two months of the heaviest flower display. Although the ideal is to collect seeds from cultivated plants, that is impossible for many species at this point. Seeds often must be field collected. Stripping an area of seeds of selected species is never justifiable. Plant communities and the wildlife they support exist in fragile equilibrium. Removal of most of the seed of one species can result in the population boom of another, less desirable species. A resulting loss of wildlife habitat, soil erosion, and the general deterioration of an ecosystem can follow. Collecting seeds from large, healthy populations and removing only a small percentage of the total yield per area will have very little effect upon established native-plant communities. Collect with a conscience.

Color, hardness, and easy separation from the plant are indices of harvestable seed, all subject to the judgment acquired through experience. Color is a key to maturity. Many seeds are green in color as well as disposition when they are immature, ripening to shades of tan, brown, and black, as in Winterfat, Evening Primrose, and Blackfoot Daisy respectively. Seeds enclosed in pulpy fruits have a ready index to ripeness. When the fruit is at its peak coloration, seed should be collected. Often you will be competing with other professional collectors—birds. They have the advantage of flight, so careful observation of fruit development is especially helpful when collecting seeds of delicacies like Russian Olive, Desert Olive, and the Sumacs. Texture is a further indication of maturity; when they are ripe, seeds will harden as the starches set. Ease of separation from the plant is another method of determining harvest time. Plumed seeds, like those of Clematis, Cliffrose, and Apache Plume, will detach from their receptacles at a touch when they are ripe. The whole flower head of Desert Zinnia can be removed easily by hand or with a wet-dry type vacuum cleaner. Seeds of Chamisa and Purple Aster are similar to dandelions in structure and method of dispersing, while Penstemon, Yucca, Desert Willow, and Evening Primrose seeds are easily harvested when the pods that enclose them dry and split open, releasing the mature seeds.

Timing is critical. Getting green seeds out of an unripe seedpod is more difficult than it is useful, yet once the seed head shatters and seeds fall to the ground, they should be left as lunch for local wildlife or you could collect more than you bargained for in the way of insects and disease. But what good would a rule be without a few exceptions? Acorns may be gathered off the ground, those with wormholes discarded. Honey Mesquite seeds are all but impossible to remove from the pods. Rodents gnawing on the sweet starchy pods leave cleaned seeds as trash. In both cases the seeds are large enough to separate easily from litter and examine for insect damage.

Specific collection times cannot be given, as variation in the conditions affecting seed ripening can hasten or delay maturity. Of equal importance is the location of the collection site. As a rule, northern sites, areas of higher elevation, or microclimates that are cooler due to exposure or shade will produce seed later in the season. These are simply guidelines. Nothing can compare with the knowledge born of experience. Once you begin to consistently observe the plants that are attractive to you and to collect and grow seed, you will recognize the stages in plant development and their implications. Keeping accurate notes helps—recording the time and location of collection, pretreatments used, sowing and transplanting dates, and results. If nothing else, it will provide you with a few good laughs in years to come.

## Cleaning Seeds

Ideally, seeds should be dried and stored in paper or cloth sacks after harvest and cleaned of debris and chaff as soon as it is practical to do so. An exception to the rule of drying after collection is Oak seed. Acorns either should be planted immediately after gathering or should be stored cool and moist, with attention given to preventing the growth of bacteria and fungi that are favored by such storage. Since repeated applications of fungicide can eventually interfere with germination and growth, I avoid long-term storage and sow the acorns immediately. Acorns from high elevations and northern sources usually put down a root soon after sowing but produce no top growth until the following spring, while lowland and southern acorns produce roots and shoots within weeks of sowing.

Seed cleaning is a time-consuming and sometimes messy process. The chore of hand cleaning Desert Zinnia, detaching seeds from the dried petals, is a fine winter pastime for days too miserable for outdoor activity. Accompanied by a Rodrigo guitar concerto and a fire in the hearth, seed cleaning can offer the same promise of spring available, at greater cost, by perusing seed catalogs. Machine cleaning Zinnia, ounce for ounce, takes about as long, stirs up more dust, and results in less viable seeds, since some seeds are broken in the process and the machine doesn't discard wormy seeds.

Cleaned seed is preferable, especially when seeding is to be done indoors in seed flats. Seed free of debris minimizes disease problems and reduces the effect of germination inhibitors and insect larvae present in the chaff. An ounce of prevention is worth several pounds of fungicide.

Commercial seed-cleaning equipment is available for processing large seed lots. For the hobbyist or small commercial grower, patience and a set of screens of graduated-size mesh are adequate. Mesh sizes are determined by the sizes of seeds to be cleaned: one mesh large enough for the seeds and fine debris to pass through and a second, smaller mesh to catch the seed but filter out fine debris. This works well for seed of Broom Dalea, Penstemon, Scorpionflower, Phlox Heliotrope, and other seeds that are distinct in size and weight from accompanying chaff. Mesh sizes most useful are 1/16" standard window-screen material and 1/8" hardware cloth. Hardware cloth is available in 1/4" and 1/2" mesh also. Sieves, colanders, and strainers made of 1/16" mesh are available in many houseware departments and serve as ready-made seed cleaners.

Small seeds equipped with a pappus, fine hairs or bristles at the tip of the seed coat, as found on Broom Baccharis, Aster, or Chamisa, can be sown without removing the pappus. Take care to maintain sanitary conditions in the seed flat to avoid damping off, a disease characterized by constriction of the stem just above the soil and rapid wilting and death of the seedling. A fungicide drench is advisable.

Seeds that are considerably heavier than the chaff and poorly shaped for screening can be cleaned by threshing in an open, shallow box or basket on a gently breezy day (10 mph or less). This works as well as anything on the woody, angular, and hooked seed coat of Blackfoot Daisy. The dried seeds of Butterflyweed detach easily from the silky pappus "parachutes." The silks float away on the breeze, leaving the cleaned seeds in the threshing box. Seed cleaning is not always necessary, but storage should include precautions against insects. Storing a no-pest strip-type insecticide bar in the seed-storage container (one strip will keep a 100-gallon storage can pest-free for a year or more) or mixing the seeds with diatomaceous earth before packaging them for storage are both effective. Seeds for sowing large field areas can be left uncleaned. The chaff keeps the seeds from blowing around and acts as a mulch. I also broadcast the trash from seed-cleaning wherever I'd like a few more plants—one year I had more Scorpionflower from the trash than in my prepared seedbed.

## Pretreating Seeds

Pulpy or winged seeds, like those of Desert Olive, Russian Olive, Sumac, Saltbush, and Sand Verbena, can be cleaned and pretreated to induce germination in an acid bath. Concentrated sulfuric acid (ninety percent +) dissolves chaff and softens hard seed coats in a process known as scarification. Use glass or very heavy plastic containers. Lab beakers, canning jars, or large glass peanut-butter jars work nicely. Place seeds in the container, pour acid over the seeds, and stir with a glass rod, dowel rod, or bamboo chopstick. The length of the treatment depends upon the hardness of the seed coat and can vary from year to year on the same species from the same source. Overprocessing will damage the embryo. Either test a few seeds from each seed lot first or examine seeds in the process. Seed coats should be scarred and pitted, papery husks (like Sand Verbena) will look burnt, but the acid reaction should be stopped before it reaches the smooth, starchy surface beneath the seed coat.

### Acid Scarification

Acid is extremely caustic. Wear protective clothing (a heavy apron or lab coat, rubber gloves, and goggles). I usually scarify seeds outdoors, as fumes from the acid reaction are irritating. Never splash water into the acid, as a violent reaction producing intense heat and steam will result. To stop the acid reaction, carefully drain off the acid (I strain it into another jar and reuse the acid several times), add water slowly, and rinse the seeds thoroughly. Add baking soda (one tablespoon per quart of water) to neutralize the acid and rinse again to remove all residue. You can then sow the seeds or give them a further cold-moist treatment if necessary. Hard seed coats can also be mechanically scarified— tumbled with coarse sand or rubbed between sheets of sandpaper. Again, take care to stop short of injuring the embryo. Scarification is the pretreatment used when the limiting factor is a hard seed coat that prevents water penetration and gas exchange or physically restricts the growth of the embryo. Scarification is the horticultural equivalent of passing through the digestive tract of birds, rodents, or other animals or washing along a watercourse in the wild.

### Hot Water Soak

Seeds with impermeable seed coats but without pulpy residues, like Bush Morningglory and Rose Locust, can be treated by soaking in boiling water. Bring water to a boil, remove from the heat, drop the seeds into the water, and leave them to soak as the water cools. Generally the seeds will begin to swell rapidly. Rose Locust often begins to germinate before the water cools entirely. While this pretreatment is less hazardous than an acid bath and is particularly effective on seeds of legumes, take care that the seeds are not overheated. The water should not continue to boil once the seeds are introduced, and seeds should not remain soaking in water lacking oxygen. If seeds are soaked for extended periods, change the water periodically. In most cases, prolonged soaking (longer than twenty-four hours) will do more harm than good. If seeds don't respond to a hot-water bath, try an alternate pretreatment. Soaking Bush Morningglory and Mariola seeds for an hour in three percent hydrogen peroxide after a hot-water soak will accelerate germination. These techniques, like scarification, have the advantage of destroying some fungi and bacteria.

**ACID SCARIFICATION:** Seeds that have thick, pulpy, or papery impermeable seed coats often germinate better if they are pretreated with sulfuric acid.

Wearing rubber gloves and protective goggles, pour concentrated sulfuric acid over seeds in glass jars.

Stir with a dowel rod as acid acts on seed coats. When seed coats are partially dissolved, pour off acid.

Rinse seeds thoroughly with water.

Add baking soda and water to seeds to neutralize acid.

Rinse again, then drain.

These Juniper seeds, shown clean of all pulp (**bottom center**) and with pulp charred and soft (**middle center**) are ready for mid-summer sowing. A warm-moist period, followed by a cold-moist period, is needed to germinate many Juniper species.

Before and after: the papery, woody seed coats of Sand Verbena. After an acid bath, seeds can be dried and stored for several months before sowing.

## Afterripening

Immaturity of the embryo is sometimes the limiting factor in germinating arid-land seeds—a defense against premature emergence during unfavorable growing conditions. Many native seeds require a period of afterripening. Dry storage at cool temperatures allows time for chemical inhibitors to deteriorate without otherwise affecting seed viability. To afterripen seeds, store the dry seeds in a cool, dry place. Enclosing a packet of silica gel or powdered milk will help absorb any excess moisture. Many Penstemon species germinate well after a year in storage, and this is the preferred long-term storage for most native seeds.

## Stratification

Some seeds require a cold-moist pretreatment to redistribute the growth regulators that are active in stimulating germination. This pretreatment, called stratification, involves storing seeds for varying lengths of time at temperatures around 40 F in a medium that will provide constant dampness in the presence of oxygen. I prefer mixing seeds with damp vermiculite or fine perlite in polyethylene (oxygen-permeable plastic) bags and storing them in the refrigerator. Put the medium in a colander, wet it, and allow excess moisture to run off before mixing in the seeds. Sumac requires three months of such moist chilling, while Four O'Clock requires one month and Gayfeather only two weeks. Penstemons require one to three months and will germinate in the refrigerator when they are ready. I check the bags every few days after the first month and sow the germinating seeds when the radicles (seed roots) are 1/8" long. While stratification is a relatively simple and foolproof procedure, it is wise to check the seeds

regularly to avoid a buildup of heat due to lack of oxygen and/or excess moisture at the interior of the seed mass and to remove seeds promptly if they start to germinate. If mold or fungus is a problem, remove the seeds and treat them with a fungicide. If you are using the same refrigerator that you use for food storage, spray seeds lightly with chlorine bleach rather than using a prepared fungicide. My Sumac seeds always mold, and it doesn't seem to affect germination at all. On the other hand, I lost an entire crop of Four O'Clocks to careless pretreating. That's eight hours' collecting and cleaning time, two hundred miles of travel, and a year without Four O'Clocks.

The easier method of stratifying seeds is to sow them directly in beds outdoors in the fall. Keep the seedbed damp (not soggy wet) through the winter, and as spring progresses your seeds will begin to germinate. The disadvantages of this method are that winds can carry off your seeds and winter-hungry rodents and birds may make your seedbed their local diner. In the fall I sow seeds that are inexpensive, readily available, or respond better to outdoor sowing, while I pamper the gems, seeds preferred by winter scavengers, and tiny seeds that need to be sown on or very near the surface. Common sense is your best guide.

## Leaching

This is a technique sometimes used in reducing the potency of germination inhibitors when time or circumstance do not allow afterripening or scarification. The seeds, enclosed in a container that permits the free flow of water, are repeatedly flushed with cold water. A canning jar with a screen lid (like an alfalfa or mung-bean sprouter) or a section of nylon stocking with the

**MECHANICAL SCARIFICATION BY ABRASION:** An alternate method of scarifying tough seed coats is by abrasion (**1**). Here, Threeleaf Sumac seeds are rubbed with coarse-grit sandpaper (**2**). Whatever method of scarification is used, care must be taken to stop short of damaging embryos (**3**).

ends tied off and a garden hose left trickling over the seeds makes an easy leaching setup. Set the leacher under an established shade tree and the runoff won't be wasted. Leaching can be much more effective than soaking, as the water dilutes and carries off the inhibitor. Since many arid-land seeds are sensitive to low oxygen levels, leaching with running water eliminates the risk of destroying seeds due to poor aeration.

The study of the chemistry of germination inhibitors is still in its infancy. The synthesis and deterioration of these chemicals is as yet poorly documented. The methods I use for overcoming dormancy are, by process of trial and error, those I have found to be effective, but they are by no means absolutes. The volume of answers found is proportionate to the number of interested growers posing questions. Welcome to the club.

## Sowing Seeds

Since all pretreatments with the exception of after-ripening are intended to directly stimulate germination, they should be timed to coincide with whatever follow-up method is desired for seedling production. When seeds are limited by availability or cost, sowing in seed flats in a greenhouse or cold frame for later transplanting gives you greater control over moisture, temperature, and pests. Seeding can be done up to three months prior to transplanting. February or early March sowing nets transplantable seedlings when outside temperatures moderate in late April and May.

Field sowing of pretreated seeds should be done when soil begins warming but air temperatures are not yet high enough to interfere with seedling development. My best results, in sandy soil, in south central New Mexico, have been with mid-March sowing dates. Covering the seedbed with a sheet of corrugated fiber glass keeps the seedbed evenly moist. Mid-March sowing outdoors has worked best on seeds preferring midrange temperatures. Cool-weather lovers like the Artemisias can be sown up to a month earlier, and warm-weather lovers like Desert Willow and Bird of Paradise can be sown six weeks to two months later.

Seeds have specific temperature and/or light preferences that limit germination. The chart (pg. 72–73) gives the optimum temperatures and other specifics that growers will find useful. Desert Willow responds more evenly to warm soils and air temperatures (70–85 F), while the Sages prefer temperatures of 55–65 F for germination. These are the upper ranges. Most seeds respond better to fluctuating day-night temperatures than to a constant temperature. Plants that prefer warm soils for germination and growth are often frost-sensitive when they are young. Delay field-sowing heat lovers until all danger of frost is past. Scorpion-flower, Evening Primrose, and Fern Verbena all germinate better without light and can be covered with up to ¼" of soil. Very fine seeds and those that germinate best in bright light, like Chamisa, should be covered very lightly or not at all. The trick then is to keep the seeds damp enough to sprout. Outdoors, covering the seedbed with a sheet of corrugated fiber glass or plastic, weighted down against the wind, solves the problem. Once daytime temperatures are consistently in the 70s, germination diminishes under cover, probably because the fiber glass/plastic traps heat and warms the soil beyond optimum range.

The procedures for seeding arid-land natives in flats are similar to those for any other cultivated plant. Bright light (or darkness), moderate warmth, ventilation, and moisture are all necessary. I prefer fine-grade perlite or a fifty-fifty mixture of perlite and vermiculite top-dressed with time-release fertilizer as a planting medium. Because perlite and vermiculite are manufactured at temperatures of 1,200 F or more, they tend to be sterile provided they've been stored dry. (If the bag is torn or waterspotted, assume that they are no longer sterile.) These products provide the rapid drainage and aeration essential for young seedlings.

Recently I began using hinged-lid styro containers, like those used by restaurants for take-out orders, as seed flats. I adapted a technique developed by New Mexico State University and the U.S. Forest Service for producing pine-tree seedlings for revegetation. I use a 9" × 9" × 3"-size container, puncturing the bottom half to allow drainage. After filling the bottom half with perlite or a fifty-fifty mix, I broadcast the seeds evenly on the surface. The 9" × 9" × 3" size easily accommodates 500 Penstemon or Chamisa-size seeds, 200 Butterfly-weed or Allium, or 100 Gayfeather. Do not overcrowd the seeds, as competition among seedlings can result in greater losses and fewer transplants. Drench the seeded trays with fungicide, label them with a waterproof marker (include the date for future reference), and close the lid. Small seeds will wash down into the perlite when it is drenched. I push larger seeds into the medium or cover them lightly with more of the same.

Given the expected germination time (Propagation From Seeds chart, pg. 72–73), I stack the trays by expected germination time, with those preferring darkness at the bottom, those requiring light on top, heat lovers in a warm spot, etc. I then check the trays every few days, and when germination is well underway I open the tray and cut off the lid, growing the seedlings on in the trays until they are ready for transplanting. Most seeds will sprout within three weeks, and the trays will not need watering while they are closed. Germination rates are very high due to the evenly moist conditions in the tray. Germination times will often be half those given on the chart, as those expectations are based on open-flat sowing where the surface is liable to dry out enough to delay sprouting. Most new seedlings require bright light to develop properly. Spindly, "stretched" seedlings will transplant poorly. The hinged-lid trays offer the greatest flexibility in meeting the germinating and early growing requirements of native seeds.

## PROPAGATION BY CUTTINGS

The alternative to using seeds as a method of reproduction is vegetative propagation, or cutting. There are both advantages and drawbacks to this means of regeneration. The techniques used in producing plants from cuttings aim to produce rapid rooting before the cutting material deteriorates.

The same foliage characteristics that minimize moisture loss in established plants are a decided advantage in the survivability of leafy softwood cuttings, allowing successful rooting of Desert Olive and Saltbush without mist at some times of the year. Plants that are variable in size, form, leaf, quality of fruit, or flower color can be selected for desirable characteristics by cutting from parent stock that displays such traits. Where seeds are difficult to handle or unavailable, cuttings can fill production gaps. Cherry Sage and Four O'Clock produce few seeds, but cuttings root easily. Cuttings sometimes produce finished plants more rapidly than seeds, and therefore reduce unit costs. Despite these advantages, it should be said that using cuttings exclusively limits the gene pool. Improvement of cutting stock by introducing "new blood" with desirable traits should be a constant, ongoing process. Likewise, selection for desirable characteristics must be broad in scope; improving appearance at the expense of drought or disease resistance is no improvement.

As a rule, success in rooting cuttings involves effective combinations of timing and cutting material. Season and plant response determine whether hardwood or softwood is used. (Hardwood cuttings are dormant woody-stem sections taken in early spring, cut from the last year's new growth. Soft or semi-softwood cuttings are tip cuttings taken from the new growth during the growing season either while it is still very soft or just as the stem tissue becomes woody.)

Consistent with selective breeding is the necessity of using the best available parent stock—average four- to seven-inch stem sections with the greatest diameter possible, cut from unshaded portions of the plant. Cutting material from unshaded plant parts has higher carbohydrate and hormone levels and will produce strong roots more rapidly. Young wood is consistently easier to root; plant material that has had adequate moisture to produce healthy new growth will root and grow more rapidly than cutting stock that has been dependent solely upon natural rainfall. When cuttings are taken from plants in the wild, results will vary with the current weather and other local conditions but will always be poorer than rooting of cuttings from cultivated stock.

# PROPAGATION FROM SEEDS

TEMPERATURE: Data given indicates optimum temperatures in most cases. Germination time and % figures are based upon the given temperatures; higher or lower temperatures may increase germinating time or lower percentages. Where % given is low, experiment; you may find an optimal range. If seeds require light (L) or darkness (D) for germination, it is noted here.
GERMINATION TIME & AVERAGE %: Figures represent estimates based upon experiments using good quality seeds treated as indicated. Results can vary depending upon seed source, storage, and treatment.

Average % indicates the number of seedlings after one month. Some seeds with a germination % less than 50% will germinate up to 90% eventually. Disturbing the soil to transplant out seedlings often results in a flush of germination, perhaps due to aeration of the growing medium.
BLANKS INDICATE INCONCLUSIVE RESULTS OR DATA OTHERWISE UNOBTAINABLE AT THIS TIME.

| PLANT NAME | PRETREATMENT | TEMPERATURE | GERMINATION TIME | SEEDS PER OUNCE | AVERAGE % GERMINATION | COMMENTS |
|---|---|---|---|---|---|---|
| **TREES** | | | | | | |
| Arizona Sycamore *Platanus wrightii* | CST 3 mo. | | erratic | 8,400 | | |
| Desert Olive *Forestiera neomexicana* | none | 65°-80°F | 3 weeks | 4,500 | 50% | SC old or uncleaned seeds |
| Desert Willow *Chilopsis linearis* | none | 70°-80°F | 5 to 10 days | 5,000 | 50% | seeds mature over a long period; use only ripe seeds |
| "King Red" Russian Olive *Elaeagnus angustifolia* | none | 65°-80°F | 3 weeks | 350 | 70% + | SC old or uncleaned seeds |
| Mesquite *Prosopis glandulosa* | BWS-fresh SC-dried | 70°-80°F | 7 to 30 + days | 250 unhulled | 40% | fresh seeds germinate well before drying |
| Oak *Quercus species* | fresh seed | outdoors Sept.-Oct. | 2 to 4 weeks | varies by species | 70% + | seed crops every 2-5 years |
| Rose Locust *Robinia neomexicana* | BWS | outdoors June | 2 weeks | 1,250 | 80% + | sow directly in beds or gallon containers |
| Soaptree Yucca *Yucca elata* | none | outdoors July-Aug. | 10 days | | 80% + | |
| **SHRUBS** | | | | | | |
| Apache Plume *Fallugia paradoxa* | fresh seed | 70°F | 5 days | 33,000 | 30-40% | damps off easily |
| Bigleaf Sage *Artemisia tridentata* | CST 2 mo. | 65°F | up to 4 weeks | 185,000 | 80% | |
| Bird of Paradise *Caesalpinia gilliesii* | none | outdoors Apr.-May | 2 weeks | 200 | 80% | new seedlings are not cold hardy |
| Broom Baccharis *Baccharis emoryi* | none | 65°-80°F | 7 to 10 days | 35,000 unclean | varies | |
| Cliffrose *Cowania mexicana* | CST 2-3 mo. | outdoors Nov.-March | erratic | 4,000 | erratic | |
| Creosote Bush *Larrea tridentata* | SC | 50°-90°F | 1 to 4 weeks | 10,000 | 40-60% | afterripening for 1 to 2 years may improve germination |
| False Indigo *Dalea scoparia* | BWS | 65°-90°F | 7 to 30 days | | | |
| Fernbush *Chamaebatiaria millifolium* | CST 2 mo. | 65°-80°F | erratic | | | |
| Fourwing Saltbush *Atriplex canescens* | SC | 65°-75°F | 7 to 21 days | 3,400 | 50% | |
| Golden Currant *Ribes aureum* | CST 3 mo. | 40°-75°F | 3 months | 13,000 | 60% in 3 mo. | |
| Littleleaf & Threeleaf Sumac *Rhus species* | SC CST 3 mo. | 65°-85°F outdoors June | 1 to 3 weeks | 4,200 | 50-70% | sow directly in beds or gallon containers |
| Mountain Mahogany *Cercocarpus montanus* | CST 2-3 mo. | 50°-70°F | 2 to 3 weeks | 3,000 | 70% | cover with 1/4" soil |
| Rabbitbrush Chamisa *Chrysothamnus nauseosus* | none | 65°-70°F (L) | 5 days | 30,000 unclean | 20-40% | |
| Winterfat *Ceratoides lanata* | none | 65°-85°F | 1 to 5 days | 5,500 | 80% | results are better using uncleaned seeds |

## GROUND COVERS  Flowering Plants, Vines, Grasses

| PLANT NAME | PRETREATMENT | TEMPERATURE | GERMINATION TIME | SEEDS PER OUNCE | AVERAGE % GERMINATION | COMMENTS |
|---|---|---|---|---|---|---|
| Beardtongue *Penstemon species* | AR 1 to 6 yrs. | 35°-70°F | 2 to 3 weeks | 22,000 | 50% | sometimes CST increases germination % on new seeds |
| Blackfoot Daisy *Melampodium leucanthum* | fresh seed | 70°F | 1 to 3 weeks | | 50% | once seeds dry it is difficult to get them to germinate |
| Blue Flax *Linum lewisii* | none | 55°F | 3 to 4 weeks | 21,000 | 70%+ | |
| Blue Grama *Bouteloua gracilis* | none | 60°-90°F | 3 weeks or less | 45,000 | 50% | seeding rate 8-12 lb. per acre 1-2 tb. per 1,000 sq. ft. |
| Buffalograss *Buchloe dactyloides* | buy treated seed | 60°-90°F | lawn density in 2-3 mo. | 17,000 | 50%+ | "Texoka" or "Sharps Improved" |
| Bush Morningglory *Ipomoea leptophylla* | BWS | outdoors mid April | 2 weeks | 200 | 75% | sow directly in place or in gallon containers |
| Cherry Sage & others *Salvia species* | CST 3 to 5 weeks | 68°-80°F (L) | 10 to 14 days | 15,000-25,000 | erratic | seeds need light to germinate |
| Cinquefoil *Potentilla species* | CST 2 mo. | 50°-70°F | 2 weeks to 1 month | 80,000 | 70% | very fine seeds, sow on surface |
| Coneflower/Mexican Hat *Ratibida columnaris* | none | 60°-75°F | 2 to 3 weeks | 75,000 | 50%+ | broadcast where plants are to grow |
| Desert Marigold *Baileya multiradiata* | none | outdoors Oct.-Dec. | erratic | 45,000 | erratic | larvae destroy seeds in storage—fumigate |
| Desert Zinnia *Zinnia grandiflora* | none | 70°-80°F | 10 to 30 days | 7,000 | 30-50% | |
| Fern Verbena *Verbena bipinnatifida* | AR 1 to 3 yrs. | 70°F (D) | 3 to 4 weeks | 10,000 | 30-50% | |
| Fringe Sage *Artemisia frigida* | none | 55°-65°F | 7 to 10 days | 125,000 | 70% | keep evenly moist |
| Gayfeather *Liatris species* | CST 2 wks. | 75°-80°F | 3 to 5 days | 8,500 | 96% with 14-hr. day length | |
| Giant Four O'Clock *Mirabilis multiflora* | CST 1 mo. | 55°-75°F | 10 days to 3 months | 400 | 30% | |
| Globemallow *Sphaeralcea coccinea* | SC CST 2 mo. | 65°-75°F | 2 to 3 weeks | 30,000 | 50%+ | |
| Indian Ricegrass *Oryzopsis hymenoides* | SC | 50°-70°F | erratic | 10,000 | erratic | 7 to 9 lb. per acre; may take 2 yrs. to develop a good stand |
| Paperflower *Psilostrophe tagentina* | CST 2 mo. | 50°-70°F | erratic | | 50% | |
| Purple Aster *Machaeranthera bigelovii* | none | outdoors Oct.-Dec. | erratic | 30,000 unclean | 50%+ | sow directly where plants are to grow |
| Purple Prairieclover *Petalostemon purpureum* | BWS | outdoors Feb. | 2 to 6 weeks | 18,000 | 50%+ | |
| Sand Verbena *Tripterocalyx (Abronia)* | SC | outdoors Feb. | erratic | 1,000 scarified | 60% | |
| Scorpionflower *Phacelia integrifolia* | none | outdoors Aug.-Oct. (D) | erratic | 14,000 | erratic | needs darkness to germinate—may take 2 yrs. to establish a stand |
| Silver Groundsel *Senecio longilobus* | none | 65°-75°F | 2 to 3 weeks | 30,000 unclean | 30-50% | |
| Western Virginsbower *Clematis ligusticifolia* | CST 2 mo. | | | 18,500 | | |
| White Evening Primrose *Oenothera caespitosa* | CST 2 mo. | 60°-70°F (D) | erratic | 54,000 | 30%? | darkness improves germination |

*SEEDS PER OUNCE:*
Figures indicate cleaned seeds unless noted otherwise. It is difficult to get an accurate seed count on species that cannot be thoroughly cleaned, and those quantities are not given here.

*PRETREATMENT ABBREVIATIONS:*
BWS—pour boiling water over seed and allow to cool
SC—scarification with sulfuric acid

CST —cold moist stratification at 35°-40°F for prescribed time
AR —cool dry storage afterripening

**HARDWOOD CUTTINGS:** Cut from previous season's new growth of greatest girth possible.

Recut so top of cuttings have a viable bud at the tip and another bud at the base. Dip stems in rooting hormone.

Stick into a prepared bed of sand.

Tamp earth around cutting.

# Hard- & Softwood Cuttings

Hardwood cuttings are taken when the plant is dormant, using the previous year's growth. Woody cuttings should be greater than ¼" in diameter and 4–6" in length. The cuttings are inserted vertically in the rooting medium, entirely covering the cutting. Be sure that the cutting is inserted with the growing tip upward, root end down. Softwood cuttings are taken using the newest growing tips, partially stripped of foliage. The portion of the stem inserted into the growing medium should be defoliated, and the tip should be handled carefully to preserve some leaf surface, as maintaining photosynthesis accelerates root production. An advantage is gained with natives that have chlorophyll in their stems, as photosynthesis is possible even when leaves have been lost. A balance must be struck between food-synthesizing surface and evaporative surface.

Hardwood cuttings can be stuck directly into a well-prepared (tilled and raked), well-drained garden plot outdoors or stored in damp perlite in polyethylene bags in the refrigerator. Coarse-grade perlite with the addition of 18–6–12 time-release fertilizer is a suitable rooting medium for softwood cuttings. Rooting hormones, used as a stimulus for rooting, are especially effective on difficult to root species like Junipers or when rapid root initiation is essential, as when softwood cuttings are taken without mist. The easier a plant is to root, the lower the concentration of hormone required. IBA talc (Indole 3 Butyric Acid in powdered form) is an easily obtained rooting hormone available in several strengths from .3% for easily rooted cuttings (Baccharis and Desert Willow) to .8% (Santolina, Saltbush, and Forestiera) to 2.0% for the most difficult to root species (Junipers, table legs, and maybe Cliffrose).

Cuttings should be inserted into the rooting medium

## GROUND COVERS — Flowering Plants, Vines, Grasses

| PLANT NAME | PRETREATMENT | TEMPERATURE | GERMINATION TIME | SEEDS PER OUNCE | AVERAGE % GERMINATION | COMMENTS |
|---|---|---|---|---|---|---|
| Beardtongue *Penstemon species* | AR 1 to 6 yrs. | 35°-70°F | 2 to 3 weeks | 22,000 | 50% | sometimes CST increases germination % on new seeds |
| Blackfoot Daisy *Melampodium leucanthum* | fresh seed | 70°F | 1 to 3 weeks | | 50% | once seeds dry it is difficult to get them to germinate |
| Blue Flax *Linum lewisii* | none | 55°F | 3 to 4 weeks | 21,000 | 70%+ | |
| Blue Grama *Bouteloua gracilis* | none | 60°-90°F | 3 weeks or less | 45,000 | 50% | seeding rate 8-12 lb. per acre 1-2 tb. per 1,000 sq. ft. |
| Buffalograss *Buchloe dactyloides* | buy treated seed | 60°-90°F | lawn density in 2-3 mo. | 17,000 | 50%+ | "Texoka" or "Sharps Improved" |
| Bush Morningglory *Ipomoea leptophylla* | BWS | outdoors mid April | 2 weeks | 200 | 75% | sow directly in place or in gallon containers |
| Cherry Sage & others *Salvia species* | CST 3 to 5 weeks | 68°-80°F (L) | 10 to 14 days | 15,000-25,000 | erratic | seeds need light to germinate |
| Cinquefoil *Potentilla species* | CST 2 mo. | 50°-70°F | 2 weeks to 1 month | 80,000 | 70% | very fine seeds, sow on surface |
| Coneflower/Mexican Hat *Ratibida columnaris* | none | 60°-75°F | 2 to 3 weeks | 75,000 | 50%+ | |
| Desert Marigold *Baileya multiradiata* | none | outdoors Oct.-Dec. | erratic | 45,000 | erratic | broadcast where plants are to grow |
| Desert Zinnia *Zinnia grandiflora* | none | 70°-80°F | 10 to 30 days | 7,000 | 30-50% | larvae destroy seeds in storage—fumigate |
| Fern Verbena *Verbena bipinnatifida* | AR 1 to 3 yrs. | 70°F (D) | 3 to 4 weeks | 10,000 | 30-50% | |
| Fringe Sage *Artemisia frigida* | none | 55°-65°F | 7 to 10 days | 125,000 | 70% | keep evenly moist |
| Gayfeather *Liatris species* | CST 2 wks. | 75°-80°F | 3 to 5 days | 8,500 | 96% with 14-hr. day length | |
| Giant Four O'Clock *Mirabilis multiflora* | CST 1 mo. | 55°-75°F | 10 days to 3 months | 400 | 30% | |
| Globemallow *Sphaeralcea coccinea* | SC CST 2 mo. | 65°-75°F | 2 to 3 weeks | 30,000 | 50%+ | |
| Indian Ricegrass *Oryzopsis hymenoides* | SC | 50°-70°F | erratic | 10,000 | erratic | 7 to 9 lb. per acre; may take 2 yrs. to develop a good stand |
| Paperflower *Psilostrophe tagentina* | CST 2 mo. | 50°-70°F | erratic | | 50% | |
| Purple Aster *Machaeranthera bigelovii* | none | outdoors Oct.-Dec. | erratic | 30,000 unclean | 50%+ | sow directly where plants are to grow |
| Purple Prairieclover *Petalostemon purpureum* | BWS | outdoors Feb. | 2 to 6 weeks | 18,000 | 50%+ | |
| Sand Verbena *Tripterocalyx (Abronia)* | SC | outdoors Feb. | erratic | 1,000 scarified | 60% | |
| Scorpionflower *Phacelia integrifolia* | none | outdoors Aug.-Oct. (D) | erratic | 14,000 | erratic | needs darkness to germinate—may take 2 yrs. to establish a stand |
| Silver Groundsel *Senecio longilobus* | none | 65°-75°F | 2 to 3 weeks | 30,000 unclean | 30-50% | |
| Western Virginsbower *Clematis ligusticifolia* | CST 2 mo. | | | 18,500 | | |
| White Evening Primrose *Oenothera caespitosa* | CST 2 mo. | 60°-70°F (D) | erratic | 54,000 | 30%? | darkness improves germination |

*PRETREATMENT ABBREVIATIONS:*
BWS —pour boiling water over seed and allow to cool
SC —scarification with sulfuric acid

CST —cold moist stratification at 35°-40°F for prescribed time
AR —cool dry storage afterripenning

*SEEDS PER OUNCE:*
Figures indicate cleaned seeds unless noted otherwise.
It is difficult to get an accurate seed count on species that cannot be thoroughly cleaned, and those quantities are not given here.

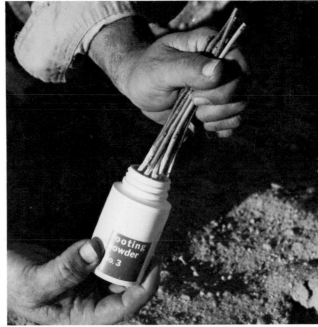

**HARDWOOD CUTTINGS:** Cut from previous season's new growth of greatest girth possible.

Recut so top of cuttings have a viable bud at the tip and another bud at the base. Dip stems in rooting hormone.

Stick into a prepared bed of sand.

Tamp earth around cutting.

## Hard- & Softwood Cuttings

Hardwood cuttings are taken when the plant is dormant, using the previous year's growth. Woody cuttings should be greater than ¼" in diameter and 4–6" in length. The cuttings are inserted vertically in the rooting medium, entirely covering the cutting. Be sure that the cutting is inserted with the growing tip upward, root end down. Softwood cuttings are taken using the newest growing tips, partially stripped of foliage. The portion of the stem inserted into the growing medium should be defoliated, and the tip should be handled carefully to preserve some leaf surface, as maintaining photosynthesis accelerates root production. An advantage is gained with natives that have chlorophyll in their stems, as photosynthesis is possible even when leaves have been lost. A balance must be struck between food-synthesizing surface and evaporative surface.

Hardwood cuttings can be stuck directly into a well-prepared (tilled and raked), well-drained garden plot outdoors or stored in damp perlite in polyethylene bags in the refrigerator. Coarse-grade perlite with the addition of 18–6–12 time-release fertilizer is a suitable rooting medium for softwood cuttings. Rooting hormones, used as a stimulus for rooting, are especially effective on difficult to root species like Junipers or when rapid root initiation is essential, as when softwood cuttings are taken without mist. The easier a plant is to root, the lower the concentration of hormone required. IBA talc (Indole 3 Butyric Acid in powdered form) is an easily obtained rooting hormone available in several strengths from .3% for easily rooted cuttings (Baccharis and Desert Willow) to .8% (Santolina, Saltbush, and Forestiera) to 2.0% for the most difficult to root species (Junipers, table legs, and maybe Cliffrose).

Cuttings should be inserted into the rooting medium

Primrose have tuberous roots that can be cut into 2–4" or larger segments. The thicker the tuber, the shorter the cutting can be. I dip the bottom end into rooting hormone immediately, so I'm sure which end is up when I begin potting. If for some reason you can't tell which end is up, lay the cuttings in flats or in an outdoor cutting bed vertically. It may take several months for the cuttings to form new terminal buds. Resist the urge to dig them up and don't overwater them. You've done most of your work—let time and the cuttings take care of the rest.

## Layering

Layering is an almost foolproof method of producing new plants, because the cutting is rooted before it is severed from the parent plant. This technique eliminates the problem of maintaining high humidity and affords more leeway in soil moisture and timing. Choose a healthy lower branch of the plant to be layered and cut a notch in the stem about ten inches from the tip just below a node (the point where a leaf is attached to the stem). Bend the stem down to the ground and loosen the soil where the notched stem contacts the soil. Push the stem into the soil so that the growing tip is exposed but the notched portion is buried. Pin the stem in place with a heavy wire loop (coat-hanger wire works well), or place a large stone over the buried stem. Keep the soil around the layer damp. Resist the urge to disturb the layer for at least six months. It may take six months to two years for a good root system to develop. When the layer is well rooted, sever it from the parent plant and transplant it to its permanent place in the landscape. Most plants that can be rooted from hardwood or softwood cuttings will layer easily.

## Division

Clump-forming perennials, plants that have a matted growth habit or form offshoots from a central crown, can be increased by dividing established specimens. Dig up the entire plant and split it into sections with a sharp knife or pull sections away by hand. A portion of the plant can then be reset in its original location, and the others transplanted elsewhere. Since the plant is uprooted in the process, dividing should be done while the plant is dormant, in spring for summer- and fall-blooming species and in autumn for spring-blooming species. Division is a quick, easy, and economical way to increase wild flowers for bedding, borders, and massed ground-cover areas. Done carefully every few years, it has a rejuvenating effect on the original plants. Yarrow, Fringe

**DIVISION:** Lift from the soil and gently pull apart sections of the original plant (here a clump of Indian Ricegrass), then reset divisions.

Sage, Indian Ricegrass, Blanketflower, the mat-forming Penstemons, and Verbenas can be divided easily. Gayfeather, Paperflower, Blackfoot Daisy, and the shrubby Penstemons are taprooted with central crowns that should not be divided.

Seeds, hardwood cuttings, and softwood cuttings are the best sources of large numbers of new plants. Root cuttings, layering, and division are easy and economical means of producing small numbers of plants from established landscape stock. Any type of propagation gives the grower a rewarding sense of participation in nature. In a time of extraterrestrial travel and nuclear power, the process of acorn to Oak tree is as reassuring as it is awesome.

# PROPAGATION FROM CUTTINGS

| PLANT NAME | TYPE OF CUTTING | APPROX. TIME | HORMONE | AVERAGE ROOTING TIME | AVERAGE ROOTING % | COMMENTS |
|---|---|---|---|---|---|---|
| **TREES** | | | | | | |
| Cottonwood & Aspen *Populus* species | hardwood | Feb.–Mar. | .1% or .3% IBA | 1 month | 80% | easy—select male trees |
| Desert Olive *Forestiera neomexicana* | semi-softwood | Aug. | .8% IBA | 7 to 14 days | 70% | easy without mist |
| Desert Willow *Chilopsis linearis* | hardwood softwood | April July–Aug. | .3% or .8% IBA | 1 month | 70% | easy way to guarantee flower color |
| Russian Olive *Elaeagnus angustifolia* | hardwood | March | .3% IBA | 1 month | 90% | easy way to guarantee fruit quality |
| Tamarisk *Tamarix pentandra* | hardwood | March | .3% IBA | 1 month | 90% | easy—select for dark color |
| **SHRUBS** | | | | | | |
| Apache Plume *Fallugia paradoxa* | softwood | Apr. or Aug. | .8% to 2.0% IBA | 7 to 10 days | 50% | very succulent tips root best but are extremely perishable |
| Bigleaf Sage *Artemisia tridentata* | leafy tips | Feb.–Apr. | 2.0% IBA | 1 month | variable | |
| Broom Baccharis *Baccharis emoryi* | semi-soft tips | Aug. | .3% IBA | 7 to 10 days | 80% | easy |
| Fourwing Saltbush *Atriplex canescens* | semi-soft tips | Aug. | .8% IBA | 2 to 3 weeks | 70% | some rooting anytime with intermittent mist |
| Littleleaf & Threeleaf Sumac *Rhus* species | semi-softwood | Aug. | .8% IBA | 2 to 3 weeks | 75% | |
| **GROUND COVERS** (Perennials and Vines) | | | | | | |
| Beardtongue *Penstemon* species | semi-soft side shoots | after flowering | .3%–.8% IBA | 1 to 2 weeks | 50% | *P. ambiguus* hardwood cuttings mid–March from close to crown |
| Blackfoot Daisy *Melampodium leucanthume* | semi-soft almost woody | Aug.–Sept. | .8% IBA | 7 to 10 days | 50% | |
| Cherry Sage *Salvia* species | soft & semi-soft tips | June–Sept. | .8% IBA | 14 days | | Aug.–Sept. cuttings root easiest |
| Coyotebush *Baccharis pilularis* | semi-softwood | Feb.–Aug. | .3% IBA | 7 to 10 days | 50–70% | August is better |
| Giant Four O'Clock *Mirabilis multiflora* | soft tips | May | .1% to .3% IBA | 2 weeks–1 with mist | 50% | stronger hormone seems to inhibit rooting |
| Fringe Sage *Artemisia frigida* | growing tips | Feb.–May | .1% to .3% IBA | 2 to 3 weeks | 70% | |
| Globemallow *Sphaeralcea* species | soft side shoots | Mar.–Apr. | .8% IBA | 2 to 3 weeks | | |
| Lavender Cotton *Santolina* | growing tips | mid Mar. or Aug. | .8% IBA | 7 to 10 days | 75% | very specific as to time |
| Western Virginsbower *Clematis ligusticifolia* | semi-softwood | dormant or Aug. | .3% IBA | varies | varies | can select for male or female |
| Woodbine/Creeper *Parthenocissus inserta* | any | anytime | none | 10 days to 1 month | 50–90% | easy |

*HARDWOOD:  Cuttings can range in length from 3 to 6 inches; the largest girth of previous year's growth is optimal.*

*SEMI-SOFT:  Judging maturity is largely a matter of observation and experience. Stems should be the greatest girth possible of 4- to 6-inch growing tips, new growth beginning to harden (become woody).*

*SOFTWOOD:  Growing tips should snap off the plant cleanly. Timing is critical.*

*PERCENTAGES:  Based upon results obtained in the time indicated without intermittent mist. Given the benefit of mist for 3 to 7 days, most cuttings will root faster. Using mist and bottom heat may increase rooting percentages and shorten rooting time. In any case, these figures may vary quite a bit depending upon growing conditions and the quality of the growing material.*

*RECOMMENDED ROOTING MEDIUM IS COARSE-GRADE PERLITE PLUS 1-OZ. TIME RELEASE 18–6–12 FERTILIZER PER 21" × 10" × 2.5" FLAT.*

# 6 🐝 CONCLUSION: SURVIVING COMPROMISE, THE GOURMET'S GARDEN

Not everyone is a born gardener, but we are all born hungry. It might help to simplify this survey of arid-landscape options if you consider your garden in culinary terms. Whatever your taste, there are arid-land natives that will satisfy it. This is then a cookbook of sorts, and your landscape plan is a recipe. You may just be adding finishing touches to an established landscape, so your plan is a recipe for "frosting on the cake." You may be looking for low-maintenance solutions to hot, dry problem areas, so your plan is a low-calorie formula. Perhaps yours is a raw site in need of development, so your plan is a recipe for "the whole enchilada." Arid-land native landscaping is the nouvelle cuisine of Southwestern gardening. The critics' choice is a garden that is light yet satisfying, low maintenance but livable. The ingredients and how they are blended determine the success of the recipe. While it is possible to create a landscape that requires no maintenance, it will not have the subtle flavor of a selectively maintained garden.

Personally, I hate peeling vegetables and pulling weeds. I prefer the hearty appearance and greater vitamin content of home fries still in their skins. My compromise is using tender-skinned new potatoes, retaining the appearance and nutrients without sacrificing flavor and texture. In the garden, I prefer tilling and pruning to the drudgery of weeding and shoveling gravel. Tilling offers a promise of harvest that is invigorating, especially since a good Rototiller does most of the work. Pruning is the gardener's signature on the landscape, a means of improving on nature the way basting improves a roast, bringing out the best in the raw ingredients. Again, there is a choice in technique. Shearing takes time, doesn't yield any insight into the nature of the plant, and creates the need to repeat the chore at regular intervals. Selective pruning, on the other hand, requires careful observation of each plant being worked on and yields an understanding of how the plant grows. It also takes time, but guarantees less work as the plant matures.

Watering requires further compromise. The selection of plants that can be established and then totally ignored in the hottest parts of the desert Southwest is very limited. "Zoning," grouping plants according to their moisture requirements, gives the arid-land gardener a wider range of ingredients with which to work. The end products are reduced water use and a more interesting landscape, a rare instance of having your cake and eating it too. The choices line up like this:

## OASIS PLANTS-THE LUSH, MOISTURE-LOVING ONES:

**TREES:**
Arizona Sycamore
Cottonwoods
Desert Olive
Quaking Aspen

**EVERGREENS:**
Afghan Pine
Arizona Cypress
Junipers

**SHRUBS:**
Broom Baccharis

Golden Currant
Shrubby Cinquefoil

**VINES:**
Western Virginsbower
Woodbine

**WILD FLOWERS:**
Blue Flax
Butterflyweed
Cherry Sage
Creeping Mahonia
Flowering Onions

## TRANSITIONAL PLANTS-THE ADAPTABLE ONES:

**TREES:**
Desert Olive
Desert Willow
Oaks
Rose Locust
Russian Olive
Tamarisk

**EVERGREENS:**
Afghan Pine
Arizona Cypress
Junipers
Piñon

**SHRUBS:**
Apache Plume
Bigleaf Sage
Chamisa
Cliffrose
Fernbush
Fourwing Saltbush
Mariola
Mountain Mahogany
Sumacs

Threadleaf Sage

**VINES:**
Western Virginsbower
Woodbine

**WILD FLOWERS:**
Blanketflower
Cherry Sage
Coneflowers
Creeping Mahonia
Desert Zinnia
Gayfeather
Giant Four O'Clock
Penstemons
Purple Aster
Purple Prairieclover
Santolina
Verbena
Yellow Evening Primrose

**GRASSES:**
Blue Grama
Buffalograss

## HEAT- AND DROUGHT-LOVING PLANTS—THE SELF-SUFFICIENT ONES:

**TREES:**
Desert Willow

Mesquite
Tamarisk

EVERGREENS:
Afghan Pine
Junipers  some
Piñon

SHRUBS:
Bird of Paradise
Broom Dalea
Creosotebush
Fourwing Saltbush
Mariola
Threadleaf Sage
Winterfat

WILD FLOWERS:
Blackfoot Daisy
Bush Morningglory

Bush Penstemon
Desert Marigold
Desert Zinnia
Fringe Sage
Mexican Evening Primrose
Paperflower
Purple Aster
Sand Verbena
Santolina
Scarlet Globemallow
Silver Groundsel
Verbena
White Tufted Evening
Primrose

GRASSES: Indian Ricegrass

Prairie Sage
Purple Prairieclover
Sand Verbena
Santolina
Scarlet Globemallow
Shrubby Cinquefoil

Silver Groundsel
Spreading Junipers
("Broadmoor,"
"Buffalo," "Tam,"
and "Blue Rug")

## PLANTS FOR MEADOWS:

Blackfoot Daisy
Blanketflower
Blue Flax
Blue Grama
Calliopsis
Coneflower
Desert Marigold
Desert Zinnia
Evening Primrose
Fringe Sage
Gayfeather

Indian Ricegrass
Paperflower
Penstemons
Prairie Sage
Purple Aster
Purple Prairieclover
Sand Verbena
Scarlet Globemallow
Silver Groundsel
Verbena

Given these moisture zones, here are some suggested uses, based on the form and adaptability of the plants.

## PLANTS FOR HEDGES, WINDBREAKS, AND SCREENS:

TREES:
Afghan Pine
Arizona Cypress
Desert Olive
Desert Willow
Junipers
Rose Locust
Russian Olive
Tamarisk

SHRUBS:
Apache Plume
Broom Baccharis
Chamisa
Cliffrose
Fourwing Saltbush
Mountain Mahogany
Sumacs

## PLANTS FOR PARKWAYS AND LOW BORDERS:

Blackfoot Daisy
Blanketflower
Broom Dalea
Bush Morningglory
Cherry Sage
Coneflower
Creeping Mahonia

Desert Zinnia
Fringe Sage
Giant Four O'Clock
Paperflower
Penstemons (especially
Pineleaf, "Bandera," and
Bush)

## PLANTS FOR SHADE:

Cinquefoils
Creeping Mahonia

Western Virginsbower
Woodbine

## ACCENT SPECIMENS:

Bigleaf Sage
Cliffrose
Creosotebush
Desert Olive

Desert Willow
Piñon
Russian Olive
Soaptree Yucca

Style is a personal ingredient that ultimately defines the direction your landscape plans will take. The same ingredients, combined differently, can result in a barbeque or a formal dinner party. The success of either depends on whether the people served (including yourself) enjoy the results. Straight lines, geometrical patterns, and symmetrical balance impart a sense of formality; flowing lines, asymmetry, and splashes of color lend a more casual tone to the landscape. The choices are yours to make, and while it may be more complicated than deciding what to have for lunch, a well-designed native landscape, with all its considerations and compromises, is an enriching investment.

# PLANT
# PROFILES

White Evening Primrose/*Oenothera coronopifolia*

# PLANT PROFILES

The Profiles section lists plants in general–use categories: Trees, Shrubs, and Ground Covers, including annuals, perennials, and grasses. Plants are listed alphabetically by common name within these categories. Mastering plant names, common and scientific, can be as much of a challenge as growing the plants.

Although plant names are meant to be descriptive, sometimes they reveal more about the personal or professional alliances of the name givers than they do about the qualities of the vegetation. Common names vary locally—Chamisa up north is Saltbush down south, Cherry Sage is also Autumn Sage (and isn't really a Sage at all). Scientific names are more consistent but *Caesalpinia* used to be *Poinciana* and *Eurotia* has only been *Ceratoides* for a few years now. In the spirit of compromise, plants are identified here by as many names as are in current usage, the most common and/or descriptive common name first. The Index of Plants by both their common names and scientific names will enable readers to locate plants in all categories according to the system with which they are most comfortable.

In the text that follows, each plant is described as to its origin and adaptations, appearance and use, and cultivation—propagation and maintenance. Origins are included because they are a clue to plant preferences and adaptability. Plants that have a broad distribution on many soils and exposures will be more adaptable in the landscape than those with an affinity for sandy or rocky soils—unless, of course, your site is sandy or rocky. Appearance is an important consideration, but not the only one. So many landscapes are groupings of individually pretty plants, landscape "10s" whose combined effect is −3. Not every plant in a landscape can be a star, a focal point demanding attention. An accent or specimen plant is offset by less showy, contrasting fillers as backdrop and foreground. Placement of these fillers is the form or line of the design that sets the tone and endures the seasons. Color and texture are facets of appearance. In the Southwest, color is both amplified and muted. The tans, grays, and blue greens of sand, adobe, rock, and "sage" are excellent color foils for vivid flower colors, which are intensified by altitude and clear blue skies.

Use, as described in the Profiles, is closely related to appearance but is also dependent upon individual growth requirements and site conditions. Aside from looking good, a low-maintenance landscape should function as outdoor living space with a minimum of upkeep. Shade trees and vine-covered trellises function as "ceilings"; hedges, screens, and windbreaks as "walls"; mass plantings, fillers, and ground covers as carpeted "floors." Accent plantings give focus and drama to a landscape as artworks and fine furnishings do inside a structure. Low-maintenance planning involves filling these categories with plants that will fulfill the function on a particular site and also adapt well to specific on-site conditions.

Cultivation, the propagation and maintenance of arid-land plants, is included in their profile description. Although you may not want to start plants from seeds or cuttings, knowing their methods of reproduction will give you an idea of the potential for and control of weediness—unruly behavior in otherwise useful plants can be avoided by placing them with discretion. Groundsel, a dense silver-leafed perennial that produces a profusion of yellow daisies on 12"–18" stems from May through October, becomes a sparse, lanky mess if it is planted where it will receive more than natural rainfall. Groundsel is an ideal choice for dry, hot spots in a landscape but adapts poorly to kinder growing conditions. Plants whose seeds require specific pretreatment usually have less potential for weedy "volunteering." Easy-to-root species are often easier to transplant, as they initiate roots readily.

Maintenance is the bottom line. Guidelines indicate the native's potential for long-term well-kept appearance by traditional horticultural standards. As I have discussed under watering, soils, and nutrition in Chapter 4, a healthy microorganism population promotes the vitality of coexisting plant life. Nitrogen-fixing plants often contribute to the nutrient requirement of associated plantings. If you are interested primarily in minimal maintenance, select plants described as most adaptable and drought tolerant. If you are interested in reduced maintenance with color and style, select plants for their ornamental value and seasonal impact as well as for general self-sufficiency. Compromise.

# TREES

## ARIZONA SYCAMORE
### Buttonwood

*PLATANUS WRIGHTII*     *Sycamore-Platanaceae*

### ORIGIN AND ADAPTATIONS

**Native Distribution:**   Central and southeast Arizona, southwest New Mexico south to Mexico.
**Elevation:**   2,000–7,000'.
**Topography:**   Along streams and lakes, moist canyons, and bottomland.
**Soil Preference:**   Cobblestone, well drained.
**Drought Tolerance:**   Fair.
**Salt Tolerance:**   Poor.

### DESCRIPTION AND USE

**Mature Height:**   To 80'.
**Spread:**   To 80'.
**Growth Rate:**   Moderate.
**Form:**   Wide-spreading heavy branches, broad open crown; conspicuous bark—thin sheets of brownish gray peeling and curling to reveal a smooth white marbled tan inner layer.
**Flower:**   Inconspicuous compared to most, monoecious; male flowers are dark red borne along the branchlets, females are light green at the tips.
**Foliage:**   Maple-shaped foliage, palmate with long, slender "fingers" (5 x 3"), apple green with lighter underside, russet in autumn.
**Fruit:**   Round balls (2–5 per stem) consisting of many single-seeded achenes that resemble tiny tacks and accompanying fluff. Fruits persist after leaves fall, and their interesting appearance is responsible for the common name "Buttonwood."
**Landscape Use:**   The thirsty giant of the natives, along with the cottonwoods, Arizona Sycamore is more adaptable to heat and alkalinity than the other sycamores. If trained early as a multiple-trunk specimen by removing the terminal bud and forcing basal branching, Arizona Sycamore remains a shorter, easier to maintain landscape specimen. The attractive bark and seed make the Sycamore interesting throughout the year. It is a wonderful shade and specimen tree on sites large enough to accommodate its mature size.

### PROPAGATION AND MAINTENANCE

**Seeds:**   Clean seeds average 135,000 seeds per pound. Cold, moist stratification for 3 months enhances germination. Seeds should be collected after leaf drop. Seedlings and liners should be root-pruned regularly to aid transplant adaptability.
**Vegetative:**   Layering or softwood cuttings under intermittent mist with .8% to 2% IBA talc.
**Watering:**   Arizona Sycamore requires abundant, consistent groundwater for optimum growth. Size can be controlled on well-established trees by limiting moisture to that necessary for maintenance—still more water than many natives require. Planting in low areas that trap runoff can help satisfy moisture requirements.
**Nutrient Requirements:**   Application of chelated iron annually and modest application of a balanced fertilizer on young trees are recommended.
**Pruning:**   Thin to shape young plants and remove weak wood periodically.
**Insect/Disease Susceptibility:**   Chlorosis is easily controlled with chelated iron.

## ASH
### Fresno

*FRAXINUS* species     *Olive-Oleaceae*

### ORIGIN AND ADAPTATIONS

**Native Distribution:**   West Texas west to California, Colorado and Utah south to Mexico. *F. anomala, F. cuspidata, F. velutina. F. anomala* and *velutina* have a broader distribution.
**Elevation:**   2,000–7,000'.
**Topography:**   Piñon-Juniper belt along streams and washes.
**Soil Preference:**   Deep, well drained, with consistent availability of groundwater.

**Drought Tolerance:** 15+" annual precipitation.
**Salt Tolerance:** Fair to poor.

## DESCRIPTION AND USE

**Mature Height:** To 40', usually 20–30'.
**Spread:** 30'.
**Growth Rate:** Moderate to rapid.
**Form:** In the wild, generally shrubby and multiple trunked, but usually cultivated as a single-trunked standard with a rounded crown.
**Flower:** Usually inconspicuous except for *F. cuspidata*, which has fragrant, showy flowers with petals in early spring (March–April).
**Foliage:** Deciduous, with 3–7 leaflets per leaf; crisp bright green, sometimes with paler undersides, turning a beautiful gold in October. Foliage tends to drop rapidly and uniformly in mid-October, which makes cleanup easier.
**Fruit:** When present, small, winged one-seeded fruits hang in clusters. Cultivated varieties are mostly seedless.
**Landscape Use:** While the native species are attractive, horticultural varieties have been developed that are more uniform in growth. "Modesto" Ash (*F. velutina*) is a readily available variety maturing to a height of 30–40'. The fresh green foliage, gold fall color, and inbred seedlessness make it an exceptional shade tree. The cultivar "Rio Grande" is reportedly more drought- and alkali-tolerant, but less commonly available. Because the ash is a clean, relatively small shade producer, it is valuable for residential landscape use.

## PROPAGATION AND MAINTENANCE

**Seeds:** Collect seeds when winged fruits turn from green to brown, usually in September, about 20,000 seeds per pound (clean). Germination is best when seeds are pretreated. A warm, moist stratification (70 F) for one month followed by a cold-moist stratification (40 F) for three months greatly increases germination percentage.
**Vegetative:** Most horticultural cultivars are grafted.
**Watering:** Once established, Ash requires regular, deep waterings for optimum growth. A weekly trickle irrigation of 30 gallons over a 12-hour period easily maintains a 15', 4"-caliper tree during hot, dry weather where groundwater is unavailable.
**Nutrient Requirements:** An annual application of zinc chelate prevents chlorosis. Ash responds well to dilute applications of nitrogen, especially on sandy soils.
**Pruning:** Thinning weak or dead wood to promote attractive shape and wind resistance is advisable every two years on rapidly growing trees; every five years when trees reach maturity.
**Insect/Disease Susceptibility:** Anthracnose has been a problem in California but is not common in New Mexico.

# COTTONWOOD

*POPULUS FREMONTII* and subspecies        *Willow-Salicaceae*

## ORIGIN AND ADAPTATIONS

**Native Distribution:** Southwestern Utah, Nevada, northern California, Arizona, and New Mexico.
**Elevation:** To 6,500'.
**Topography:** Along stream beds and where abundant groundwater is available.
**Soil Preference:** Adaptable.
**Drought Tolerance:** Poor.
**Salt Tolerance:** Fair.

## DESCRIPTION AND USE

**Mature Height:** 40–100'.
**Spread:** 50–100'.
**Growth Rate:** Rapid.
**Form:** Tree with a broadly rounded crown and widely spreading branches which provide dense shade over an extended area.
**Flower:** Reddish 3"-long catkins, April–May, male and female on separate trees.
**Foliage:** 2–3" in length and width, broadly triangular, spade-shaped, shiny, crisp green turning bright yellow in autumn.
**Fruit:** Seed dispersal June–July from ½"-long egg-shaped capsules with abundant cottony seeds.
**Landscape Use:** The Cottonwood is an excellent shade tree where space permits. It is too large for the average city lot but valuable for parks and large commercial buildings where the Cottonwood's large size is not out of scale. Dense shade, heavy leaf drop, and self-pruning twig drop limits growth of plants within the drip line.
**Other Uses:** Cottonwoods are useful for erosion control along watercourses.

## PROPAGATION AND MAINTENANCE

**Seeds:** With a cottony dispersal mechanism, the seeds average more than 2 million seeds per pound.

**Vegetative:**  Easily propagated from hardwood cuttings, no hormone needed. Male trees do not produce cotton and so are preferred.

**Watering:**  Ample groundwater is necessary. Deep watering is advisable when planted as a lawn tree.

**Nutrient Requirements:**  None.

**Pruning:**  Summer pruning reduces suckering.

**Insect/Disease Susceptibility:**  Plants stressed by lack of water, compacted soils, excess salts, etc., are more prone to disease and insect problems, including wetwood (slime flux), borers, and tent caterpillars.

## DESERT OLIVE
### New Mexico Privet. New Mexico Mountain Ash, Paloblanco

*FORESTIERA NEOMEXICANA*    Olive-Oleaceae

### ORIGIN AND ADAPTATIONS

**Native Distribution:**  Texas, New Mexico, and Colorado.

**Elevation:**  3,000–7,000'.

**Topography:**  Hillsides, mesas, and moist valleys.

**Soil Preference:**  Widely adapted, found wild in sand, loam, clay, and lava. Under cultivation soil type seems to make little difference except in watering technique.

**Drought Tolerance:**  Drought deciduous, defoliates when stressed for moisture. 10–20" annual precipitation.

**Salt Tolerance:**  Moderate. Foliage salt burns.

### DESCRIPTION AND USE

**Mature Height:**  To 15'.

**Spread:**  8–10'.

**Growth Rate:**  Rapid while young if moisture is available, otherwise moderate; slow when mature.

**Form:**  Deciduous, upright woody shrub or small tree. Stiff, vaselike, multiple trunked, suckering at base.

**Flower:**  Small, fragrant cream-colored in clusters before plants leaf out in spring, usually mid-March in the Albuquerque area.

**Foliage:**  Small, bright apple green (1 1/2 x 1/2") contrasts nicely with almost black coloration of new growth of stems. Foliage is dense when moisture is available, defoliates under severe moisture stress. Yellow gold fall color.

**Fruit:**  Small blue black fruit matures in June–July, a favorite of songbirds. If you want to harvest seed, observe development closely, as birds will rapidly strip plants of fruit.

**Landscape Use:**  Forestiera has an interesting stiff vaselike form when lower growth is removed and it is trained as a small specimen tree. It shears well to form a dense hedge, windbreak, or screen. The small, bright green, crisp foliage is clean and attractive. Drought and cold-tolerant Forestiera is a good container specimen in large tubs, etc. As the common names indicate, this plant is quite adaptable, even on severe sites. The compact size is a particular advantage in urban areas.

**Other Uses:**  Useful erosion control, Forestiera prevents washing along streams and arroyos. It is excellent wildlife cover.

### PROPAGATION AND MAINTENANCE

**Seeds:**  4,500 to 6,000 seeds per ounce. 70 F soil and air temperatures (65–85 F range) provide best germination (50% or better) in 3 weeks. Fall or early February seeding outdoors results in germination in May. Stratification for 30 days at 40 F accelerates germination. Old seeds may require a boiled water soak to speed uptake of water.

**Vegetative:**  .8% IBA talc-treated semi-softwood tips will root in 7–14 days without mist in August. Hardwood dormant cuttings of previous year's growth taken in early spring also root well.

**Watering:**  Regular deep watering accelerates growth. Forestiera develops a deep taproot and is extremely drought tolerant once established.

**Nutrient Requirements:**  Forestiera responds well to nitrogen fertilizers, especially while it is young and growing rapidly.

**Pruning:**  Shearing results in a dense, privet-like hedge. Removal of suckers and low branches reveals an interesting specimen tree.

**Insect/Disease Susceptibility:**  Poor air circulation and high soil moisture levels, especially in clay soils, can cause mildew on foliage. This is a localized problem resulting from site problems rather than a propensity of the plant. Wild populations that are the understory in Cottonwood/bosque habitats are susceptible to mistletoe.

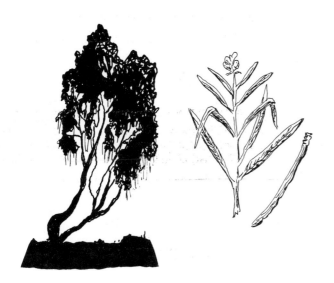

## DESERT WILLOW
### Flor de Mimbres

*CHILOPSIS LINEARIS*     Catalpa-Bignoniaceae

### ORIGIN AND ADAPTATIONS

**Native Distribution:**   Central Texas west to southern California, Albuquerque south to Chihuahua.
**Elevation:**   1,500–5,000'.
**Topography:**   In washes and arroyos.
**Soil Preference:**   Porous sandy soil, but will tolerate any soil that is fairly well drained.
**Drought Tolerance:**   Excellent when established, 8-15" annual precipitation.
**Salt Tolerance:**   Very good.

### DESCRIPTION AND USE

**Mature Height:**   To 25'.
**Spread:**   To 15'.
**Growth Rate:**   Rapid, may grow 2–3' in a month during summer rains.
**Form:**   Tree or large shrub with an open, rounded crown, usually multiple trunked, with characteristic gnarled growth.
**Flower:**   Large, orchidlike blossoms in clusters, deep purple to pink to white in color, light pink most common in the wild. Blooms profusely mid-June to September. Attractive to hummingbirds.
**Foliage:**   Long, narrow (5 x 1/8") willowlike leaves, bright green. Desert Willow is a heat lover, leafs out late in spring. Foliage produces a light, airy effect, excellent textural contrast.
**Fruit:**   Long, slender pods typical of the Catalpa family, split along the side to release seeds.
**Landscape Use:**   The interesting form when grown as a tree creates an airy accent or open background planting. Desert Willow is useful in windbreaks and screens and as a textural contrast. The long bloom period provides color most of the summer and is very attractive mass-planted in groves.
**Other Uses:**   Desert Willow is useful as erosion con-

trol in arroyos. The unpalatable foliage is eaten only when more attractive forage is unavailable.

### PROPAGATION AND MAINTENANCE

**Seeds:**   Approximately 5,000 seeds per ounce, the fairly large (1/2 x 1/8") winged but thin and light seeds germinate best at warm soil and air temperatures (70–80 F) in light, well-drained soil. Seeds ripen from October on and should be collected as they ripen. Germination averages 50%.
**Vegetative:**   Hardwood cuttings in April, stuck directly in beds outdoors, and softwood cuttings in July and August, both treated with .3% or .8% IBA talc, root easily.
**Watering:**   Young plants given frequent water and nutrients grow rapidly, blooming within 18 months from seed. A 4' tall, 5-gallon containerized plant can be grown from seeds or cuttings in 24–30 months with ample water. Plants should be hardened off early in fall, as new growth is very cold sensitive.
**Nutrient Requirements:**   Desert Willow responds well to dilute applications of nitrogen in early summer. Established plants of mature size do not require feeding.
**Pruning:**   Thin and remove suckers to accentuate form on mature trees. Tip prune and remove frost-damaged branches in early summer on young plants.
**Insect/Disease Susceptibility:**   Aphids on new growth at times; generally can be controlled by washing off with a high pressure stream of water.

## GAMBEL'S OAK
### Encino

*QUERCUS GAMBELII*     Beech-Fagaceae

### ORIGIN AND ADAPTATIONS

**Native Distribution:**   Northern Utah east to southern Wyoming, Texas west to Arizona.
**Elevation:**   4,000–8,000'.
**Topography:**   Slopes and valleys in mountains, foothills, and plateaus.
**Soil Preference:**   Well drained, adapts to various soil textures.

**Drought Tolerance:**    15 + " annual precipitation.
**Salt Tolerance:**    Undetermined.

## DESCRIPTION AND USE

**Mature Height:**    6–50', commonly 15-20'.
**Spread:**    Groves of 40+'.
**Growth Rate:**    Slow.
**Form:**    Large shrub to tree with rounded crown usually found in dense groves in association with pine and juniper. Rough grey bark is smooth when young, furrowed on older trees.
**Flower:**    Dioecious, male and female catkins.
**Foliage:**    Deciduous, deeply lobed, dark green foliage (2–7" in length, 1.5–3.5" in width).
**Fruit:**    Broadly oval acorns (1 x 1/2"), the cup enclosing up to half of the acorn.
**Landscape Use:**    Gambel's Oak is excellent in background or accent plantings. The slow growth rate prevents plants from outgrowing the landscape rapidly. Characteristic leaf shape and russet fall color are valuable additions to the landscape.
**Other Uses:**    Fence posts and firewood are cut from oak stands. The Indians preferred to eat these because they are sweet. Oaks are good browse plants for deer and excellent wildlife shelter.

## PROPAGATION AND MAINTENANCE

**Seeds:**    Best germination is on very fresh seeds sown in September and October. Seeds should not be allowed to dry in storage; therefore, unless a rather sophisticated storage facility is available, seeds are best planted immediately. Seed crops are abundant every 2–5 years.
**Watering:**    Oaks require additional irrigation at lower elevations. The growth rate may be accelerated a little by regular, deep watering. Regular watering is imperative on seedlings.
**Nutrient Requirements:**    In extremely alkaline soils, chelated iron may be required.
**Pruning:**    Light tip-pruning forces branching when a shrub form is desired. Removal of suckers enhances tree form.
**Insect/Disease Susceptibility:**    None observed to date.

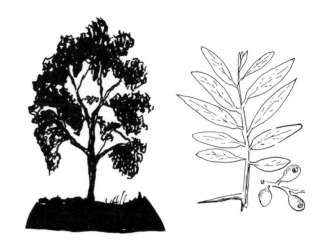

# "KING RED" RUSSIAN OLIVE

*ELAEAGNUS ANGUSTIFOLIA "KING RED"*          Olive-
                                                                                  Oleaceae

## ORIGIN AND ADAPTATIONS

**Native Distribution:**    Southern Europe and western Asia-type locations, as Afghanistan. Naturalized in western United States (light-colored fruit).
**Elevation:**    3,000–7,000'.
**Topography:**    Along streams, drainage ditches, and seasonal watercourses.
**Soil Preference:**    Sandy to sandy loam where groundwater is abundant. Adapts to most soils under cultivation. Possibly longer-lived where soil is well drained.
**Drought Tolerance:**    Good once established but requires relatively heavy watering at first. 10–30 + " annual precipitation.
**Salt Tolerance:**    Excellent.

## DESCRIPTION AND USE

**Mature Height:**    To 25'.
**Spread:**    To 20'.
**Growth Rate:**    Rapid, 3–4' annually under irrigated conditions.
**Form:**    Usually multiple-trunked tree or large shrub with rounded crown. Some selections are less thorny.
**Flower:**    Small yellow- to cream-colored flowers more obvious for their sweet fragrance than for conspicuous flower show—profuse in May.
**Foliage:**    Small (2 x 1/2"), oblong to elliptical, dark green with white, scurfy on topside, light to silvery white on underside.
**Fruit:**    Extremely variable due to cross-pollination with light buff-colored wild species, ranging from crabapple-sized and cherry red to pea-sized and russet. Large-fruited types with good coloration should be vegetatively propagated.
**Landscape Use:**    The naturalized Russian Olive is widely used as a specimen accent and small shade tree, for windbreaks, sheared or unsheared hedges, and screens. The attractive form and foliage are effective

as a color foil; the dormant silhouette, gray to black shredding bark, and coppery-bronze new growth are seasonally effective. Specimens with large, colorful fruit offer additional color in autumn.

**Other Uses:** Russian Olive is a good soil stabilizer along streams and washes and is good bee forage when it is flowering. Naturalizing along streams, the common Russian Olive is replacing less competitive native species and changing, often for the worse, our limited riparian habitats.

## PROPAGATION AND MAINTENANCE

**Seeds:** Averages 3,000 seeds per pound cleaned. A sulfuric acid bath is an effective cleaning as well as germination pretreatment. Germination is usually better than 70% on cleaned seeds in a moist medium. 50% germination average in 3 weeks from sowing when soil and air temperatures are in 65–85 F range.

**Vegetative:** Since "King Red" cannot be reliably reproduced from seed within the naturalized range of the common Russian Olive, selections should be made by hardwood cuttings treated with .3% IBA talc and stuck directly into outdoor beds in March.

**Watering:** "King-Red" requires regular deep watering unless it is rooted into a high water table. Once established, Russian Olives are quite drought tolerant but require regular deep waterings during hot, dry, and windy weather.

**Nutrient Requirements:** Russian Olives are nitrogen-fixing in light soils where conditions are right for development of soil bacteria. Excessive fertilization is detrimental.

**Pruning:** Removal of suckers and periodic thinning when used as a tree; periodic severe pruning when grown as a windbreak (2–3 years) or hedge (annually).

**Insect/Disease Susceptibility:** Russian Olives are fairly short-lived trees even under optimum conditions (40 years), as compared with Oaks, etc. Abuse or recurrent stress from over- or under-watering or excess fertilization can further shorten the normal life-span.

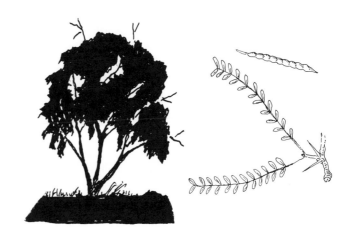

# MESQUITE

*PROSOPIS GLANDULOSA*    *Pea-*
(Honey Mesquite),    *Leguminosae*

*PROSOPIS PUBESCENS*
(Screwbean or Tornillo)

## ORIGIN AND ADAPTATIONS

**Native Distribution:** Kansas, Texas, Colorado, New Mexico, and Arizona south into Sonora, Mexico.
**Elevation:** 2,000–6,000'.
**Topography:** Along streams and arroyos up onto alluvial hills.
**Soil Preference:** Deep, well-drained.
**Drought Tolerance:** Excellent.
**Salt Tolerance:** Fair.

## DESCRIPTION AND USE

**Mature Height:** To 20'.
**Spread:** To 20'.
**Growth Rate:** Moderate.
**Form:** Deciduous large shrub to small tree, usually thorny with deep taproots and gnarled multiple-trunked branches forming a spreading, rounded crown.
**Flower:** White to yellow peduncles in late March through May are not showy as are Acacias but are attractive to bees (*P. glandulosa*) and useful honey plants. Pollen of *P. pubescens* is toxic to honeybees, however.
**Foliage:** Finely cut bipinnate foliage, dark green and deciduous, gives an airy, lacy look to the plants.
**Fruit:** *P. glandulosa* has a long, narrow (6 x 1/2") flat seedpod, straw to rose-mottled in color *P. pubescens* has short, tightly coiled (2 x 1/4") "screw beans" in clusters.
**Landscape Use:** The thorny branches make effective barrier plantings. Given abundant moisture, Mesquites grow to small trees with interesting gnarled trunks, useful as accent or specimen plants. Because they are deep rooted once established, they are a good

choice for highway and other minimal maintenance landscapes.

**Other Uses:**   Rootwood is used for fuel, especially cooking. Good for barbecueing and smoking meats. Native Americans used pods for food and later as feed for livestock.

## PROPAGATION AND MAINTENANCE

**Seeds:**   The 10,000 seeds per pound are hard coated and require scarification. Seeds germinate best at warm soil and air temperatures (80 F). Pods drop from the tree when they are ripe and are quickly foraged by birds, rodents, and livestock.

**Vegetative:**   No reliable method.

**Watering:**   Mesquite needs deep intermittent watering to establish, but once the desired size and form have been attained, it can be left unattended except in extreme, prolonged drought.

**Nutrient Requirements:**   Nitrogen fixing.

**Pruning:**   Thorns make this an unwelcome task. Luckily, except for shaping, which reveals sculptured trunks, little is required.

**Insect/Disease Susceptibility:**   Honey Mesquite is sometimes attacked by a stem-girdling insect that causes tip dieback on affected trees.

## QUAKING ASPEN

*POPULUS TREMULOIDES*     *Willow-Salicaceae*

### ORIGIN AND ADAPTATIONS

**Native Distribution:**   Alaska east to Labrador, south to Virginia; Rocky Mountains south to New Mexico and Arizona. Most widely distributed tree in North America.

**Elevation:**   6,500–10,000'.

**Topography:**   In the West, usually in almost pure stands below spruce-fir belt in mountain areas.

**Soil Preference:**   Sandy to gravelly but quite adaptable.

**Drought Tolerance:**   Fair for a poplar.

**Salt Tolerance:**   Poor.

## DESCRIPTION AND USE

**Mature Height:**   50–100'.

**Spread:**   10'.

**Growth Rate:**   Rapid.

**Form:**   Tall tree with narrow, rounded crown and smooth white bark.

**Flower:**   Brownish catkins.

**Foliage:**   Nearly round, short, pointed shiny green foliage with dull lighter undersides. Gold yellow in autumn.

**Fruit:**   Light green woody capsules.

**Landscape Use:**   A beautiful accent when planted in clumps, at lower elevations Aspen will tolerate heat well if soil is shaded with a low to medium height ground cover. Excellent fall color, distinctive dormant appearance, and animated summer foliage are landscape pluses.

**Other Uses:**   Revegetation of burned areas within its range, timberwood, and Native American ceremonial use.

## PROPAGATION AND MAINTENANCE

**Seeds:**   Aspen averages 3.5 million seeds per pound when produced.

**Vegetative:**   Division of suckers, root cuttings, and hardwood stem cuttings are alternatives to seed production.

**Watering:**   At low elevations in New Mexico, Aspens require ample groundwater, as do all Poplars and Willows.

**Nutrient Requirements:**   None, once established.

**Pruning:**   None.

**Insect/Disease Susceptibility:**   Leaf scorch at lower elevations if grown too dry.

## ROSE LOCUST

*ROBINIA NEOMEXICANA*     *Pea-Leguminosae*

### ORIGIN AND ADAPTATIONS

**Native Distribution:**   Trans-Pecos Texas west through

New Mexico and Arizona, north to Colorado, Utah, and Nevada.

**Elevation:**  4,000–8,500'.

**Topography:**  In moist soil, along streams in sun and on dry, rocky slopes.

**Soil Preference:**  Sandy loam to gravelly—adapts to most soil types and to lower elevations.

**Drought Tolerance:**  In dry soils, plants are dwarfed, rarely exceeding 3' in height. 12 + " annual precipitation.

**Salt Tolerance:**  Fair.

## DESCRIPTION AND USE

**Mature Height:**  To 24'.

**Spread:**  15–20'.

**Growth Rate:**  Rapid, especially while young. Plants can grow to gallon container size in 6 months.

**Form:**  Thicket forming small tree or shrub. Rhizomatous and freely suckering, mature plants suckering less. Rounded crown, stiff, arching branches.

**Flower:**  Showy rose pink pendant racemes (like Wisteria) 2–4" long, borne most profusely in early summer but sporadically April–August.

**Foliage:**  Leaves pinnate and small (1 x 1/2"), individual leaflets oval, dark gray green in color.

**Fruit:**  Small (2 x 1/2"), flat pod enclosing the seed.

**Landscape Use:**  Rose Locust has been used as an ornamental in the United States since 1881, when it was also introduced into European horticulture. Valuable for its flower and general adaptability as well as for its impenetrable thorny habit when used as a windbreak or hedge, it can become invasive if watered heavily, difficult to move once established. Rose Locust is best planted in low-traffic, minimum-care areas where aggressiveness can be controlled by limiting the availability of water.

**Other Uses:**  Excellent soil binder on slopes and along waterways. Robinia provides browse for livestock and is used locally in herbal dyes.

**Other Useful Species:**  *R. pseudoacacia*, Black Locust, is a large, spiny tree with white flower clusters, native to the eastern United States but naturalized in the Southwest. Uses and care are similar to Rose Locust.

## PROPAGATION AND MAINTENANCE

**Seeds:**  Mature in September–October, 3–8 seeds per pod, 20,000 per pound. Seeds are collected before the pods open by stripping off branches, beating in a bag to release seed, and fanning to remove debris. Pretreat by soaking in boiling water. Fairly fresh seeds (1–4 years from harvest) will swell rapidly. Properly stored seeds will last 10 years in viable condition. Sow outdoors in spring in rows or containers. Germinate rapidly if pretreated.

**Vegetative:**  Suckering roots can be divided and reset while plants are dormant.

**Watering:**  Occasional deep watering once plants are established is recommended.

**Nutrient Requirements:**  Nitrogen fixing, Robinia

needs no fertilizing once it is established. Young plants, especially containerized stock, benefit from regular light feeding.

**Pruning:**  Thorny growth makes pruning a pain! Better to locate plants where they can grow unattended.

**Insect/Disease Susceptibility:**  Borers may attack plants, especially when plants are stressed.

# SHRUB LIVE OAK
## Encino

*QUERCUS TURBINELLA*      *Beech-Fagaceae*

## ORIGIN AND ADAPTATIONS

**Native Distribution:**  Texas west to California and south into Mexico.

**Elevation:**  4,500–8,000'.

**Topography:**  Dry slopes.

**Soil Preference:**  Gravelly, well drained.

**Drought Tolerance:**  12–25" annual precipitation.

**Salt Tolerance:**  Undetermined.

## DESCRIPTION AND USE

**Mature Height:**  3–15', often less than 12'.

**Spread:**  To 20'.

**Growth Rate:**  Slow.

**Form:**  Densely branched, rounded crown, shrub or small tree, evergreen.

**Flower:**  Catkins.

**Foliage:**  Small, blue green, holly-shaped leaves, evergreen.

**Fruit:**  Small, elongated acorns, caps covering about 1/3 of the acorn.

**Landscape Use:**  Shrub Live Oak is an excellent specimen tree for those with *patience*. Small plants are best used mass planted as fillers or background.

**Other Uses:**  Acorns are relished by wildlife.

## PROPAGATION AND MAINTENANCE

**Seeds:**  Fresh seeds should be planted immediately. (See *Q. gambelii*.)

**Watering:**  Although more drought tolerant than Gambel's Oak, once established, *Q. turbinella* will grow a little faster if it is given additional, regular water. Oaks should never stand in water. Good drainage is essential.

**Nutrient Requirements:**  None.

**Pruning:**  None.

**Insect/Disease Susceptibility:**  Nutgalls.

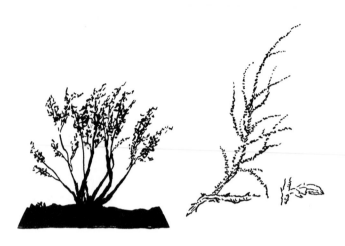

## TAMARISK
### Salt Cedar

*TAMARIX PENTANDRA*    Tamarisk-Tamaricaceae

### ORIGIN AND ADAPTATIONS

**Native Distribution:**  Southeastern Europe and Central Asia, naturalized in Utah, New Mexico, and west Texas.

**Elevation:**  Usually below 8,000'.

**Topography:**  Along watercourses or where periodic flooding occurs and watertable is shallow.

**Soil Preference:**  Adaptable to most soils.

**Drought Tolerance:**  8 + " annual precipitation.

**Salt Tolerance:**  Excellent.

### DESCRIPTION AND USE

**Mature Height:**  20–25'.

**Spread:**  25'.

**Growth Rate:**  Rapid.

**Form:**  Shrub or small tree.

**Flower:**  Feathery pink plumes in April and often in late summer. Darker flower color (a deep rose pink) is showier, and selections propagated vegetatively should be made more available.

**Foliage:**  Soft, ferny blue green turning gold in autumn, deciduous. Leaf litter from Salt Cedar may inhibit growth of other plants and can be corrosive to metals. The shiny red bark of new growth and interesting texture of old wood give the tree ornamental value while it is dormant.

**Fruit:**  Inconspicuous.

**Landscape Use:**  The same qualities, tenacity and adaptability, that can make the plant a problem in the wild make the Salt Cedar a useful windbreak and soil stabilizer on harsh sites. The ferny foliage and flowers make it an interesting textural contrast. Salt Cedar has warm gold fall color and is attractive while dormant when it is pruned judiciously (minimally). It shears well for a medium to tall hedge. A useful and attractive plant when it is well placed.

**Other Uses:**  A controversy over water loss versus erosion control, especially in the Middle Rio Grande-Rio Abajo area, has been raging for years. Tamarisk has naturalized aggressively, choking out less vigorous and sometimes more valuable plant life in the habitat, and is difficult to irradicate once it is established. It is important bee forage in the Southwest, yielding tons of baker's honey annually.

### PROPAGATION AND MAINTENANCE

**Seeds:**  Seeds are minute, windborne, and germinate without pretreatment. Because plants grown from cuttings develop faster, this is the preferred method of propagation.

**Vegetative:**  Hardwood cuttings taken in March, stuck directly in soil beds outdoors after dipping in .3% IBA talc, produce plants 3' tall by October.

**Watering:**  Responds to ample water with rapid growth. Salt Cedar should be watered deeply to promote rapid establishment of a deep root system, making for a more drought-tolerant planting.

**Nutrient Requirements:**  None necessary once the plant is well established.

**Pruning:**  Salt Cedar can be thinned and lower branches removed to train it as a small tree or it can be sheared as a hedge. If dormant appearance is valued, thinning and restrained pruning prevent heavy suckering that is unattractive without foliage.

**Insect/Disease Susceptibility:**  None observed.

# SHRUBS

## APACHE PLUME

*FALLUGIA PARADOXA*     *Rose-Rosaceae*

### ORIGIN AND ADAPTATIONS

**Native Distribution:**  West Texas west to California; Chihuahua, Mexico, north to Colorado.
**Elevation:**  3,000–8,000'.
**Topography:**  Along and in arroyos in full sun.
**Soil Preference:**  Dry, gravelly, or sandy soil, but will tolerate most soil types as long as they are reasonably well drained and dry between waterings.
**Drought Tolerance:**  8–20" annual precipitation.
**Salt Tolerance:**  Fair.

### DESCRIPTION AND USE

**Mature Height:**  2–8', average 5'.
**Spread:**  2–6'.
**Growth Rate:**  Moderate, seed to 1-gallon size in 18 + months.
**Form:**  Densely twiggy, mounding, semi-evergreen shrub, branches and suckers at base.
**Flower:**  Small (1"), single, white wild-rose flowers with yellow stamens, May to October, with greatest profusion in May and again after rains, on new growing tips.
**Foliage:**  Small (3/4" x 1/2"), deeply lobed, dark green with a reddish underside. Foliage persistent into winter, develops a dark bronzy cast which contrasts with the silver white twigs (newest growth).
**Fruit:**  Showy pink seed heads, in clusters, soft and feathery (hence the common name, Apache Plume). Plumes dry from pink to straw white and seed is thus wind dispersed.
**Landscape Use:**  Year-round interest is provided by this shrub—dark foliage, silvery twigs, profuse white flowers, and perhaps the most striking, showy pink plumes. Apache Plume can be used effectively as a background, accent, and foundation planting, or as a hedge, screen, or low windbreak.
**Other Uses:**  Apache Plume acts as a soil binder against wind and water erosion and affords excellent cover for wildlife.

### PROPAGATION AND MAINTENANCE

**Seeds:**  Seeds are produced in midspring and/or late summer; approximately 420,000 seeds per pound. Best germination is in the 60–78 F range, diminishes rapidly above 85 F, and the best germination reported during testing was at a constant 72 F (in 4–10 days at 60 F). 30–40% germination is average. Seedlings are somewhat prone to damping off; good air circulation and a well-drained medium are essential. Collect seeds when styles (plumes) fade to white and detach easily from receptacle.
**Vegetative:**  Layering and division are the easiest methods when only a few plants are needed. Stem cuttings of very soft wood in spring or August–September, treated with 0.8–2.0% IBA talc, root reasonably well.
**Watering:**  Intermittent deep watering in summer will keep the shrub in flower. Avoid constantly wet soil in winter.
**Nutrient Requirements:**  Fertilizing is probably unnecessary on established plants in light soil.
**Pruning:**  No pruning is necessary to maintain dense, attractive form, but Apache Plume can be sheared as a hedge. Suckers remain close to the base of the plant and are not invasive.
**Insect/Disease Susceptibility:**  Spider mites are sometimes attracted to Apache Plume in hot, dry weather, but are easily controlled by washing the foliage with a water stream from the hose.

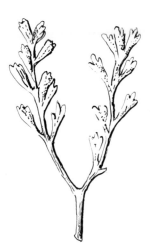

## BIGLEAF SAGE

*ARTEMISIA TRIDENTATA*     *Sunflower-Compositae*

### ORIGIN AND ADAPTATIONS

**Native Distribution:**  Dakotas south to the Rockies, Sierra Nevada, and Cascades, predominant in the Great Basin area.
**Elevation:**  1,500–10,600'.

**Topography:**   Low elevation rangeland to mountain slopes.
**Soil Preference:**   Deep, well-drained soil of variable texture, adaptable.
**Drought Tolerance:**   10–18" annual precipitation.
**Salt Tolerance:**   Low to moderate.

## DESCRIPTION AND USE

**Mature Height:**   3–8'.
**Spread:**   4–6'.
**Growth Rate:**   Rapid with moisture.
**Form:**   Medium to tall shrub, evergreen with a stiff and irregular growth habit and deep, spreading root system.
**Flower:**   Inconspicuous green to yellow in August–September, earlier further south.
**Foliage:**   Three-lobed, small, soft gray green leaves are evergreen.
**Landscape Use:**   Sage is picturesque as a specimen or accent planting due to characteristic form. The evergreen foliage is attractive as a color contrast, especially with Piñon, Baccharis, and Junipers.
**Other Uses:**   It is effective erosion control and provides browse, cover, and nesting for wildlife. Many Artemisias are historically important as medicinal plants.
**Other Useful Species:**   *A. tridentata* ssp. *nova*, Black Sage is a smaller version of Bigleaf Sage, adapted to shallower soils. It seems to be less adaptable than its larger counterpart. *A. filifolia* is most common on sandy soils, smaller in stature (4' x 4'), and more refined in texture. Like many shrubby Artemisias, Sand Sage looks windblown even when the air is still.

## PROPAGATION AND MAINTENANCE

**Seeds:**   Seeds ripen in late September. Germination is best at cool temperatures (60 F). Seeds are cleaned by threshing and blowing to remove debris. 2.5 million seeds per pound.
**Vegetative:**   Take stem cuttings February–April. 2.0% IBA talc necessary for acceptable rooting percentages.
**Watering:**   Occasional, deep irrigation during hot, dry weather is helpful.
**Nutrient Requirements:**   Artemisias will fix nitrogen when soil contains a proper microorganism balance.
**Pruning:**   Periodic heavy pruning increases new growth and improves overall appearance (browsing wildlife perform this function in the wild).
**Insect/Disease Susceptibility:**   None observed.

# BIRD OF PARADISE

*CAESALPINIA (POINCIANA) GILLIESII*     *Pea-Leguminosae*

## ORIGIN AND ADAPTATIONS

**Native Distribution:**   Argentina, escaped cultivation and naturalized in Texas, New Mexico, and Arizona.
**Elevation:**   Below 6,000'.
**Topography:**   Sunny flats and washes, very heat tolerant.
**Soil Preference:**   Well drained, adapts well to most soils.
**Drought Tolerance:**   Excellent.
**Salt Tolerance:**   Good.

## DESCRIPTION AND USE

**Mature Height:**   4–6', can grow to 15'.
**Spread:**   3–6'.
**Growth Rate:**   Rapid, seed to gallon container in one season.
**Form:**   Coarse, stiff branches and open, asymmetrical habit.
**Flower:**   Unusual and showy, yellow pea-shaped flowers with many long red stamens which are borne in terminal racemes.
**Foliage:**   Feathery bipinnate leaves give the plant an airy, open quality.
**Fruit:**   A pod encloses large, flat, shiny brown seeds, and opens with an audible "pop" when ripe.
**Landscape Use:**   Grown mostly for its unusual flowers, it makes a striking accent or specimen plant. As an open hedge or screen it is extremely showy in bloom. Mass planted where limited moisture is available, it is a minimal-care filler. Produces quite a bit of litter (spent blooms, seedpods, and autumn foliage); raking under plants in midsummer and autumn produces a more cultivated appearance.

## PROPAGATION AND MAINTENANCE

**Seeds:** Sow when soil warms in spring, in containers or where the plants are to grow; germinate without pretreatment in 2–3 weeks. Germination percentage often exceeds 80%. Seedlings are cold sensitive when young: 1-month-old seedlings will freeze at 22 F, while 10-month-old seedlings can tolerate 8 F.

**Watering:** Deep, infrequent irrigations increase foliage density.

**Nutrient Requirements:** Nitrogen-fixing, requires no additional fertilizer.

**Pruning:** Removal of spent blooms extends the flowering period.

**Insect/Disease Susceptibility:** None observed.

## BROOM BACCHARIS

*BACCHARIS EMORYII*    *Sunflower-Compositae*

### ORIGIN AND ADAPTATIONS

**Native Distribution:** West Texas, New Mexico, Arizona, California, Nevada, Utah, and Colorado.

**Elevation:** 500–5,000'.

**Topography:** Moist soils along streams and canals.

**Soil Preference:** Silty loam.

**Drought Tolerance:** 10–16" annual precipitation.

**Salt Tolerance:** Good.

### DESCRIPTION AND USE

**Mature Height:** 3–12'.

**Spread:** To 5'.

**Growth Rate:** Rapid with abundant moisture.

**Form:** Loosely branched, generally erect, vase-shaped shrubs with an extensive spreading root system.

**Flower:** Loose panicle, pale green to white disc flowers in late summer to fall. Male and female flowers on separate plants.

**Foliage:** Bright green, evergreen, individual leaves are 2" x 1/4", slightly thick and rubbery. Foliage assumes a reddish blush in cold weather. Foliage density is improved by periodic tip pruning or shearing.

**Fruit:** Seed heads on female plants are snowy white (pappus) and persistent, contrasting with reddish green winter foliage.

**Landscape Use:** The vivid green foliage is unusual in arid-land natives and is especially welcome being evergreen. Broom Baccharis prefers readily available groundwater but adapts well to heat and drought if it is encouraged to root extensively. It provides an effective mid-sized screen or filler, especially where periodic deep waterings are possible.

**Other Uses:** Erosion control along streams and other watercourses.

## PROPAGATION AND MAINTENANCE

**Seeds:** Collect in October–November and seed in trays in late January indoors for transplanting to containers. Seeds are very small and difficult to keep moist when seeded outdoors, as they must be seeded on the soil surface or only lightly covered. Seedlings transplant easily, but well-established plants are difficult to move successfully.

**Vegetative:** Semi-soft tip cuttings taken during August rains or under intermittent mist root easily with .3% IBA talc.

**Watering:** Once established Baccharis is quite drought tolerant, but intermittent deep watering during hot, dry weather improves foliage density. Being evergreen, plants transpire moisture during winter months and should be watered periodically to avoid winter burn.

**Nutrient Requirements:** If plants are watered abundantly to promote rapid growth and extensive rooting, periodic fertilizing is useful. Once they are established, if grown relatively dry, little fertilization is needed.

**Pruning:** Light tip pruning or periodic shearing of established plants improves foliage density. Seed heads can be removed from female plants in December, or male plants can be grown to avoid seed-head litter.

**Insect/Disease Susceptibility:** Spittle bugs have been observed on plants in the wild. Aphids can be a problem in early spring but are easily washed off with a high-pressure stream of water.

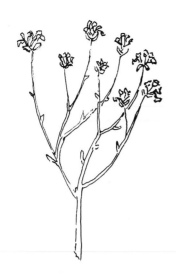

## BROOM DALEA
### False Indigo

*DALEA SCOPARIA    Pea-Leguminosae*

### ORIGIN AND ADAPTATIONS

**Native Distribution:**  El Paso County, Texas. Sand hills along the Rio Grande watershed in New Mexico.
**Elevation:**  2,000–6,000'.
**Topography:**  Sand hills or sandy bottomland.
**Soil Preference:**  Sandy and dry; may not tolerate other soil types, especially clay.
**Drought Tolerance:**  6–12" annual precipitation.
**Salt Tolerance:**  Fair to poor.

### DESCRIPTION AND USE

**Mature Height:**  3'.
**Spread:**  3–4'.
**Growth Rate:**  Moderate.
**Form:**  Low mounding habit, rounded crown; taprooted with few laterals, must be container grown to transplant; densely twiggy.
**Flower:**  Small (to 1/2") individual flowers borne in clusters at the tips of slender stems. Intense royal blue or violet blue in June, most profuse in August–September. Very fragrant, sweet.
**Foliage:**  Usually absent. Occasionally after rains or when it is irrigated, Dalea produces very small blue green leaves. Photosynthesis takes place in the stems, as leaves are present only when moisture is abundant.
**Fruit:**  Small, dry capsules, inconspicuous.
**Landscape Use:**  False Indigo is an excellent ground cover for areas where no maintenance is desired and soil is well drained. The flower color is intense and unusual (combines well with Desert Marigold). Flowers are very small but so profuse and fragrant that a mass planting is quite showy.
**Other Uses:**  Bees will travel long distances to forage Dalea. Twiggy growth slows the flow of flash floodwaters in dry washes and traps and holds sand, slowing wind erosion.

**Other Useful Species:**  Feather Dalea (*D. formosa*) is a small shrub, 2' height and spread, mostly evergreen with tiny, dark green compound leaves. It flowers April–October, reddish purple with feathery appendages on the seed coat. This species occurs infrequently on gravelly slopes to 6,500' elevation.

### PROPAGATION AND MAINTENANCE

**Seeds:**  Dalea germinates easily at a wide range of temperatures (65–90 F). Collect in October, store cool and dry.
**Watering:**  No supplemental watering is necessary, but occasional deep watering in summer encourages heavy flowering. Dalea declines rapidly if overwatered.
**Nutrient Requirements:**  Dalea fixes nitrogen in sandy soils.
**Pruning:**  None.
**Insect/Disease Susceptibility:**  None observed.

## CHAMISA
### Rabbitbrush

*CHRYSOTHAMNUS NAUSEOSUS    Sunflower-Compositae*

### ORIGIN AND ADAPTATIONS

**Native Distribution:**  Western North America: western Canada south to California, Texas, and northern Mexico.
**Elevation:**  3,000–8,000'.
**Topography:**  Dry, open areas, grassland, or open woodland, in dry washes.
**Soil Preference:**  Medium to coarse texture, alkaline, very adaptable.
**Drought Tolerance:**  8–16" annual precipitation.
**Salt Tolerance:**  Moderate.

### DESCRIPTION AND USE

**Mature Height:**  To 5'.
**Spread:**  To 5'.
**Growth Rate:**  Rapid.
**Form:**  Dense, erect, multi-branched deciduous to

mostly evergreen with a mounding, rounded crown. Chamisa is interesting and attractive all year.

**Flower:** Sulfur to gold yellow dense clusters of feathery disc flowers are showy from 2–4 weeks depending on weather in September and October. Blooms fade to straw color.

**Foliage:** Blue green linear leaves, often partially evergreen. Stems are woolly white, a nice contrast to the foliage.

**Fruit:** Airborne seed with pappus attached.

**Landscape Use:** Can be used as an accent, color foil, unsheared hedge or border, or mass planted. Combined with red yucca (*Hesperaloe parviflora*), the contrast of the coral yucca flowers and blue green foliage is attractive. Combined with the purple aster (*Machaeranthera bigelovii*), the yellow Chamisa flowers complement the aster well. Chamisa is good winter contrast to evergreens like Piñon or Cliffrose.

**Other Uses:** Erosion control, historical and contemporary use as a dye.

## PROPAGATION AND MAINTENANCE

**Seeds:** 330,000 uncleaned seeds per ounce, many sterile. Germination percentages usually 20–40% with no pretreatment. Germination is rapid (5 days at 65–70 F). Collect seeds as they ripen October–November.

**Vegetative:** Take hardwood cuttings of previous year's new growth of greatest girth in spring before plants leaf out, dip in .8% IBA talc, and stick directly in a prepared bed outdoors. Keep dry for best results.

**Watering:** Once established, periodic deep watering, especially during hot weather, encourages leafiness without forcing rank growth.

**Nutrient Requirements:** None.

**Pruning:** Periodic severe pruning, removing old wood to the crown, rejuvenates a planting.

**Insect/Disease Susceptibility:** Gall-forming insects, species specific (so much so that the insects are sometimes used to classify plant subspecies), lay eggs in stems, causing a bead-like swelling. Seldom injurious to the plant.

# CLIFFROSE

*COWANIA MEXICANA*    *Rose-Rosaceae*

## ORIGIN AND ADAPTATIONS

**Native Distribution:** United States and Mexico: southern Colorado west to southeastern California, south to Mexico.

**Elevation:** 3,000–8,000'.

**Topography:** Sunny, dry slopes of mesas or washes.

**Soil Preference:** Well-drained soil. Too wet or excess subsurface water produces rank growth that distorts the natural form.

**Drought Tolerance:** 10–25" annual precipitation.

**Salt Tolerance:** Fair.

## DESCRIPTION AND USE

**Mature Height:** 4–20'.

**Spread:** Average 5'.

**Growth Rate:** Moderate to start, then rapid when irrigated and established.

**Form:** Vase shaped and mounding, characteristic gnarled appearance when moisture is limited and exposed to wind.

**Flower:** Profuse 1" creamy white wild-rose type. Pleasant musky fragrance, most abundant in May but not uncommon April–September. Cut branches last up to 2 weeks in water indoors and are slow to shatter.

**Foliage:** Small (3/4" length and 1/2" width) deeply lobed leaves. Thick and resinous, deep blue green color, evergreen.

**Fruit:** White feathery plumes, most conspicuous in June–July but not as showy as Apache Plume.

**Landscape Use:** Cliffrose is very showy and fragrant when flowering; makes an excellent evergreen screen, foundation planting, hedge, or accent specimen. It can be pruned as a small tree for the latter use and takes shearing well.

**Other Uses:** Cliffrose is an excellent soil binder on slopes, reducing soil slippage and erosion. It is a preferred cattle browse, can be grazed to 65% of mass and recover.

## PROPAGATION AND MAINTENANCE

**Seeds:**   The seeds of the May flowering are most viable; those of later flowering are often sterile (lack of pollination?). Cold, moist stratification for 2–3 months prior to sowing improves germination. 64,000 seeds per pound.

**Vegetative:**   To date, cuttings taken of semi-softwood in spring and late summer, treated with .8% IBA talc, have failed to root.

**Watering:**   Limit water available to mature plants, as weak, rangy growth results from overwatering. Because Cliffrose is a broadleaf evergreen and continues to transpire moisture from foliage in winter, plants should be deep watered monthly during cold weather to prevent burning.

**Nutrient Requirements:**   Fertilizing is unnecessary on established plants, but low-level applications of a balanced fertilizer cut production time on young plants.

**Pruning:**   Cliffrose can be sheared or the natural gnarled form can be enhanced by judicious thinning. Light tip pruning of young plants improves early appearance, especially when plants are fed and watered.

**Insect/Disease Susceptibility:**   None observed.

## CREOSOTEBUSH
### Hediondilla

*LARREA TRIDENTATA*      *Caltrop-Zygophyllaceae*

## ORIGIN AND ADAPTATIONS

**Native Distribution:**   West Texas and New Mexico, north to Utah and Nevada, west to California, and south to Durango, Mexico.

**Elevation:**   Usually below 6,000'.

**Topography:**   Hilly, gravelly terrain.

**Soil Preference:**   Usually in soils underlain with hardpan.

**Drought Tolerance:**   6–15" annual precipitation.

**Salt Tolerance:**   Undetermined.

## DESCRIPTION AND USE

**Mature Height:**   3–6', recorded to 11'.

**Spread:**   3–6'.

**Growth Rate:**   Slow to moderate.

**Form:**   Characteristically flat topped, open spreading; has an oriental sculptured feeling that is responsible for much of its popularity as a landscape ornamental.

**Flower:**   Yellow, silky textured, about 1/2" in diameter, borne in profusion irregularly throughout the growing season, especially after rains.

**Foliage:**   Small, opposite paired leaves (1/4" in length, slightly less in width) are thick, dark green, and resinous, aromatic and evergreen.

**Fruit:**   Small, hairy seed capsules.

**Landscape Use:**   Its airy, open, oriental character and ease in maintenance (none once established) makes creosotebush especially useful as an accent or in a mass planting on harsh sites where subsequent care will be limited. Creosotebush reportedly produces toxins that limit plant growth within its drip line, so it is not advisable to use it where an understory of ground cover is desired. This may be advantageous in limiting unwanted weed growth in mass plantings, however.

**Other Uses:**   Creosotebush has traditional medicinal uses as an antiseptic dressing for wounds and a treatment for rheumatism, tuberculosis, and intestinal disorders.

## PROPAGATION AND MAINTENANCE

**Seeds:**   Seeds ripen from mid July through October. Germination is erratic. Acid-scarified seeds, field-sown in March, will germinate sporadically throughout the growing season. Overall germination is less than 50%. 170,000 seeds per pound. It has been suggested that innoculating the seedbed with symbiotic microbes by broadcasting leaf litter from mature plants over the seedbed will improve germination and growth of seedlings.

**Watering:**   Once established, creosotebush is extremely drought tolerant.

**Nutrient Requirements:**   None.

**Pruning:**   Characteristic form requires no pruning.

**Insect/Disease Susceptibility:**   None observed.

# FERNBUSH

*CHAMAEBATIERIA MILLEFOLIUM*    *Rose-Rosaceae*

## ORIGIN AND ADAPTATIONS

**Native Distribution:**   Idaho south to New Mexico, Arizona, and California (common on both rims of the Grand Canyon).
**Elevation:**   4,500–7,000'.
**Topography:**   Most common on gravelly slopes.
**Soil Preference:**   Well drained, adapts to many soils.
**Drought Tolerance:**   Good.
**Salt Tolerance:**   Fair.

## DESCRIPTION AND USE

**Mature Height:**   2–5'.
**Spread:**   3–5'.
**Growth Rate:**   Moderate.
**Form:**   Full, rounded, profusely branching aromatic shrub with shredding red bark.
**Flower:**   The creamy white, showy blossoms are small but so profuse that they are quite showy. Most abundant midsummer through fall.
**Foliage:**   The thick, leathery, finely cut ferny leaves are mostly evergreen and aromatic.
**Fruit:**   Dry pods.
**Landscape Use:**   Fernbush is effective mass planted in full sun, on banks or difficult-to-water areas, as color or textural accent, as filler in accent groupings, or as a low border.

## PROPAGATION AND MAINTENANCE

**Seeds:**   Three months of cold, moist stratification is recommended. Seeds are very fine and should be sown on the soil surface.
**Vegetative:**   Division of clumps while plant is dormant.
**Watering:**   Supplemental deep irrigation during hot, dry weather increases foliage density.
**Nutrient Requirements:**   Fernbush responds well

to periodic dilute nutrient applications, especially immediately after transplanting until plants are well established.
**Pruning:**   Removing flower heads in late winter keeps plants looking well kept. Like many native ornamentals, the dried seed heads are attractive until they are weathered.
**Insect/Disease Susceptibility:**   None observed to date.

# FOURWING SALTBUSH
## Chamiso

*ATRIPLEX CANESCENS*    *Goosefoot-*
                        *Chenopodiaceae*

## ORIGIN AND ADAPTATIONS

**Native Distribution:**   New Mexico north to South Dakota and west to California, abundant throughout the western states.
**Elevation:**   Sea level to 8,000'.
**Topography:**   Dry slopes, along washes and on salt flats.
**Soil Preference:**   Widely adaptable in alkaline, well-drained soils, easy to establish on a wide range of soils.
**Drought Tolerance:**   6–20" annual precipitation.
**Salt Tolerance:**   Excellent.

## DESCRIPTION AND USE

**Mature Height:**   2–6'.
**Spread:**   4–8'.
**Growth Rate:**   Rapid when moisture is available.
**Form:**   Densely branched, spreading, rounded semi-evergreen. Size is determined by availability of moisture and genetic variability.
**Flower:**   Small, yellowish green, and inconspicuous male and female flowers are borne on separate plants.
**Foliage:**   As with form, there is great variability in the size and shape of foliage within this species. The leaves are small (1/2–1" x 1/4–1/8" or less), rounded to linear, and blue green to light "sage" green in color. The blue green types often develop an opalescent plum

cast to the foliage in winter. Some varieties are nearly evergreen.

**Fruit:**  Papery husks remain on the plant well into winter and are attractive to small songbirds.

**Landscape Use:**  I prefer the lower growing, evergreen types as ornamentals. Fourwing can be used as color accents, mass planted as ground cover; taller selections are good hedge or screen material. Because it produces an abundance of seeds and is an aggressive competitor on disturbed soils, Fourwing Saltbush can become invasive. It is most valuable for use on harsh, dry sites.

**Other Uses:**  Because the seeds and foliage of Atriplex are relatively high in protein and very palatable and it establishes easily on disturbed sites, it is used for range and mine reclamation. Native Americans used the seeds/seed husks ground as a leavening agent. The dry seed husks are attractive in floral arrangements.

## PROPAGATION AND MAINTENANCE

**Seeds:**  22,500 cleaned seeds per pound, 30–60% germination, if properly stored retain viability well. Harvest seeds October through winter. Germination is improved by acid scarification (which is an easy way to remove the husks) and dry afterripening or leaching to lessen the effect of germination inhibitors.

**Vegetative:**  Stem cuttings in spring and summer (August if not misting) of semisoft wood tips, treated with .8% IBA talc root, in 2–3 weeks. A week of intermittent mist is optimum.

**Watering:**  Occasional deep watering will keep foliage dense. Excessive watering produces lush growth more susceptible to insect attack.

**Nutrient Requirements:**  When production-growing, light applications of nitrogen improve color and accelerate growth; otherwise, it is unnecessary.

**Pruning:**  Removal of old seed heads keeps a planting neat.

**Insect/Disease Susceptibility:**  Lush, soft growth is attractive to the gall midge, a small, gnat-like insect that lays its eggs in soft stem wood causing swollen galls, "bead-like" bulges in the stems. A native wasp preys on insect-bearing galls and controls populations in the wild.

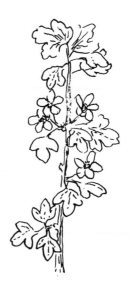

## GOLDEN CURRANT

*RIBES AUREUM*    Saxifrage-Saxifragaceae

## ORIGIN AND ADAPTATIONS

**Native Distribution:**  Western United States: Washington east to Montana and south across New Mexico and Arizona.

**Elevation:**  2,500–8,000'.

**Topography:**  Along stream banks and moist canyon bottoms.

**Soil Preference:**  Adaptable to any well-drained soil provided with intermittent watering.

**Drought Tolerance:**  15 + " annual precipitation.

**Salt Tolerance:**  Poor.

## DESCRIPTION AND USE

**Mature Height:**  3–6'.

**Spread:**  2–5'.

**Growth Rate:**  Moderate.

**Form:**  Erect, ascending branches, rounded clumping habit, suckers at base.

**Flower:**  Yellow clove-shaped blossoms, 3/4" x 1/2", borne in clusters, have a pleasant, spicy fragrance. Flowers early in the spring.

**Foliage:**  Rounded, lobed, almost scalloped looking, medium green turning scarlet to burgundy red in autumn, deciduous.

**Fruit:**  Small red currants ripen June–July, bland tasting but much relished by birds and other wildlife.

**Landscape Use:**  Golden Currant has broad ornamental appeal: showy blooms, good fall color, attractive, fresh green lobed foliage. Useful for mass plantings, hedges, and low screens, Golden Currant is a native substitute for forsythia.

**Other Uses:**  Ribes is a surface stabilizer and retainer along stream banks for erosion control, due to its vigorous sprouting. In a landscape an overzealous root system can be controlled by reducing the available moisture.

## PROPAGATION AND MAINTENANCE

**Seeds:** Approximately 350,000 cleaned seeds per pound, ripen in June–July, require 3 months cold, moist stratification at 40 F; 60% germination.

**Vegetative:** Hardwood cuttings in fall stuck directly in beds outdoors or division of suckers while plant is dormant are alternate propagation methods.

**Watering:** Golden Currant requires deep intermittent watering, especially when air temperatures are high.

**Nutrient Requirements:** Responds well to light feedings.

**Pruning:** Light tip pruning while plant is young encourages branching; mature plants take shearing well.

**Insect/Disease Susceptibility:** Aphids are attracted to early growth.

## LITTLELEAF SUMAC
### Lemita

*RHUS MICROPHYLLA*    Sumac-Anacardiaceae

### ORIGIN AND ADAPTATIONS

**Native Distribution:** Missouri west to Washington state, California east to Texas.

**Elevation:** 2,000–7,000'.

**Topography:** Open grasslands or along floodplains.

**Soil Preference:** Prefers sand or sandy loam but adapts to most soils.

**Drought Tolerance:** 10–20" annual precipitation.

**Salt Tolerance:** Fair.

### DESCRIPTION AND USE

**Mature Height:** 3–6'.

**Spread:** 2–5'.

**Growth Rate:** Moderate.

**Form:** Round crowned, densely twiggy deciduous shrub with gray bark and reddish twigs (new growth).

**Flower:** Small and yellow in clustered spikes in early spring (March).

**Foliage:** Individual bipinnate leaflets less than 1/2" in length and width, dark green, often reddish, undersides turning a plum color in autumn.

**Fruit:** Conspicuous bright orange red berries in clusters, sticky and slightly acidic, in July–August. Very attractive to birds, rarely persist past ripening in the wild.

**Landscape Use:** Littleleaf Sumac can be used like pyracantha for its conspicuous fruits, as a foundation, or for mass planting. Used as screen or hedge material it can be sheared, but the natural form is more attractive when leafless. Showy fruit provides color in midsummer.

**Other Uses:** Littleleaf Sumac is good wildlife cover, forage, and erosion control. A traditional beverage like lemonade was made with the tart berries.

## PROPAGATION AND MAINTENANCE

**Seeds:** 68,000 seeds per pound, usually ripen in August. The dry seed coat is impermeable, and germination is greatly improved by acid scarification followed by three months' cold stratification (about 35 F).

**Vegetative:** Softwood cuttings taken in mid August should be treated with 0.8% IBA talc.

**Watering:** Once established, deep watering in times of heat and drought increases leaf density and fruit development.

**Nutrient Requirements:** Dilute nutrient solutions accelerate the growth of young plants.

**Pruning:** Periodic removal of dead wood may be necessary if plants are grown with no supplemental water. If plant growth is being accelerated by fertilizer application, tip pruning long shoots will encourage early branching.

**Insect/Disease Susceptibility:** None observed.

## MARIOLA

*PARTHENIUM INCANUM*    Sunflower-Compositae

### ORIGIN AND ADAPTATIONS

**Native Distribution:** Grand Canyon area of Arizona; New Mexico, especially in the foothills above the Rio Grande and Pecos River, east into southwest Texas.

**Elevation:**  2,500–6,000'.
**Topography:**  Slopes and canyonsides.
**Soil Preference:**  Gravelly caliche, but adapts to most soils.
**Drought Tolerance:**  Excellent. 8–15" annual precipitation.
**Salt Tolerance:**  Undetermined.

### DESCRIPTION AND USE

**Mature Height:**  1–3'.
**Spread:**  To 3'.
**Growth Rate:**  Moderate.
**Form:**  Low mounding shrub, twiggy but open, lending an airy quality to a landscape.
**Flower:**  Small, white, densely clustered heads, grouped in large, flat clusters, give a lacy look to the plants in flower.
**Foliage:**  Small-lobed gray green leaves add to the overall refined texture.
**Landscape Use:**  Mariola is an effective color foil and light textural accent among coarser, more colorful plantings. Its drought and heat resistance make Mariola a good choice on harsh, demanding sites.

### PROPAGATION AND MAINTENANCE

**Seeds:**  An hour soak in 3% hydrogen peroxide prior to sowing improves germination. Best results are in the midrange temperatures (65–75 F).
**Watering:**  Mariola is very drought tolerant once established.
**Nutrient Requirements:**  None.
**Pruning.**  None.
**Insect/Disease Susceptibility:**  None observed. The cold hardiness of Mariola has not been tested, and it may winter kill where average winter low temperatures are below 0°F.

# MOUNTAIN MAHOGANY
## Palo Duro

*CERCOCARPUS MONTANUS*      *Rose-Rosaceae*

### ORIGIN AND ADAPTATIONS

**Native Distribution:**  Throughout the mountains of New Mexico, west into Nevada, north to Montana and Wyoming, and south into Mexico.
**Elevation:**  3,500–9,000'.
**Topography:**  Foothills and mountainsides.
**Soil Preference:**  Shallow, well-drained, and rocky. Adapts to most soils under cultivation as long as drainage is adequate.
**Drought Tolerance:**  Very good. 10–25" annual precipitation. Growth is faster and more dense in moister habitats.
**Salt Tolerance:**  Moderate to poor.

### DESCRIPTION AND USE

**Mature Height:**  To 12', usually 4–10'.
**Spread:**  To 6' in open locations, narrower where shaded or clustered in groves.
**Growth Rate:**  Slow to moderate.
**Form:**  Upright, vase-shaped shrub to small tree.
**Flower:**  Small and inconspicuous in May and June.
**Foliage:**  Semi-evergreen, wedge-shaped, and toothed on the upper margins, crisp dark green above with silvery undersides.
**Fruit:**  Clusters of single seeds with plumelike styles, July through October.
**Landscape Use:**  The reddish, shedding bark and twisted branches add a stark accent when Mountain Mahogany is pruned to a tree-form specimen. Planted closely (6' on center), it makes an attractive screen or hedge. The white seed plumes add a soft, textural touch in late summer.
**Other Uses:**  Erosion control, revegetation, and wildlife conservation within its native range. Traditionally, Mountain Mahogany has ceremonial and medicinal

uses as well as domestic uses as a dye plant, for fuel, and as wood for ornamental use.

**Other Useful Species:**  Curlleaf Mountain Mahogany (*C. ledifolius*) is a smaller leafed, more variable species found over a broader range in elevation.

## PROPAGATION AND MAINTENANCE

**Seeds:**  Approximately 45,000 seeds per pound with an average germination rate of 50–70%. Cold, moist stratification for 4–6 weeks or late fall/winter seeding outdoors enhances germination. The bulk of germination occurs when temperatures are mid-70°F/day and mid-50°F/night.

**Watering:**  When drainage is good, ample water during hot weather will promote faster growth and denser foliage.

**Nutrient Requirements:**  Fertilization is unnecessary when plants are grown close to native conditions, but early spring feeding while plants are young will accelerate growth.

**Pruning:**  Little pruning is needed when Mountain Mahogany is grown as a shrub. Thinning to several main stems and removing lateral branches from the bottom 1/2–2/3 of the stems will help to develop a tree-like character.

**Insect/Disease Susceptibility:**  None observed.

## SOAPTREE YUCCA
### Amole

*YUCCA ELATA*    *Lily-Liliaceae*

## ORIGIN AND ADAPTATIONS

**Native Distribution:**  Southwest Texas west to central Arizona, north to southwest Utah.

**Elevation:**  2,000–6,000'.

**Topography:**  Deserts, grasslands, mesas.

**Soil Preference:**  Well-drained soil, very adaptable except where water stands.

**Drought Tolerance:**  8–15" annual precipitation.

**Salt Tolerance:**  Moderate.

## DESCRIPTION AND USE

**Mature Height:**  To 15'.

**Spread:**  3–10', clustered.

**Growth Rate:**  Moderate, rapid when young, slowing with age.

**Form:**  Solitary, low, with grass-like heads, to tree-like stature with multiple heads.

**Flower:**  White, bell-shaped, 2"-long individual flowers borne on spikes standing 3–6' above the foliage, commonly in June.

**Foliage:**  Up to 3' long, an inch or less wide, pale blue green, flexible, with fibery, shredding margins.

**Fruit:**  Dry, woody capsule encloses seed.

**Landscape Use:**  Stereotypic of "desert landscapes," the Soaptree Yucca is a dramatic accent plant.

**Other Useful Species:**  *Y. baccata* (Datil), a low-growing (rarely to 3') broad-leafed plant with dull green foliage and white flowers followed by edible fruits. Native to higher elevations, usually above 7,000'. Perhaps the most useful (food/soap/craft) plant in the Southwest.

## PROPAGATION AND MAINTENANCE

**Seeds:**  The large, flat, black seeds germinate readily in warm soils (90% + is common). Temperatures near 80 F produce fastest results; full germination within 7–10 days.

**Watering:**  No supplemental water is required once plants are established, although intermittent watering during hot weather accelerates growth. Plants should be kept dry in winter.

**Nutrient Requirements:**  Fertilizing is unnecessary.

**Pruning:**  None.

**Insect/Disease Susceptibility:**  Yuccas are pollinated by moths (*Pronuba* or *Prodoxus* sp.) that gather pollen and place it, along with their eggs, in the stigmatic tube. Some seed (less than 20%) is consumed by subsequent larvae. Control is undesirable—no moth, no seed.

## THREELEAF SUMAC
### Lemita

*RHUS TRILOBATA*     *Sumac-Anacardiaceae*

### ORIGIN AND ADAPTATIONS

**Native Distribution:**  Missouri west to Washington state, California east to Texas.

**Elevation:**  3,100–10,000'.

**Topography:**  Rocky hillsides and ridges as well as open bottomlands.

**Soil Preference:**  Very adaptable; deep, moist soils produce lush, rapid growth.

**Drought Tolerance:**  10–20" annual precipitation.

**Salt Tolerance:**  Poor to moderate.

### DESCRIPTION AND USE

**Mature Height:**  3–8' taller with abundant moisture.

**Spread:**  6–8'.

**Growth Rate:**  Moderate to rapid.

**Form:**  Deciduous, densely branched with rounded crown, arching branches when growth is rapid.

**Flower:**  Clusters of small yellow flowers in profusion, but not really showy early in spring (April).

**Foliage:**  Deeply lobed, dark green, aromatic crisp leaves borne three per leaf stem. Fall color is a beautiful scarlet. Size varies with available moisture (1–2" overall).

**Fruit:**  Bright, sticky orange red berries borne in clusters, best color mid to late summer.

**Landscape Use:**  The dark green foliage complements the many silver and blue gray shades of other drought-tolerant plants. The compact mounding shape when plants are grown with limited moisture is excellent mass planted and as a bank cover. More moisture is required to produce a tall screen or hedge. The scarlet fall color is beautiful, especially combined with Winterfat.

**Other Uses:**  Threeleaf Sumac is a good surface stabilizer for erosion control. Birds relish the berries. A lemonade-like drink traditionally was made with the berries, water, and sugar.

### PROPAGATION AND MAINTENANCE

**Seeds:**  Fruit ripens in August–September and averages 50,000 clean seeds per pound. Acid scarification to remove pulp, followed by cold stratification (32–38 F for 3 months or more), greatly increases the percentage of germination.

**Vegetative:**  Stem cuttings of hardwood in early spring or late summer, using 0.8–2.0% IBA talc. Softwood cuttings in midsummer with 0.8% IBA talc.

**Watering:**  Irregular deep waterings improve foliage density on established plants. Sumacs grow best given some additional moisture.

**Nutrient Requirements:**  Fertilizing is not necessary on established plants, but use of dilute solutions on production stock shortens crop time.

**Pruning:**  Sumac shears well as a hedge, given additional water. Plants grown dry will develop a compact, rounded form that requires no pruning.

**Insect/Disease Susceptibility:**  Black aphids on new growth in spring can be washed off with a heavy spray of water, or use carbaryl or pyrethrins.

## WINTERFAT

*CERATOIDES LANATA*     *Goosefoot-Chenopodiaceae*

### ORIGIN AND ADAPTATIONS

**Native Distribution:**  Canada south to Mexico, eastern Rocky Mountains west to the Pacific Coast.

**Elevation:**  Sea level to 10,000'.

**Topography:**  Most common on rolling plains.

**Soil Preference:**  Very adaptable to most soils from clay to sand to gravelly types as long as the soil is fairly alkaline and moderately well drained.

**Drought Tolerance:**  Survives 4" annual precipitation, thrives at 8–15".

**Salt Tolerance:**  Fair.

### DESCRIPTION AND USE.

**Mature Height:** 12–24".
**Spread:** 6–18".
**Growth Rate:** Rapid, grows faster given free root run rather than in containers.
**Form:** Erect to spreading subshrub, herbaceous with a woody base.
**Flower:** Inconspicuous, April–August.
**Foliage:** Woolly white hairs densely cover light blue green foliage, giving the effect of silver white color. Leaves are small (1"), narrow, and closely spaced on the soft stems.
**Fruit:** Downy, plume-like seed heads are very showy September–December, and cause the slender stems to arch gracefully and look windswept even when the air is still.
**Landscape Use:** The dense, woolly, silver blue green foliage and downy white seed heads give the plant exceptional ornamental value, March–December. Winterfat is excellent as a color foil to evergreens in winter, vivid flower colors in spring and late summer, and reds of Creeper, Currant, and Sumac in autumn. Mass-planted, Winterfat is good cover in hot, dry locations.
**Other Uses:** Seed spikes (sprayed with thin lacquer, i.e., hair spray) make interesting additions to dry floral arrangements and Christmas wreaths (nice with red chile). Highly palatable, it's excellent winter forage for livestock and wildlife. It is a surface soil stabilizer and good erosion control.

## PROPAGATION AND MAINTENANCE

**Seeds:** Seeds average 90,000 per pound, germination is rapid (2–5 days) on fresh seeds. Seeds reportedly lose viability rapidly when stored (up to 50% in one year). Storage at subfreezing temperatures slows deterioration. Best results in terms of plant quality and success rate are had by seeding directly into containers or outdoor beds, March–May, using uncleaned seeds. Plants require full sun for proper development. From seeds to 1-gallon-size plants in 12 months is average production time. Greenhouse-produced plants are of inferior quality due to reduced light intensity. Can be fall seeded for range improvement at 3–5 lbs. per acre.
**Watering:** Plants grow rapidly when moisture is available. Once established, no additional water is needed for maintaining.
**Nutrient Requirements:** Fertilizing is unnecessary except for production growing, and even then only very dilute applications of a balanced nutrient solution are recommended.
**Pruning:** Cutting back to 6–8" from the ground in late winter keeps a mass planting neat.
**Insect/Disease Susceptibility:** None observed.

# GROUND COVERS
## Perennials, Annuals, Vines & Grasses

## BLACKFOOT DAISY

*MELAMPODIUM LEUCANTHUM*          *Sunflower-Compositae*

### ORIGIN AND ADAPTATIONS

**Native Distribution:** Arizona east to Kansas and south into Mexico.
**Elevation:** To 6,500'.
**Topography:** Dry plains and gravelly desert slopes.
**Soil Preference:** Dry, rocky, calcareous.
**Drought Tolerance:** 8–15" annual precipitation.
**Salt Tolerance:** Poor.

### DESCRIPTION AND USE

**Mature Height:** 6–16".
**Spread:** 10–16".
**Growth Rate:** Moderate, flowers first year from seed if started early.
**Form:** Rounded mound, almost globular, herbaceous perennial with a woody base, densely twiggy. Compact plants look sheared.
**Flower:** Profuse white-rayed daisy, 3/4–1" in diameter, with a yellow center. Flowers from May to October.
**Foliage:** Gray green, mostly evergreen, small (3/4" x 1/8") linear leaves, sometimes toothed.
**Fruit:** Foot-shaped, papery, black husk encloses small black seed.
**Landscape Use:** The natural, mounded, compact shape is excellent when mass planted with Santolina, Gaillardia, Penstemon, and other drought-tolerant natives. Useful in parkways and bordering walks, where hot, dry conditions and limited space are ideal for this native daisy.
**Other Uses:** Erosion control on slopes.

### PROPAGATION AND MAINTENANCE

**Seeds:** Freshly collected seeds germinate well. Dry,

stored seeds germinate better if acid scarified. Germination is faster at warm soil temperatures (70 F). 50% germination is optimum.

**Vegetative:**   Semi-soft cuttings treated with .8% IBA talc root easily. Stems need to approach woodiness for best cutting material.

**Watering:**   Once established, Blackfoot Daisy requires no additional watering, but deep infrequent watering in late spring and summer increases flowering. Avoid overwatering, especially during winter and on heavier soils.

**Nutrient Requirements:**   None.

**Pruning:**   None is required when plants are grown dry.

**Insect/Disease Susceptibility:**   None observed.

# BLANKETFLOWER

*GAILLARDIA* Species*      Sunflower-Compositae

## ORIGIN AND ADAPTATIONS

**Native Distribution:**   Throughout North America.

**Elevation:**   Below 7,000'.

**Topography:**   Common on disturbed sites such as roadsides.

**Soil Preference:**   Alkaline.

**Drought Tolerance:**   15+" annual precipitation.

**Salt Tolerance:**   Good.

## DESCRIPTION AND USE

**Mature Height:**   To 2'.

**Spread:**   To 2'.

**Growth Rate:**   Rapid.

**Form:**   Globular, mounding growth habit from a rosette of foliage crowned by a profusion of flowers.

**Flower:**   Red to russet globular center with rays varying from mahogany to clear yellow to pink and red yellow bicolors.

**Foliage:**   Compact, hairy, light green rosette.

**Fruit:**   Globular seed head changes in color from russet red to straw color to gray.

**Landscape Use:**   Blanketflower is a good component

of mixed perennial beds; compact varieties are good border subjects. There are several excellent cultivars— "Goblin" is a dwarf variety which clumps to 10" tall and wide, "Burgundy" is a taller copper red hybrid. *Annuals derived from *G. pulchella;* perennials derived from *G. aristata.*

## PROPAGATION AND MAINTENANCE

**Seeds:**   Large chaffy seeds germinate in 2–3 weeks at 68 F. If sown early enough, they will flower the same summer. Seeds should be covered very lightly for best results (10,000–14,000 seeds per ounce).

**Vegetative:**   Clumps may be divided.

**Watering:**   Intermittent watering is recommended to extend flowering throughout the summer and autumn.

**Nutrient Requirements:**   Plantings that are watered regularly benefit from light applications of a balanced fertilizer.

**Pruning:**   Removal of spent flowers keeps plants flowering.

**Insect/Disease Susceptibility:**   None observed.

# BLUE FLAX

*LINUM LEWISII*      Flax-Linaceae

## ORIGIN AND ADAPTATIONS

**Native Distribution:**   Alaska east to Saskatchewan, south through Kansas into west Texas and Mexico, west to California.

**Elevation:**   4,500–9,500'.

**Topography:**   On steep, sloping terrain, in conifer forests, and on dry mesas and open ridges.

**Soil Preference:**   Well drained sand to rocky.

**Drought Tolerance:**   Good.

**Salt Tolerance:**   Fair to poor.

## DESCRIPTION AND USE

**Mature Height:**   To 18".

**Spread:**   12–18".

**Growth Rate:**   Rapid.

**Form:**   Densely branched from central crown, stems

thin and wiry, arching gracefully.

**Flower:** Single, open blue flowers usually having 5 broad petals, borne in panicles. Individual flowers are short-lived but produced in abundance. Not showy in the solid-color mass sense, but an attractive color accent.

**Foliage:** Finely cut blue green foliage, light and airy.

**Fruit:** Dry seed capsule.

**Landscape Use:** Blue Flax is a useful component of low border or mixed planting with other flowering annuals and perennials that require intermittent watering.

**Other Useful Species:** *L. grandiflorum rubrum*, Scarlet Flax, is a showy, low-growing annual (to 14" height) that flowers in spring and early summer. Effective mass planted or as a meadow component, Scarlet Flax prefers light, sandy soil in full sun. 120,000 seeds per pound.

### PROPAGATION AND MAINTENANCE

**Seeds:** Average 21,000 seeds per ounce, germination in 3–4 weeks at 54 F. Blue Flax self-sows readily.

**Vegetative:** Division of large clumps while plants are dormant.

**Watering:** Periodic watering during hot, dry weather results in better overall growth and flowering.

**Nutrient Requirements:** Flax responds to dilute nutrient applications with denser growth.

**Pruning:** Remove previous year's growth at ground level.

**Insect/Disease Susceptibility:** None observed.

## BLUE GRAMA

*BOUTELOUA GRACILIS*    Grass-Gramineae

### ORIGIN AND ADAPTATIONS

**Native Distribution:** Wisconsin north to Alberta, Canada; Missouri, Texas, southern California south into Mexico. Common throughout New Mexico.

**Elevation:** 3,000–8,000'.

**Topography:** From plains-prairie to mountain grasslands and bottomlands.

**Soil Preference:** Grows on most soil types, including alkali.

**Drought Tolerance:** Excellent, tolerates 8", best suited to 12–24" annual precipitation.

**Salt Tolerance:** Fair.

### DESCRIPTION AND USE

**Mature Height:** 12–18" with seed heads.

**Spread:** Rhizomatous.

**Growth Rate:** Moderate.

**Form:** Warm season, perennial sod grass, dense mat-like cover.

**Flower:** Inconspicuous.

**Foliage:** Fine-leafed, gray green leaves cure to straw color.

**Fruit:** Seed is held in comb-like spikes, usually two per stem. Seed heads resemble eyelashes.

**Landscape Use:** Blue grama is an excellent native lawn grass where drought tolerance and minimal maintenance are considerations. Mowing periodically aids in sod formation. Since seed heads are ornamental and weediness is not a problem, allowing the grass to go to seed is an ornamental option. "Lovington" and "Hachita" are two selections made for seedling vigor, forage and seed production, and general adaptability.

**Other Uses:** Blue grama is a nutritious and palatable range grass but it should not be grazed closer than 2–3" in height while it is actively growing. Effective for erosion control when seeded in pure stands, it is an excellent soil binder and slows surface flow of water.

### PROPAGATION AND MAINTENANCE

**Seeds:** Early summer seeding when night temperatures drop to the 60s but soil is warm seems to be optimum for germination (60–90 F fluctuation). Constant cool temperatures, even when soil is relatively dry, produce poor results. Range seeding rates are 8–12 pounds per acre. 725,000 cleaned seeds per pound. 30–50% PLS (Pure Live Seed), 70–90% germination. One half pound per 1,000 square feet is a heavy seeding rate for lawn use.

**Vegetative:** Blue grama can be divided and "plugged." Coverage is faster and more uniform from seed for lawn use.

**Watering:** Moisture levels should be kept relatively high right after seeding until germination is mostly complete, then the surface should be allowed to dry between deep waterings to encourage deep rooting.

**Nutrient Requirements:** Blue grama responds well to low levels of nitrogen while actively growing, when it is used as a lawn grass. 1 1/2 to 2 lbs. 20-10-10 per 1,000 square feet nets 1/4 to 1/2 lb. nitrogen per 1,000 square feet.

**Pruning:** Mow to a height of 2–3" periodically once the sod is well developed, to encourage dense cover.

**Insect/Disease Susceptibility:** None noted to date.

# BUFFALOGRASS

*BUCHLOE DACTYLOIDES*    *Grass-Gramineae*

## ORIGIN AND ADAPTATIONS

**Native Distribution:**   Drier areas of Great Plains, eastern half of New Mexico.
**Elevation:**   3,000–7,000'.
**Topography:**   Mostly plains and prairies.
**Soil Preference:**   Especially well adapted to drier, heavy soils.
**Drought Tolerance:**   Excellent, tolerates 10", best suited to 12–24" annual precipitation.
**Salt Tolerance:**   Good to excellent.

## DESCRIPTION AND USE

**Mature Height:**   3–5".
**Spread:**   Stoloniferous.
**Growth Rate:**   Rapid in relatively dry soil.
**Form:**   Perennial, warm season, sod grass spreading by stolons to produce dense, mat-like cover.
**Flower:**   Inconspicuous, comb-like heads similar to gramas are male flowers. Male and female flowers are borne on different plants.
**Foliage:**   Fine, soft, light green foliage usually less than 5" in height and densely matted.
**Fruit:**   Female plants produce bur-like seed capsules usually at ground level or at growing tips of stolons not yet rooted.
**Landscape Use:**   One of the best native grasses for lawn use, Buffalograss produces an attractive, soft, light green turf with very little moisture. Because it spreads best when kept drier than most annual weeds can survive, Buffalograss sod competes well, overcoming weeds easily and taking moderate to heavy use. "Texoka" and "Sharp's Improved" are two selected varieties well adapted to central New Mexico.
**Other Uses:**   Buffalograss provides effective erosion control or range forage grass where soils are heavy and dry. It should not be grazed below 1–3" in height.

## PROPAGATION AND MAINTENANCE

**Seeds:**   Two pounds of treated seeds per 1,000 square feet produces a dense lawn cover. Seed May–July in warm soil and keep the seedbed moist until germination is substantial, about 7–10 days. Gradually wean the lawn of superficial watering. Encourage deep rooting and stolon production by watering thoroughly, then allowing the soil surface to dry between waterings. (30–45 minutes weekly on clay soil, 1 hour weekly on sandy soils.) 40,000 uncleaned seeds (burs) per pound.
**Vegetative:**   Well-established Buffalograss can be plugged, like Bermuda grass or Zoyzia; vigorous tillering plants should be placed on 8–12 inch centers and allowed to spread. It is not advisable to subject a new lawn to extreme drought.
**Watering:**   Buffalograss responds to extreme drought by browning out, going dormant until moisture is available, then it resumes active growth and greens up rapidly.
**Nutrient Requirements:**   Buffalograss responds well to low levels of nitrogen while actively growing. 1 1/2 to 2 pounds of a general lawn fertilizer 20–10–10 per 1,000 square feet (approximately 1/4 to 1/2 pound nitrogen per 1,000 square feet), especially when grown as a monocultural lawn planting.
**Pruning:**   Mowing is unnecessary. If a traditional mowed lawn is desirable, Buffalograss should be mowed infrequently (monthly or less) to a height of 2–3".
**Insect/Disease Susceptibility:**   None noted to date.

# BUSH MORNINGGLORY

*IPOMOEA LEPTOPHYLLA*    *Morningglory-Convolvulaceae*

## ORIGIN AND ADAPTATIONS

**Native Distribution:**   Montana and South Dakota south to Texas and New Mexico.
**Elevation:**   To 4,500'.
**Topography:**   At lower elevations, especially on plains, grasslands.

**Soil Preference:**  Sandy to sandy loam, well drained.
**Drought Tolerance:**  10–20" annual precipitation.
**Salt Tolerance:**  Poor.

## DESCRIPTION AND USE

**Mature Height:**  3'.
**Spread:**  4'.
**Growth Rate:**  Moderate.
**Form:**  Stems are erect but limber, gracefully arching, forming dense mounding clumps.
**Flower:**  Large, to 3"-diameter, magenta trumpets open morning and evening, close during the heat of the day.
**Foliage:**  Leaves are linear, 2" x ¼", and green. Dies back to ground in September.
**Fruit:**  Inconspicuous, very hard seed capsules, wedge shaped.
**Landscape Use:**  Bush Morningglory is excellent massed for color, especially useful in parkways and other dry spots where low cover is advantageous. The fleshy, tuberous root system can weigh in excess of 100 lbs. on well-established plants. Once established, plants are difficult to move.
**Other Uses:**  Bush Morningglory is an excellent soil binder for erosion control. The wiry stems traditionally were used in basket making.

## PROPAGATION AND MAINTENANCE

**Seeds:**  Use fresh seeds, as insect larvae destroy seeds. Soak in boiling water until seeds swell (4–8 hours).
**Vegetative:**  Division of tubers while dormant. Keep dry.
**Watering:**  Unnecessary once established. Supplemental watering during June and July extends blooming period.
**Nutrient Requirements:**  None.
**Pruning:**  Dead stems can be removed at ground level when plant is fully dormant, usually by mid September.
**Insect/Disease Susceptibility:**  Larvae within the seeds destroy seeds but don't seem to affect the plant.

## BUSH PENSTEMON

*PENSTEMON AMBIGUUS*      *Figwort-Scrophulariaceae*

## ORIGIN AND ADAPTATIONS

**Native Distribution:**  Texas panhandle, New Mexico, Colorado, and Utah, north to Kansas and west to California.
**Elevation:**  4,000–6,500'.
**Topography:**  Sandy mesas, grasslands, and in dry washes.
**Soil Preference:**  Well drained, fairly adaptable.
**Drought Tolerance:**  8–20" annual precipitation.
**Salt Tolerance:**  Fair.

## DESCRIPTION AND USE

**Mature Height:**  To 24".
**Spread:**  18–20".
**Growth Rate:**  Moderate, flowers first year from seed if started in fall and overwintered.
**Form:**  Shrubby, densely twiggy plant, globe shaped.
**Flower:**  Tubular pink to purple flowers borne in loose panicles, in flower from late May through mid autumn.
**Foliage:**  Fine, linear, bright green leaves, sometimes sticky, as are the many stems. Turns a golden brown in winter.
**Fruit:**  Small brown seedpods replace flowers; ornamental in dry floral arrangements.
**Landscape Use:**  Bush Penstemon can be mass planted or combined with other drought-tolerant flowers for a meadow effect. It is attractive planted with Indian Ricegrass.
**Other Useful Species:**  *P. eatonii:* 4,000–10,000', Mohave and Arizona deserts, sandy to clay soil, smooth dark green foliage, red flowers in June and September. *P. pseudospectabilis:* below 6,000' in California, Arizona, and New Mexico deserts, spoon-shaped dark green leaves, 3–4' flower stalk, hot pink flowers in late spring and late summer. *P. strictus:* at higher elevations in Wyoming, Utah, Arizona, and northern New

Mexico, strap-shaped green foliage, dark blue flowers on 2' stems in June. *P. superbus:* to 6,000' in southwest New Mexico and Arizona, large foliage rosettes look like Echeverria, 12" across, steel blue, flushed red in cold weather, coral flowers on 3–4' stems in June and October. *P. pinifolius:* an evergreen subshrub with needle-like green leaves and red flowers. *P. caespitosus:* a mat-forming small-leafed ground cover with small dark blue flowers, looks like creeping thyme.

## PROPAGATION AND MAINTENANCE

**Seeds:**  Small, brown to black, resembling coffee grounds. Require afterripening of at least one year, cool and dry, for germination of 50% or more. Germinate best at cooler temperatures (35–70 F, fluctuating night and day temperatures). 250,000 to 600,000 seeds per pound, varies with species and type location.

**Vegetative:**  Hardwood cuttings taken from thickest stems near the base of the plant, treated with .3–.8% IBA talc, root in early spring before the plant begins to leaf out.

**Watering:**  Intermittent deep watering during hot, dry weather promotes flowering, but Penstemons are longer lived if they are grown dry.

**Nutrient Requirements:**  Fertilizers are unnecessary when plants are grown moderately dry. Excessive feeding and watering shortens the life-span of some species.

**Pruning:**  Dried seedpods are ornamental, can be removed in midwinter if they begin to look weatherbeaten.

**Insect/Disease Susceptibility:**  Grasshoppers love the flower buds, and aphids can occur in early spring. Mildew can be a problem on broad-leafed species, where air circulation is poor and humidity remains abnormally high.

kota, south to Florida and west to New Mexico and Arizona.

**Elevation:**    Sea level to 7,000'.

**Topography:**    Meadows and prairies in full sun.

**Soil Preference:**    Sandy, poor soil but adapts to clay and loam.

**Drought Tolerance:**    Survives periodic drought due to a deep taproot but requires ample moisture while flowering.

**Salt Tolerance:**    Fair.

## DESCRIPTION AND USE

**Mature Height:**    To 18".

**Spread:**    To 18".

**Growth Rate:**    Rapid. Early spring seeding nets flowering specimens the same summer.

**Form:**    Erect, stout stems from the crown branch near the top.

**Flower:**    Brilliant orange red clusters in June through September given adequate moisture.

**Foliage:**    Lance-shaped, dark green leaves are crisp and fresh looking.

**Landscape Use:**    Showy long-lasting flowers attract butterflies, as the common name indicates; Butterfly Weed is an excellent textural contrast as well and is effective mass planted. It requires more moisture during the summer than many natives and should be placed accordingly.

## PROPAGATION AND MAINTENANCE

**Seeds:**    The papery thin seeds germinate well in the 65–80 F range. Cover lightly.

**Vegetative:**    Clumps can be divided while the plants are dormant.

**Watering:**    Ample moisture is necessary for flowering.

**Nutrient Requirements:**    A light feeding in late May is beneficial for plants growing in light, sandy soil but is usually not essential.

**Pruning:**    Cut back to the ground when winter takes its toll.

**Insect/Disease Susceptibility:**    Bright yellow aphids can attack with a vengeance and require regular removal or spraying to control if predators are not on the job.

## BUTTERFLY WEED

*ASCLEPIAS TUBEROSA*    Milkweed-Asclepiadaceae

## ORIGIN AND ADAPTATIONS

**Native Distribution:**    New England west to North Da-

Desert Willow/*Chilopsis linearis*; inset: closeup of flower

Desert Olive/*Forestiera neomexicana*

Black Locust/*Robinia pseudoacacia*

Bird of Paradise/*Caesalpinia gilliesii*

Fourwing Saltfush/*Atriplex canescens*

Threadleaf Sage, Purple Aster , Chamisa (**top to bottom**)/*Artemisia filifolia*, *Machaeranthera bigelovii* , *Chrysothamnus nauseosus*

Apache Plume/*Fallugia paradoxa*

Cliffrose & Gayfeather/*Cowania mexicana, Liatris punctata*

Paperflower/*Psilostrophe bakerii*

Blanketflower/*Gaillardia* hybrid

Butterfly Weed/*Asclepias tuberosa*

Coral Penstemon/*P. superbus*

Yellow Evening Primrose/*Oenothera hookerii*

Fern Verbena/*Verbena bipinnatifida*

Silver Groundsel/*Senecio longilobus*

Indian Ricegrass/*Oryzopsis hymenoides*

Giant Four O'Clock/*Mirabilis multiflora*

Blue Grama/*Bouteloua gracilis*

Western Virginsbower/*Clematis ligusticifolius*

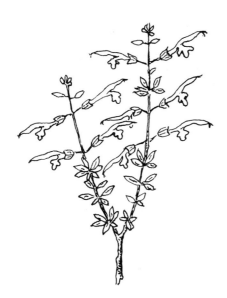

## CHERRY SAGE
### Autumn Sage

*SALVIA GREGII*      *Mint-Lamiaceae*

### ORIGIN AND ADAPTATIONS

**Native Distribution:**   Central and West Texas west and south into New Mexico and Mexico.
**Elevation:**   5,000–7,000'.
**Topography:**   Rocky, scrub-covered slopes.
**Soil Preference:**   Prefers well drained, but is tolerant of most soils, including heavy clay and alkali.
**Drought Tolerance:**   Good.
**Salt Tolerance:**   Poor.

### DESCRIPTION AND USE

**Mature Height:**   To 3'.
**Spread:**   To 3'.
**Growth Rate:**   Moderate to rapid.
**Form:**   A densely branched, mounded subshrub, dies back to the ground in 0° winters.
**Flower:**   Tubular, cherry red blossoms usually 1" long and paired on spikes; summer through fall.
**Foliage:**   Elliptical to 1" long and less than half as wide, with a leathery texture and fresh medium green color, evergreen in milder climates.
**Landscape Use:**   The showy flowers and neat growth habit of Cherry Sage make it useful for borders and ground cover on slopes. Mass planted, it is a dramatic color accent in flower from late spring through fall.
**Other Useful Species:**   *S. azurea grandiflora* is an herbaceous perennial with large gentian blue flowers on 3- to 5-foot stems. Flowers July through October. Very cold hardy. *S. leucophylla* is showy for its white stems and crinkly gray leaves. Overall size is determined by available moisture and can range from 2 to 6 feet in height and spread. Flowers are light purple and borne in whorled clusters similar to horehound, May and June. Probably not hardy below 10 F. *S. pinquefolia* is a shrubby perennial usually less than 3 feet in height

and width bearing intense royal purple flowers all summer and autumn.

### PROPAGATION AND MAINTENANCE

**Seeds:**   Germination is somewhat erratic, 7 days to 4 weeks at temperatures fluctuating from 60 to 70 F. Plants grow better at 50–60 F once transplanted from seed flats to small containers. Fall or winter seeding outdoors with natural stratification yields better results than spring–summer seeding.
**Vegetative:**   Softwood cuttings root readily using 0.3% IBA talc.
**Watering:**   Plants are quite drought tolerant once established, but need water during hot dry weather.
**Nutrient Requirements:**   Excess nitrogen will produce lush foliage at the expense of flowering.
**Pruning:**   Where plants die back to the ground in winter, cutting back as winter cleanup is recommended. Pinching back new seedlings produces sturdier transplants.
**Insect/Disease Susceptibility:**   Grown indoors as a blooming potted plant, Cherry Sage is susceptible to mealy bugs. The problem does not occur on landscape specimens.

## CONEFLOWER
### Mexican Hat

*RATIBIDA COLUMNARIS*      *Sunflower-Compositae*

### ORIGIN AND ADAPTATIONS

**Native Distribution:**   Minnesota and Arkansas west to New Mexico and Arizona.
**Elevation:**   5,000–7,500'.
**Topography:**   Roadsides and open fields, prairies and plains.
**Soil Preference:**   Calcareous soils.
**Drought Tolerance:**   Good.
**Salt Tolerance:**   Fair.

### DESCRIPTION AND USE

**Mature Height:**   1–2'.

**Spread:**  18".
**Growth Rate:**  Rapid to moderate.
**Form:**  Perennial with rounded head, branching from a central crown.
**Flower:**  Unusual shape: elongated cylindrical disk receptacle ringed with drooping yellow- or mahogany-colored ray petals, June–October.
**Foliage:**  Narrow, linear leaves.
**Fruit:**  Compressed seeds form the columnar center of the flower.
**Landscape Use:**  Coneflower is a low-maintenance component of a mixed meadow planting, and can also be used in perennial beds, borders, and parkways.

## PROPAGATION AND MAINTENANCE

**Seeds:**  75,000 seeds per ounce. Sow outdoors when soil begins to warm. Prefer cool temperatures to germinate, no pretreatment necessary. 65% germination, 60% PLS is average.
**Watering:**  Coneflower is drought tolerant once established. Too much moisture may shorten the life-span.
**Nutrient Requirements:**  None.
**Pruning:**  Meadow areas can be mowed high (4–12" blade setting) in the winter, the seed and trash left as mulch.
**Insect/Disease Susceptibility:**  None observed.

## CREEPING MAHONIA

*BERBERIS REPENS*    *Barberry-Berberaceae*

## ORIGIN AND ADAPTATIONS

**Native Distribution:**  West Texas, New Mexico, Arizona, and California, north to Nebraska and British Columbia.
**Elevation:**  4,500–10,000'.
**Topography:**  Shaded slopes, usually under a high canopy of conifer trees.
**Soil Preference:**  Well drained, sandy to rocky, acidic.
**Drought Tolerance:**  Fair to good.
**Salt Tolerance:**  Very poor.

## DESCRIPTION AND USE

**Mature Height:**  4–12".
**Spread:**  Stoloniferous.
**Growth Rate:**  Slow to moderate.
**Form:**  Spreading evergreen ground cover.
**Flower:**  Yellow racemes to 3" long at the tips of the short stems, April–June, are showy contrast to the foliage.
**Foliage:**  Evergreen, holly-shaped leaves with spiny tips, dark shiny green in warm weather turning plum to red in cold weather.
**Fruit:**  Black oval to round berry with a bluish blush, in clusters.
**Landscape Use:**  Mahonia is an excellent evergreen ground cover on *shaded sites* where *soil is not extremely alkaline*, as cover under evergreens or shade trees. Cultivated since 1882, an excellent low-maintenance evergreen ground cover when properly placed. Since it is fairly slow to cover, especially under less than optimum conditions, plants should be planted close together (on 10" centers) where immediate appearance is a consideration. Berberis growing in full sun requires abundant moisture to establish, moderate moisture to maintain.
**Other Uses:**  Erosion control; fruit can be made into jelly, attracts birds.

## PROPAGATION AND MAINTENANCE

**Seeds:**  Best results are with seeds sown immediately upon ripening or stratified and sown in the spring. Germination is enhanced by an acid scarification pretreatment. 54,000 seeds per pound.
**Vegetative:**  Semi-softwood cuttings under mist, layering on site or division of suckers while plants are dormant, are alternate propagation methods.
**Watering:**  To establish and promote spreading, soil should be kept moist but never waterlogged. A mulch of bark and pine needles or oak leaves creates a more suitable growing environment at lower elevations.
**Nutrient Requirements:**  Dilute nutrient solutions that are acidic are helpful in establishing a planting.
**Pruning:**  None.
**Insect/Disease Susceptibility:**  Resistant to black stem rust.

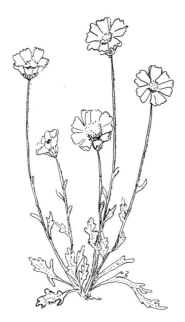

## DESERT MARIGOLD

*BAILEYA MULTIRADIATA*     *Sunflower-Compositae*

### ORIGIN AND ADAPTATIONS

**Native Distribution:**  Southwestern United States south to northern Mexico.

**Elevation:**  To 6,000'.

**Topography:**  Common along roadsides and on disturbed sites; prefers well-drained sandy or gravelly slopes.

**Soil Preference:**  Sandy or gravelly, well drained.

**Drought Tolerance:**  Excellent.

**Salt Tolerance:**  Poor.

### DESCRIPTION AND USE

**Mature Height:**  12–24".

**Spread:**  12–24".

**Growth Rate:**  Biennial, germinates fall and early winter, maintains a small rosette of foliage, growth resumes in spring.

**Form:**  Rosette of basal foliage, flowers forming on 12–24" stems, rounded mound of color by late summer.

**Flower:**  1 1/2"-diameter gold yellow disk, usually double layer of ray flowers, profuse and showy April–October, most spectacular August–September.

**Foliage:**  Indented, lobed, soft blue gray foliage densely covered with woolly hairs.

**Landscape Use:**  The white woolly foliage and compact mounding form, coupled with the profusion of vivid gold flowers, make this an excellent self-seeding naturalized ground cover on low-maintenance sites. Since Baileya is rarely preferred forage, it can be established where more palatable plants are damaged by rodents, etc. Desert Marigold is a good "mixed meadow" component with other drought-resistent plants like Indian Ricegrass (*Oryzopsis*), Blue Grama (*Bouteloua*), Bush penstemon (*P. ambiguus*), Gayfeather (*Liatris*), Purple Aster (*Machaeranthera*), Nama (*N. demissa*), Bush morningglory (*Ipomoea leptophylla*), etc. Although

Baileya self-sows readily, population density will fluctuate greatly. Disturbing the soil increases the likelihood of a good stand.

### PROPAGATION AND MAINTENANCE

**Seeds:**  With 45,000 seeds per ounce, Desert Marigold is best seeded directly where plants are to grow in fall, using previous year's seeds.

**Vegetative:**  Basal rosettes can be transplanted with care (they are taprooted) during *cold* weather. Not a reliable method for large areas, as transplants require careful watering.

**Watering:**  On tilled soil, seedbeds should be kept relatively moist until a good percentage (30–50%) of seedlings are visible, then only sporadic irrigation is optimum.

**Nutrient Requirements:**  None. Nitrogen application produces rank vegetative growth and a less attractive plant.

**Pruning:**  None. Mowing, in early winter leaving the trash to reseed, can be done where a manicured look is desired.

**Insect/Disease Susceptibility:**  None observed to date.

## DESERT ZINNIA
### Rocky Mountain Zinnia

*ZINNIA GRANDIFLORA*     *Sunflower-Compositae*

### ORIGIN AND ADAPTATIONS

**Native Distribution:**  Colorado, New Mexico, Arizona, and northern Mexico.

**Elevation:**  4,000–6,000'.

**Topography:**  Roadsides, dry mesas, hills, and plains.

**Soil Preference:**  Dry calcareous, adaptable.

**Drought Tolerance:**  Excellent.

**Salt Tolerance:**  Fair.

### DESCRIPTION AND USE

**Mature Height:**  To 8".

**Spread:**  8–10".

**Growth Rate:** Rapid growth, moderate spread.
**Form:** Low-growing perennial ground cover with a woody base. Spreads horizontally by deep (12" under surface) lateral rhizomes.
**Flower:** Showy yellow flowers with orange centers dry to straw color. In warm microclimates flowering may begin as early as May and June, is most showy August–October.
**Foliage:** Light green diminutive foliage is almost needle-like, quite densely produced.
**Fruit:** Seeds are attached to the rays of the flowers. Disk flowers usually produce empty seeds.
**Landscape Use:** Desert Zinnia is an excellent low ground cover providing dense cover and color much of the year. It can be used in parkways and medians, on banks, and as low, wide borders as well as mass planted.
**Other Uses:** In the wild, Zinnia contributes much to controlling erosion as a soil binder. Since plants are easily and rapidly grown from seed and difficult to transplant from the wild successfully, transplanting is not recommended.

## PROPAGATION AND MAINTENANCE

**Seeds:** Flower heads detach from plants when seeds are ripe. Approximately 6,000 to 8,000 cleaned seeds per ounce. Seed cleaning is tedious and for direct seeding outdoors is probably unnecessary. When seeding in flats for container growing, clean seeds should be used to prevent bacterial and fungal infections. Seeds germinate at warm temperatures (70–80 F). Direct seeding is best in early May. Germination percentages are usually less than 50%.
**Vegetative:** Young cultivated plants can be divided.
**Watering:** Some additional moisture accelerates coverage. Once established, Zinnia will grow and flower well with 6–8" annual precipitation.
**Nutrient Requirements:** None.
**Pruning:** Root pruning by cutting vertically with a sharp shooter shovel around plants for the first few years will thicken a stand more rapidly.
**Insect/Disease Susceptibility:** Insects lay eggs in flowers, the larvae feeding on seeds. Control might be desirable when plants are grown for large-scale seed production.

# DWARF COYOTEBRUSH

*BACCHARIS PILULARIS*      *Sunflower-Compositae*

## ORIGIN AND ADAPTATIONS

**Native Distribution:** California coast—Sonoma to Monterey counties.
**Elevation:** Undocumented.
**Topography:** Wet, almost swampy sites to dry, rocky slopes.
**Soil Preference:** Adaptable.
**Drought Tolerance:** Good.
**Salt Tolerance:** Undocumented. Native origin along coast would indicate some salt tolerance.

## DESCRIPTION AND USE

**Mature Height:** Matted to 12".
**Spread:** 4–6'.
**Growth Rate:** Rapid.
**Form:** Dense, billowy mat of vivid green.
**Flower:** Inconspicuous.
**Foliage:** Small, toothed leaves (1/2" length and width), light bright green, densely cover wiry stems.
**Fruit:** Inconspicuous.
**Landscape Use:** Dwarf Coyotebrush is an excellent ground cover, especially good cover on slopes and hot exposed sites where dense cover is desirable. Reported hardy to 0°F, but may require a warm microclimate north of Truth or Consequences in New Mexico, or at higher elevations in the warm desert such as Flagstaff, Arizona.
**Other Uses:** Erosion control.

## PROPAGATION AND MAINTENANCE

**Vegetative:** Semisoft tip cuttings root easily (0.3% IBA talc). The variety "Twin Peaks" is said to be denser and more cold tolerant.
**Watering:** On slopes, drip irrigation is preferable; otherwise, periodic deep watering maintains heavy foliage cover and best overall appearance.

**Nutrient Requirements:** Light applications of nitrogen speed cover and encourage foliage density.

**Pruning:** Periodic severe pruning rejuvenates plant. Remove oldest, coarsest growth.

**Insect/Disease Susceptibility:** The June 1984 issue of *Sunset* magazine describes a condition called Baccharis "decline," spotty dying back of mature plantings possibly caused by overwatering in winter. A new interspecific hybrid of *B. pilularis* and *B. sarothroides* called "Centennial" that has been developed and tested at the University of Arizona, Tucson, seems immune. "Centennial" will need test planting in high desert locations to determine cold hardiness.

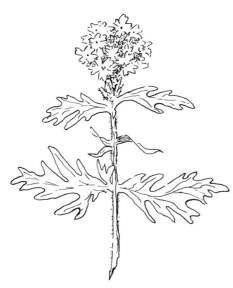

## FERN VERBENA

*VERBENA BIPINNATIFIDA*     *Vervain-Verbenaceae*

### ORIGIN AND ADAPTATIONS

**Native Distribution:** South Dakota south and east to Alabama, west to Arizona, and south to northern Mexico.

**Elevation:** 5,000–10,000'.

**Topography:** Open Piñon and Ponderosa Pine forests to sandy roadsides.

**Soil Preference:** Sandy to gravelly.

**Drought Tolerance:** Excellent.

**Salt Tolerance:** Undocumented.

### DESCRIPTION AND USE

**Mature Height:** 12" or less.

**Spread:** To 18".

**Growth Rate:** Rapid.

**Form:** Perennial ground cover, bedding plant, matlike growth in full sun.

**Flower:** Umbels of lavender purple florets.

**Foliage:** Finely-cut dark green, softly hairy.

**Fruit:** Inconspicuous.

**Landscape Use:** Fern Verbena is very effective mass planted as a low bedding ground cover for color and textural interest. There are many improved varieties of verbena seed and bedding plants commercially available that provide a mass of color with limited moisture. Attractive with Fringed Sage, the verbena provides color while the sage provides contrast.

**Other Useful Species:** *V. cilliata* has reddish purple flowers all season on plants 12" tall and at least as wide. *V. tenuisecta* has pinkish purple flowers spring through midsummer on plants 2' tall. *V. rigida* has deep purple flowers and large, dark green, coarse foliage on plants 10–18" tall and at least as wide. *V. goodingii* has warm pink flowers on 18" tall spreading plants, is short-lived but reseeds readily.

### PROPAGATION AND MAINTENANCE

**Seeds:** 10,000 cleaned seeds per ounce. Require cool, dry afterripening of a year or longer. Germinate best in the dark at 70 F. 30–50% germination within 3–4 weeks is average.

**Watering:** Water deeply and allow the surface to dry between waterings to encourage deep rooting. Flowering is best when watered regularly during hot weather.

**Nutrient Requirements:** Light applications of a balanced fertilizer can improve performance in some soils.

**Pruning:** Removal of top-growth when killed by frost.

**Insect/Disease Susceptibility:** None observed, although cultivars are attractive to aphids.

## FLOWERING ONION

*ALLIUM GEYERI, ALLIUM CERNUUM*   Lily-Liliaceae

### ORIGIN AND ADAPTATIONS

**Native Distribution:**   Throughout the western United States.
**Elevation:**   4,500–10,000'.
**Topography:**   Varied with species from mountain forests to gravelly foothills and plains.
**Soil Preference:**   Adaptable to most well-drained sites.
**Drought Tolerance:**   Most showy, given 15–25" annual precipitation.
**Salt Tolerance:**   Fair.

### DESCRIPTION AND USE

**Mature Height:**   12–18".
**Spread:**   To 12".
**Growth Rate:**   Slow, at least 18 months from seed to flowering.
**Form:**   Grassy clumps from bulb-like root systems.
**Flower:**   Umbels of white, pink, or yellow bell-shaped flowers, June–October depending upon species.
**Foliage:**   Fine, narrow to broad, strap-like leaves.
**Fruit:**   Dried seed heads are long lasting and ornamental.
**Landscape Use:**   Alliums are a light textural addition to meadows, perennial borders, and beds. Onion odor is not strong unless the foliage is crushed. The dried flower heads of some species add interest to the dormant landscape.

### PROPAGATION AND MAINTENANCE

**Seeds:**   Black, flat to wedge-shaped seeds germinate readily under a broad range of conditions. Cool temperatures.
**Vegetative:**   Division of clumps while dormant.
**Watering:**   While many species are quite drought tolerant, the Onions are showiest when given regular deep waterings. Lack of water will dwarf otherwise healthy plants.

**Nutrient Requirements:**   Light applications of nitrogen accelerate growth and enhance flowering.
**Pruning:**   None.
**Insect/Disease Susceptibility:**   None observed.

## FRINGED SAGE

*ARTEMISIA FRIGIDA*   Sunflower-Compositae

### ORIGIN AND ADAPTATIONS

**Native Distribution:**   Western United States from Canada south to Mexico.
**Elevation:**   3,000–11,000'.
**Topography:**   Mountains and plains.
**Soil Preference:**   Widely adaptable.
**Drought Tolerance:**   8–12" annual precipitation.
**Salt Tolerance:**   Fair.

### DESCRIPTION AND USE

**Mature Height:**   8–18", including flower stems.
**Spread:**   12".
**Growth Rate:**   Rapid with moderate water.
**Form:**   Herbaceous with a woody base, stems hug the ground producing a mat-like cover.
**Flower:**   Small yellow disk flowers, inconspicuous individually but are borne in profusion on nodding stems, hence the common name, Fringed Sage.
**Foliage:**   Finely cut, soft, matted foliage, silvery gray in color and evergreen.
**Landscape Use:**   Introduced into horticulture in 1883, Fringed Sage is an excellent choice for borders, as a color foil and evergreen ground cover. It resembles "Silvermound" but does *not* brown out in the center during hot dry weather like "Silvermound" can do. Best in full sun or partial shade, Fringed Sage grows fastest if it is kept moderately dry. Combined plantings with Blue Flax, Blackfoot Daisy, *Liatris* (Gayfeather), Zinnia, and *Penstemon ambiguus* in a perennial bed and/or border will provide year-round color and interest.
**Other Uses:**   Erosion control. All Artemisias have been used medicinally for various ailments.

**Other Useful Species:**   Prairie Sage (*A. ludovichiana*), with its coarse white foliage on sprawling stems to 2' tall, is an excellent color foil and textural contrast.

## PROPAGATION AND MAINTENANCE

**Seeds:**   Seeds are small, 4.5 million seeds per pound, and difficult to separate from chaff. They germinate best at relatively cool temperatures—55–65 F. Low temperatures and thrashy seeds increase problems with damping off. Seeds ripen in late September.

**Vegetative:**   Stem cuttings in February–May, with 0.1% IBA talc, root easily. The entire plant can be divided and reset during cold weather.

**Watering:**   Moderate watering will promote rapid cover; too much water will slow growth, resulting in uneven cover.

**Nutrient Requirements:**   Mycorhizzal relationship has been observed, and in well-drained soil Artemisia is nitrogen-fixing when compatible microorganisms are present.

**Pruning:**   Removal of flower stems in midsummer and late fall keeps the plant neat and increases herbaceous growth.

**Insect/Disease Susceptibility:**   If overwatered in heavy soil, fungus may be a problem.

## GAYFEATHER
### Cachana

*LIATRIS PUNCTATA*   *Sunflower-Compositae*

### ORIGIN AND ADAPTATIONS

**Native Distribution:**   Manitoba, Canada, south to Texas; most common in New Mexico in the northeast quarter.

**Elevation:**   Usually 5,000–8,000'.

**Topography:**   Open plains and prairies, open meadows at higher elevations.

**Soil Preference:**   Adapts to most soils, shallow or heavy loam.

**Drought Tolerance:**   15 + " annual precipitation.

**Salt Tolerance:**   Fair.

### DESCRIPTION AND USE

**Mature Height:**   1–2'.

**Spread:**   12–18".

**Growth Rate:**   Moderate.

**Form:**   Herbaceous perennial, branching from a central crown with a short thick corm and thick tuberous taproot.

**Flower:**   Spikes of pinkish purple, feathery disk flowers followed by purplish feathery seed plumes August–October.

**Foliage:**   Somewhat succulent or leathery narrow, linear leaves, 2–6" long and 1/8" wide.

**Fruit:**   Feathery seed plume.

**Landscape Use:**   Gayfeather can be used mass planted alone or with other drought-tolerant perennials and annuals in a "meadow"-type ground cover area. It combines well with *Penstemon ambiguus*, Blue Flax, Purple Aster, Baileya, Gaillardia, Indian Ricegrass, and Evening Primrose, as mixed meadow or bordering Bigleaf Sage as color contrast interplanted with Fringed Sage.

### PROPAGATION AND MAINTENANCE

**Seeds:**   8,500 seeds per ounce. Seeds stratified cold and moist for two weeks then sown at temperatures between 75–80 F, 14 hours of day length, can germinate up to 96%.

**Vegetative:**   Division of tubers in early spring.

**Watering:**   Excess moisture and nutrients, once established, can produce unruly vegetative growth at the expense of flowering. Plants have nicer compact form when they are grown dry.

**Nutrient Requirements:**   Minimal, once established.

**Pruning:**   Can be mowed off at ground level when foliage dies back in winter.

**Insect/Disease Susceptibility:**   None observed.

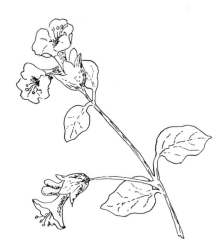

## GIANT FOUR O'CLOCK

*MIRABILIS MULTIFLORA*   *Four O'Clock-Nyctaginaceae*

### ORIGIN AND ADAPTATIONS

**Native Distribution:**   Southern California east to southern Colorado and New Mexico.

**Elevation:** To 8,000'.
**Topography:** Open, sandy areas, Juniper and Piñon desert grasslands.
**Soil Preference:** Sandy, porous to rocky, adapts to most soils.
**Drought Tolerance:** Excellent.
**Salt Tolerance:** Fair.

## DESCRIPTION AND USE

**Mature Height:** 18".
**Spread:** 4–6 square feet.
**Growth Rate:** Rapid.
**Form:** Dense green cover, stems trail but do not root adventitiously. One plant will completely cover a 4–6-square-foot area, develops a fleshy root system.
**Flower:** Profuse magenta tubular flowers 1" in diameter are very showy, close during the hottest part of the day. April–September.
**Foliage:** Almost heart-shaped, bright green, lush foliage dies back to the ground in winter and during extreme drought.
**Fruit:** Seed is enclosed in a papery calyx-like covering with the faded flowers.
**Landscape Use:** Desert Four O'Clock is a very showy flowering perennial ground cover. Best massed in monocultural stands rather than mixed in plantings with other ground covers, as it may choke out slower or less vigorous plants. It is a good ground cover under pines and junipers, a natural association.
**Other Uses:** Four O'Clock provides effective erosion control and soil stabilization due to its extensive tuberous root system.

## PROPAGATION AND MAINTENANCE

**Seeds:** Mirabilis seeds are fairly large, almost round, reddish brown in color, and not abundant. Some years, little or no seeds are produced. The seed coats are thick and impermeable. Acid scarification and cold moist stratification for 1 month softens seed coats and enhances germination. 50% germination is good—many seeds are sterile. 8,000 seeds per pound.
**Vegetative:** Soft cuttings root well under intermittent mist, dipped in .3% IBA talc (stronger hormone concentrations may inhibit rooting). Division of tuberous root system may be done while plant is dormant.
**Watering:** Supplemental water extends bloom period from May continuously to September.
**Nutrient Requirements:** None.
**Pruning:** Mow off at ground level when stems die back in October.
**Insect/Disease Susceptibility:** Mexican steel blue flea beetles can defoliate plants, but they are unusual in urban areas.

## INDIAN RICEGRASS

*ORYZOPSIS HYMENOIDES*     *Grass-Gramineae*

## ORIGIN AND ADAPTATIONS

**Native Distribution:** Throughout the western United States.
**Elevation:** 2,000–9,000'.
**Topography:** Dry foothills, ridges, and rocky slopes.
**Soil Preference:** Sandy and/or rocky soils, sometimes in clay loams.
**Drought Tolerance:** Excellent, 5–12" annual precipitation.
**Salt Tolerance:** Fair.

## DESCRIPTION AND USE

**Mature Height:** 12–24".
**Spread:** 8–12".
**Growth Rate:** Moderate.
**Form:** Clumping cool-season perennial bunchgrass with attractive seed heads.
**Flower:** Inconspicuous.
**Foliage:** Fine, wiry, light green leaves. Cures to a yellow straw color.
**Fruit:** Loose, wiry seed heads support hard round to oval seeds enclosed in hairy sheaths.
**Landscape Use:** The airy, light quality of Indian Ricegrass and its extreme drought tolerance make this grass an ideal low, accent filler in mixed plantings with Bush Penstemon and other drought-tolerant perennials. Since it is not a sod-forming grass, it is not recommended for lawn use, although mass planted it is an extremely attractive monocultural ground cover. "Nezpar" was selected for low percentage of hard seeds and seedling vigor. "Paloma" was selected for longevity and vigor.
**Other Uses:** Indian Ricegrass is excellent winter forage—seeds are a good protein source and attract mourning doves, pheasant, and other wildlife as well as livestock. It is commonly used as a filler in dried

floral arrangements, wreaths, etc. The seeds were a food source for many Native American peoples.

## PROPAGATION AND MAINTENANCE

**Seeds:** Recommended seeding rate for range use is 7–9 pounds of pure live seeds per acre. Seeds germinate very unevenly, and it can take 2 years to establish a good stand. Acid scarification of seeds afterripened for a year produces more controlled results. Seeding rate for ornamental use is 1 pound per 1,000 square feet. 160,000 cleaned seeds per pound.

**Vegetative:** Clumps can be divided while plants are dormant. Since the grass is relatively short-lived, it is best to divide young clumps, establishing a seed-producing stand that will renew itself.

**Watering:** Once established, Indian Ricegrass requires no supplemental watering where annual rainfall is 8 inches or more.

**Nutrient Requirements:** None—excess feeding may shorten life-span.

**Pruning:** None.

**Insect/Disease Susceptibility:** None noted to date.

## LAVENDER COTTON

*SANTOLINA CHAMAECYPARISSUS*     *Sunflower-Compositae*

## ORIGIN AND ADAPTATIONS

**Native Distribution:** Mediterranean area of Europe and the Middle East.
**Elevation:** Undocumented.
**Topography:** Sandy and rocky slopes.
**Soil Preference:** Well drained.
**Drought Tolerance:** Excellent.
**Salt Tolerance:** Good.

## DESCRIPTION AND USE

**Mature Height:** 1–2'.
**Spread:** 1–2'.
**Growth Rate:** Moderate to rapid depending upon available moisture.

**Form:** Dense, compact, mounded subshrub.
**Flower:** Small (1/2" diameter), buttonlike, yellow gold disk, blooms in June.
**Foliage:** Soft, finely divided gray silver aromatic leaves, evergreen.
**Fruit:** Dry, brown, buttonlike seed head.
**Landscape Use:** Santolina is an excellent compact ground cover, bank cover, and low clipped border hedge. Good in parkways as it does not obstruct vision and requires comparatively little moisture once it is established. Santolina is compatible with drought-tolerant, sun- and heat-loving natives.
**Other Uses:** Dried seed heads, spray tinted (natural color is bleak gray) or bleached, are used in floral arrangements.

## PROPAGATION AND MAINTENANCE

**Seeds:** 50,000 seeds per ounce, germinate best at 60–70 F, in 2–3 weeks. Generally faster results are obtained by growing plants from cuttings.
**Vegetative:** Softwood cuttings of new growth can be taken in spring or from the flush of growth following flowering (August), with or without mist, using .8% IBA talc.
**Watering:** Santolina requires intermittent water to establish and looks best if deep watered in times of hot, dry weather.
**Nutrient Requirements:** None, once established.
**Pruning:** Removal of seed heads in July–August, annual cutting back in spring, encourage new growth and keep planting young and vigorous.
**Insect/Disease Susceptibility:** None observed to date.

## PAPERFLOWER

*PSILOSTROPHE TAGENTINA*     *Sunflower-Compositae*

## ORIGIN AND ADAPTATIONS

**Native Distribution:** West Texas, New Mexico, Arizona, south to northern Mexico.
**Elevation:** 4,000–7,000'.

**Topography:**    Open plains, mesas, and roadsides.
**Soil Preference:**    Adapts well to most soils.
**Drought Tolerance:**    Excellent.
**Salt Tolerance:**    Fair.

## DESCRIPTION AND USE

**Mature Height:**    To 12".
**Spread:**    To 12".
**Growth Rate:**    Rapid.
**Form:**    Perennial, mounding head from basal rosette.
**Flower:**    Yellow disk and ray flowers, small (1/2") diameter, but so profuse they cover the plant. Blooms April–October if given moderate, intermittent watering and spent blooms are removed periodically.
**Foliage:**    Densely woolly basal rosette, sparse foliage on flower stems.
**Fruit:**    Flowers fade to papery texture, tan color, enclosing seed.
**Landscape Use:**    Paperflower can be used in low borders, massed as a ground cover, or mixed with other drought-tolerant flowering plants in beds or meadow areas. Since seed production is abundant and seed germinates readily, Paperflower may prove weedy in some situations. The species *P. bakeri* is less weedy and more ornamental, with larger flowers. Removal of seed heads reduces potential for weediness and stimulates further flowering.
**Other Uses:**    Erosion control.

## PROPAGATION AND MAINTENANCE

**Seeds:**    Plants are easily produced from seeds sown where plants are to grow when soil and air temperatures are moderately warm. To stimulate flowering, plants may require cold temperatures ("vernalization," a cold period necessary in the development of some plants that promotes the synthesis of hormones required for flowering). Seeds do not need to be cleaned—whole, dry flower heads planted like seeds produce good results. If storing seeds, fumigate.
**Watering:**    Periodic deep watering during growing season, once established, prolongs the bloom cycle.
**Nutrient Requirements:**    None.
**Pruning:**    The removal of spent flower stalks at ground level lengthens the bloom cycle; the tops can be mowed off (3–4" blade setting) November–February to reveal basal rosettes.
**Insect/Disease Susceptibility:**    None observed.

# PURPLE ASTER

*MACHAERANTHERA BIGELOVII*    *Sunflower-Compositae*

## ORIGIN AND ADAPTATIONS

**Native Distribution:**    Colorado, New Mexico, and Arizona.
**Elevation:**    3,000–7,000'.
**Topography:**    Varies from rocky slopes to prairie sage grassland and along roads.
**Soil Preference:**    Adapts to most soil types; establishes easily on disturbed sites.
**Drought Tolerance:**    Excellent.
**Salt Tolerance:**    Good.

## DESCRIPTION AND USE

**Mature Height:**    To 3 1/2'.
**Spread:**    To 3 1/2'.
**Growth Rate:**    Rapid.
**Form:**    Several long stems produced from a central crown, forms a billowy mound.
**Flower:**    Narrow-petaled purple daisy with a yellow center, average flower size 1" in diameter. Blooming in masses at branched ends of the long stems, showiest in mid September–mid October.
**Foliage:**    Narrow, grooved, soft, dark gray green leaves.
**Fruit:**    Downy seed heads are wind dispersed, leaving a golden brown and tan star that remains attractive well into winter.
**Landscape Use:**    Versatile as a tall temporary border, a component of a mixed meadow, or a tall filler, Purple Aster is also showy bordering or interplanted with Rabbitbrush, as they flower at about the same time. Topping plants in mid July results in a shorter, denser planting.
**Other Uses:**    Source of a purple dye.
**Other Useful Species:**    *M. tanacetifolia*, Tahoka Daisy, is a ferny-leafed, low-growing (to 18") biennial with purple daisy-like flowers, blooming May–August.

## PROPAGATION AND MAINTENANCE

**Seeds:**  30,000 uncleaned seeds per ounce. Seeds germinate in very early spring and require a prolonged cold period to flower later in the season. Once plants have become established, they self-sow readily.

**Watering:**  A moderate amount of supplemental watering increases the size of the plants and profuseness of the flowers.

**Nutrient Requirements:**  None.

**Pruning:**  Removal of entire plant any time from midwinter until early spring is recommended. Remove plants before they go to seed to control an overpopulation.

**Insect/Disease Susceptibility:**  None observed.

## PURPLE PRAIRIECLOVER

*PETALOSTEMON PURPUREUM*      Pea-Leguminosae

### ORIGIN AND ADAPTATIONS

**Native Distribution:**  Indiana north to Saskatchewan, south and west to Texas and central Arizona.

**Elevation:**  3,500–7,000'.

**Topography:**  Plains and prairies, especially in tallgrass uplands.

**Soil Preference:**  Deep, well drained.

**Drought Tolerance:**  16" or more annual precipitation.

**Salt Tolerance:**  Good.

### DESCRIPTION AND USE

**Mature Height:**  1–2'.

**Spread:**  To 2'.

**Growth Rate:**  Rapid.

**Form:**  Deep-rooted, warm-season perennial characterized by slender, upright branches.

**Flower:**  Conical head densely covered with individual, intense pink florets in a crown around the cone, May–June.

**Foliage:**  Short, finely cut, branch-like leaves.

**Fruit:**  Dense, compacted seeds on cone.

**Landscape Use:**  Purple Prairieclover is a good com-

ponent of meadow mixtures for early summer color where some irrigation is possible.

**Other Uses:**  It provides nutritious, high-protein forage.

## PROPAGATION AND MAINTENANCE

**Seeds:**  18,000 seeds per ounce. Prairieclover self-sows readily.

**Watering:**  Requires supplemental watering during hot, dry weather.

**Nutrient Requirements:**  Nitrogen fixing.

**Pruning:**  None.

**Insect/Disease Susceptibility:**  None observed.

## SAND VERBENA

*TRIPTEROCALYX (ABRONIA)* species      *Four O'Clock-Nyctaginaceae*

### ORIGIN AND ADAPTATIONS

**Native Distribution:**  West Texas west to California, some species north to Montana.

**Elevation:**  Below 6,500'.

**Topography:**  Sandy dunes.

**Soil Preference:**  Well-drained, deep sand, may not adapt well to heavy soils.

**Drought Tolerance:**  Excellent.

**Salt Tolerance:**  Fair.

### DESCRIPTION AND USE

**Mature Height:**  To 2'.

**Spread:**  To 3' radius.

**Growth Rate:**  Rapid.

**Form:**  Annual ground cover, rarely perennial.

**Flower:**  Umbels of pink (sometimes white) tubular florets.

**Foliage:**  Usually 1 1/2" long to 1" wide, glaucous to hairy; light green internodes are large (to 2"), but foliage is abundant enough to appear dense.

**Fruit:**  Seeds are enclosed in showy pink to salmon bracts more ornamental than the flowers.

**Landscape Use:**  Seeds are large and easy to handle.

Direct seeding where plants are to grow. Results in fast, showy coverage of large areas with little water.

**Other Uses:**   Seeds attract quail, doves, and other wildlife.

## PROPAGATION AND MAINTENANCE

**Seeds:**   Seeds collected as they ripen, August–October, germinate best when scarified with sulfuric acid and sown directly in beds before mid February.

**Watering:**   Moderate watering results in larger, showier plants.

**Nutrient Requirements:**   None.

**Pruning:**   Removal of entire plant when it is killed by frost is recommended.

**Insect/Disease Susceptibility:**   Several insects can be found on the plant throughout the growing season, none of which seems to do much damage.

# SCARLET GLOBEMALLOW

*SPHAERALCEA COCCINEA*     *Mallow-Malvaceae*

## ORIGIN AND ADAPTATIONS

**Native Distribution:**   Texas west to California and Canada south to Mexico.

**Elevation:**   3,000–8,000'.

**Topography:**   Dry, grassy prairies, mesas, and roadsides, among boulders on hillsides.

**Soil Preference:**   Gypsum or caliche soils—sandy clay or gravelly limestone. Widely adapted.

**Drought Tolerance:**   Good.

**Salt Tolerance:**   Fair to good.

## DESCRIPTION AND USE

**Mature Height:**   To 10".

**Spread:**   To 10".

**Growth Rate:**   Moderate.

**Form:**   Stems radiate out from a central crown, generally prostrate with flowering tips standing upright.

**Flower:**   Five petals, usually bright coral, rarely more than 3/4–1" in diameter. Blooming summer through autumn.

**Foliage:**   Gray green segmented foliage, 5 segments each three-lobed. Overall impression given is that of a finely scalloped, lacy appearance that is quite ornamental.

**Fruit:**   Seeds are enclosed in a papery capsule that resembles a pleated crown. Individual capsules about 1/4" in diameter are clustered along the flower stem.

**Landscape Use:**   Scarlet Globemallow, because of its attractive lacy foliage and flowers, is effective as a mono-cultural ground-cover planting. Other Globemallow species are useful components of mixed meadows and perennial borders.

**Other Useful Species:**   This family, which includes cotton, okra, and hollyhock, contains many species of globemallow varying in height from nearly prostrate to 4–5 feet tall and includes flower colors of white, pink, coral, lavender, and burgundy. Some species are more weedy than ornamental.

## PROPAGATION AND MAINTENANCE

**Seeds:**   30,000 seeds per ounce; acceptable germination rates without pretreatment, 2–3 weeks at temperatures between 65–75 F. Light mechanical scarification (rubbing between sheets of sandpaper) increases germination, especially when seeds have been dried and are more than a year old. Keep the seedbed evenly moist until germination is completed. Seeds begin to ripen in July.

**Vegetative:**   Division of crown, stem cuttings with .8% IBA talc in spring.

**Watering:**   Once established, only intermittent deep waterings during hot, dry weather are required.

**Nutrient Requirements:**   None.

**Pruning:**   Dry seed heads are ornamental and persist late into winter; can be removed when they are weathered or as growth resumes in the spring.

**Insect/Disease Susceptibility:**   Some species are affected by a disfiguring black mold on the foliage. Infected plants should be uprooted and discarded. Plants grown dry are less prone to attack.

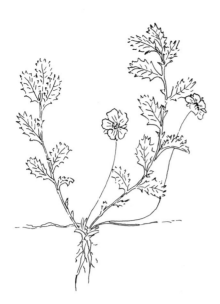

## SILVER CINQUEFOIL

*POTENTILLA ANSERINA*　　*Rose-Rosaceae*

### ORIGIN AND ADAPTATIONS

**Native Distribution:**　New Mexico mountains west to California.
**Elevation:**　7,000–10,000'.
**Topography:**　Wet meadows and open woodlands.
**Soil Preference:**　Moist loam.
**Drought Tolerance:**　15 + " annual precipitation.
**Salt Tolerance:**　Poor.

### DESCRIPTION AND USE

**Mature Height:**　To 6".
**Spread:**　Rhizomatous.
**Growth Rate:**　Moderate.
**Form:**　Low ground cover, central rosettes radiate outward by runners.
**Flower:**　Bright yellow, "buttercup-like," single flowers.
**Foliage:**　Silvery white finely-cut leaves, ferny in appearance, forming dense, matted rosettes.
**Fruit:**　Inconspicuous.
**Landscape Use:**　Potentilla use is limited to sites where moisture is available. It is especially well suited to ground cover use at higher elevations, but attractive enough to merit consideration anywhere that some additional moisture is available.
**Other Useful Species:**　*P. fruticosa*, a small (to 4'), densely twiggy shrub with an almost nationwide distribution. Yellow flowers are profuse throughout the summer where moisture is available. This Potentilla has been in the nursery trade since the late 1800s, and many improved forms are available. Suffers heat stress at lower elevations. *P. thurberii*, a low-growing rosette of dark green foliage with orange red flowers on stems to 18" tall, blooms July–September.

### PROPAGATION AND MAINTENANCE

**Seeds:**　Stratification for 2 months enhances germi-

nation. Seeds sown outdoors in the fall germinate the following spring when soils begin to warm.
**Vegetative:**　Division of rhizomes while dormant is an alternate method.
**Watering:**　At lower elevations, Silver Cinquefoil requires consistently moist soil during warm weather. At higher elevations, infrequent watering speeds coverage.
**Nutrient Requirements:**　Although questionable at higher elevations, a balanced fertilizer application annually in the spring is recommended in the lowlands.
**Pruning:**　None.
**Insect/Disease Susceptibility:**　None observed. *P. fruticosa* is sometimes host to spidermite. Periodically washing the dust off the foliage is an effective control.

## SILVER GROUNDSEL

*SENECIO LONGILOBUS*　　*Sunflower-Compositae*

### ORIGIN AND ADAPTATIONS

**Native Distribution:**　Arizona and New Mexico, southern Utah and Colorado south into northern Mexico.
**Elevation:**　2,500–7,500'.
**Topography:**　Sandy washes and dry gravelly stream beds.
**Soil Preference:**　Well drained.
**Drought Tolerance:**　Excellent.
**Salt Tolerance:**　Fair.

### DESCRIPTION AND USE

**Mature Height:**　18–24".
**Spread:**　To 2'.
**Growth Rate:**　Rapid.
**Form:**　Mound shaped, dense, and semi-succulent.
**Flower:**　1" diameter, lemon yellow, daisy-like flowers. Profuse after summer rains but produced irregularly late spring through fall.
**Foliage:**　Densely covered with matted, woolly hairs; narrow, succulent leaves.
**Fruit:**　White pappus seed-dispersal mechanism.

**Landscape Use:**   Mass planted, Groundsel is particularly showy in early fall. The silvery white foliage is an attractive color foil, good combined with other drought-tolerant perennials. Avoid disturbing soil and limit numbers to prevent weedy reproduction.
**Other Uses:**   Erosion control.

## PROPAGATION AND MAINTENANCE

**Seeds:**   Seeds are fine with pappus attached, easy to germinate in fall or spring at 65–75 F.
**Watering:**   Once established, little extra water is necessary. Overwatering produces rank, weedy growth. The form is more attractive when grown dry.
**Nutrient Requirements:**   None required.
**Pruning:**   Remove spent flowers in winter.
**Insect/Disease Susceptibility:**   None observed.

## WESTERN VIRGINSBOWER

*CLEMATIS LIGUSTICIFOLIA*      Buttercup-
                              Ranunculaceae

## ORIGIN AND ADAPTATIONS

**Native Distribution:**   Western Canada south to North Dakota, New Mexico and Arizona west to California; in New Mexico, generally found at higher elevations.
**Elevation:**   4,000-8,500'.
**Topography:**   Wet locations, along roadsides and in moist canyons.
**Soil Preference:**   Fertile, light, loamy soil but adapts well to most soils.
**Drought Tolerance:**   12–30" annual precipitation.
**Salt Tolerance:**   Good.

## DESCRIPTION AND USE

**Mature Height:**   18–20'.
**Spread:**   Vining.
**Growth Rate:**   Rapid, if given water.
**Form:**   Woody climbing vine, usually small stemmed and herbaceous with a woody base.
**Flower:**   Small white flowers in profuse branched clusters, flowering May–September with male and female flowers on separate plants. Male flowers with their many stamens are the showiest. Flowers are sweetly fragrant.
**Foliage:**   Lush (with moisture) medium green, deciduous.
**Fruit:**   Female flowers produce plumed seed heads, similar to Apache Plume.
**Landscape Use:**   This Clematis provides good shade for patios and window lattices where winter sun is desirable, and cover for wire fences and screening where vertical height is desirable but horizontal space is limited. It can be used as a sprawling bank cover (best with drip irrigation). Where seed litter would involve extra maintenance, only male plants should be used.
**Other Uses:**   A traditional sore-throat remedy, this Clematis was also used to treat burns and wounds on horses.

## PROPAGATION AND MAINTENANCE

**Seeds:**   300,000 cleaned seeds per pound. Best germination results when seeds are cold-moist stratified for 60 days prior to seeding. 50% average germination.
**Vegetative:**   Cuttings of semi-soft wood root easily with .3% IBA talc. Clematis also layers easily and can be divided once it is fairly large.
**Watering:**   Abundant moisture, especially in hot, dry weather, produces the best coverage and overall vigor.
**Nutrient Requirements:**   Annual application of dilute nitrogen solution is recommended, especially when vines are watered frequently.
**Pruning:**   Severe pruning every 2–5 years rejuvenates the vine.
**Insect/Disease Susceptibility:**   None noted to date.

## WHITE EVENING PRIMROSE

*OENOTHERA CAESPITOSA*          *Evening Primrose-*
                               *Onograceae*

### ORIGIN AND ADAPTATIONS

**Native Distribution:**   Minnesota west to Washington, New Mexico west to California.
**Elevation:**   4,000–7,500'.
**Topography:**   Roadsides and dry, rocky slopes.
**Soil Preference:**   Well drained.
**Drought Tolerance:**   Fair to good.
**Salt Tolerance:**   Poor.

### DESCRIPTION AND USE

**Mature Height:**   10–12".
**Spread:**   14–18".
**Growth Rate:**   Rapid.
**Form:**   Central basal rosette, sometimes branching at ground level to form a cluster of rosettes.
**Flower:**   Large (to 3" in diameter) white blossoms open late in the day and remain open until the heat of the following day, fading to pink upon closing. Most profuse in spring and fall, but will flower all summer if watered regularly.
**Foliage:**   Leaves to 5" in length, 1/2" in width; lanceolate and slightly toothed, dark green with reddish undersides, white downy cast in full sun. Dies back to the ground in November, resprouting February–March depending on elevation.
**Fruit:**   Seed capsules resemble gerkins while they are green and mature to a tough, woody, straw-colored capsule.
**Landscape Use:**   The compact growth habit and showy flowers make White Evening Primrose an excellent bedding perennial, border planting, or patterned ground cover. Good for areas used during the cooler times of the day (e.g., patios, courtyards), where the flower display can be fully appreciated.

**Other Uses:**   Seed is attractive to many wild birds (mourning doves, quail, etc.).
**Other Useful Species:**   *O. missouriensis,* yellow flowers, requires more moisture, perennial. *O. hookeri,* yellow flowers on tall stems, biennial. *O. speciosa,* pink flowers, spreads by rhizomes, very drought tolerant, will cover a large area. *O. coronopifolia,* white flowers on 18" stems, mounded habit, perennial.

### PROPAGATION AND MAINTENANCE

**Seeds:**   Collect as they ripen June–October. Germinate erratically, best results in the absence of light and relatively cool (60–70 F). 75,000 seeds per pound.
**Vegetative:**   *O. pallida* and *O. speciosa* can be divided in early spring.
**Watering:**   New plantings should be kept moist, but soil should never become waterlogged. Once plants are established, intermittent deep watering keeps them flowering throughout the summer. Good drainage is essential.
**Nutrient Requirements:**   Evening Primrose, especially as a young plant, responds well to dilute fertilizer solutions.
**Pruning:**   Old foliage can be trimmed off when it dies back. At lower elevations, the central rosette often will remain green throughout the winter.
**Insect/Disease Susceptibility:**   Subject to Mexican steel blue flea beetle infestations. This seems to be a localized problem, rare in urban reas. Carbaryl controls the problem but should be used carefully in deference to foraging quail and doves.

## WOODBINE
### Creeper

*PARTHENOCISSUS INSERTA*          *Grape-Vitaceae*

### ORIGIN AND ADAPTATIONS

**Native Distribution:**   Texas, New Mexico, Wyoming, and California.
**Elevation:**   4,000–8,000'.

**Topography:**   Moist canyons, streambanks, and roadsides in full sun.
**Soil Preference:**   Adaptable.
**Drought Tolerance:**   Moderate.
**Salt Tolerance:**   Fair.

## DESCRIPTION AND USE

**Mature Height:**   To 40'.
**Spread:**   Vining.
**Growth Rate:**   Rapid with water.
**Form:**   Woody, deciduous vine without suction-clinging mechanism. The lack of an adhesive device and a less aggressive growth habit (which may be a response to environment—less available moisture and more intense sunlight) seem to be the major distinctions between Western Woodbine and the more invasive Eastern Virginia Creeper.
**Flower:**   Small, greenish flowers in open clusters bloom June–July.
**Foliage:**   Five-fingered dark green deciduous leaves with shiny surfaces turn scarlet in the fall—very showy.
**Fruit:**   Grapelike clusters of blue black fruit (to 1/4" in diameter), ripen August–September and persist into winter if not consumed by birds.
**Landscape Use:**   Creeper provides good shade in summer without sacrificing winter sunshine. Clean crisp cover anywhere fast growth is desirable and moisture is available. Fall color is exceptionally fine.
**Other Uses:**   Fruits attract songbirds.

## PROPAGATION AND MAINTENANCE

**Seeds:**   Scarification of fruits to remove pulp and soften seed coats will improve germination.
**Vegetative:**   Easily grown from cuttings, any time, no hormone necessary.
**Watering:**   Abundant groundwater produces lush growth.
**Nutrient Requirements:**   Minimal once established; too much nitrogen may produce rank growth.
**Pruning:**   Thinning is recommended periodically (2 years or so) once coverage has reached desired limits.
**Insect/Disease Susceptibility:**   Cabbage loopers and flea beetles may be a localized problem. *Bacillus thuringiensis* is a non-toxic control for cabbage loopers.

# ADDENDUM: THE GOOD, THE BAD, AND THE TOO-SOON-TO-TELL

The plants profiled here are by no means the only arid-land natives of ornamental value, but they are among the best and the most available. Curious and persistent growers are adding many new plants to the list. Several plants mentioned in the text or included in the landscape layouts are not described in detail. Some are natives that already enjoy broad landscape use: the Junipers, Arizona Cypress, Ponderosa Pine, Piñon Pine, and Calliopsis. Some are plants limited either in use or availability: Picklebush, Kinnikinnick, Ocotillo, Beargrass, the true Willows, Scorpionweed, Nama, and Phlox heliotrope. Others are adaptable introductions—the good, the bad, and the too-soon-to-tell. Coralberry, drought tolerant despite its Eastern and Midwestern origins, deserves broader landscape use. The Siberian Elm is a problem solver turned pest, a mistake from which we should learn. The Afghan Pine is a recent introduction that shows great promise as a fast-growing evergreen for low-desert areas. These plants, described briefly below, are examples of the promise and pitfalls of arid-land natives.

**AFGHAN PINE** (*Pinus eldarica*) is a recently introduced species from the Middle East that appears to be well adapted to much of the desert Southwest. Because it grows continuously throughout the year, it is subject to winter injury in cold portions of the high desert. Exact winter hardiness guidelines have not yet been established, but many Afghan Pines, well-established in the Albuquerque area, have survived 0°F winters without damage. A tall, columnar, medium green evergreen, the Afghan Pine is especially valuable for its drought and heat tolerance and its rapid growth rate.

**AILIANTHUS/TREE OF HEAVEN** (*Ailianthus altisoima*) was introduced in the Southwest from China by way of the Eastern United States because it could survive heat, dust, drought, and smog. Tree of Heaven is now viewed as unacceptable because it is invasive. The female of the species produces an abundance of viable seeds, and the male produces ample allergy-causing pollen and a disagreeable odor.

**ARIZONA CYPRESS** (*Cupressus arizonica*) is a large evergreen tree. Dense foliage and a rapid growth rate make it an excellent choice for windbreaks where space is available. Usually available in 1- and 5-gallon containers, young Arizona Cypress are a poor choice for foundation planting due to their massive (40' × 20') mature dimensions. Cutting-grown selections should be used where uniformity is desirable, as seedlings are quite variable in appearance.

BEARGRASS (*Nolina microcarpa* and *N. erumpens*) is a native lily, the foliage resembling clumps of coarse-bladed grass and the tiny flowers borne on stout stems in dense clusters. Papery seed husks remain on the plant well into autumn. Usually found on rocky slopes above 3,000 feet, landscape use is similar to that of low-growing Yucca species, as accents and for textural interest.

CACTUS, the stereotypic desert plant, is mentioned as an example of several drought defenses. Whole books are devoted to the description of this valuable family of natives. In the landscape, cacti require careful placement. While most are extremely drought tolerant, relatively few can survive our coldest winters. Soil must be well drained and winter moisture minimal. The spines tend to collect windblown trash and leaves, and periodic cleanup is, quite literally, a pain. Young children, active pets, and cactus spines are rarely a welcome combination. In raised beds or containers, combined with drought-tolerant annual and perennial ground covers, cold-hardy cacti provide "Southwestern character" with almost no care. Their sculptural qualities and contrasting flowers place this family among the gems of the plant world.

CALLIOPSIS (*Coreopsis tinctoria*) is a prolific summer and fall flowering annual. Among the varieties available are a red yellow bicolor (24" height) and a dwarf red (to 8" height). Calliopsis is a good mixed-meadow component, as it competes well with grasses and self-sows readily on light soils in full sun. 1,400,000 seeds per pound.

COLUMBINE (*Aquilegia* species) is one of the most widely cultivated North American wild flowers. More than thirty species exist and countless hybrids have been developed from them, ranging in color from clear blue to purple, pink, red, and yellow, including several bicolors. Height is variable, from matted alpine species to 3-foot giants where moisture is ample. Although they are widespread, Columbines are neither drought nor heat tolerant.

CORALBERRY (*Symphoricarpos orbiculatus*), related to the native montane Snowberry, is a pink-fruited, deciduous, thicket-forming shrub. Very heat- and drought-tolerant once established, Coralberry is useful for mass planting, where fruit-laden stems assume a graceful, nodding character. It has been available, mostly through Mid-Western conservation nurseries, for at least fifty years.

GILIA (*Gilia* species) is a large genus of the Phlox family (100 species ±) of Western annuals, biennials, and perennials in many colors and forms. Some species have been used extensively in gardens; others, long admired

in the wild, deserve cultivation. Still others have been renamed Ipomopsis and remain old favorites despite the new name. One common feature is the tendency to begin life as a basal rosette of foliage.

INDIAN PAINTBRUSH (*Castilleja* species) is one of the best known Western wild flowers. Its scarlet-, orange-, and rose-colored calyx and bracts brighten roadsides and mountain meadows April through September. Most Indian Paintbrushes are partially parasitic on the roots of other plants, especially Gramas, and consequently are difficult to grow independently from seeds.

JUNIPER (*Juniperus* species) is mentioned several times throughout the text and appears as evergreen ground cover in the design section. Our Rocky Mountain Juniper, *J. scopulorum*, is the source of many beautiful cultivars. Junipers are available in a range of heights from a matlike 6 inches to 40-foot trees. Foliage color ranges from blue green to emerald, silver gray to plum in winter. *Sunset* magazine's *Western Gardens* book contains an excellent descriptive breakdown of varieties generally available in the trade.

KINNIKINNICK/BEARBERRY (*Arctostaphylos uva-ursi*) is a native of high-altitude Spruce-Fir forests in New Mexico, where soils are relatively low in pH, summers are relatively cool, and winters are snow covered. Low-maintenance use is limited to similar habitats.

NAMA (*Nama demissa*) is a lovely tuft of green covered with purple, bell-shaped flowers. This early annual, native intermittently throughout the Southwest on sandy or clay soils, has no bad qualities except that seeds are not commercially available. Seeds are minute and difficult to harvest. Plantings are readily established by pulling up spent plants and mulching with them in areas where they are desired.

OCOTILLO (*Fouquieria splendens*) is an interesting native of the warmer desert climates that is reliably hardy as far north as Albuquerque. The slender, whip-like, thorny stems are drought deciduous, leafy only when moisture is readily available. Red tubular flowers tip the branches in spring and after summer rains. An excellent textural interest, Ocotillo combines well with cacti and the most drought-hardy of arid-land wild flowers.

PALO VERDE (*Cercidium* species) is a remarkable small tree with fragrant yellow flowers in early spring, colorful bark, and a graceful growth habit. It is drought deciduous and leafless much of the year; photosynthesis occurs in the smooth blue green or yellow green bark. Unfortunately, this attractive specimen is very sensitive to cold and hardy only to about 10 F.

PHLOX HELIOTROPE (*Heliotropium convolvulaceum*) is a "well-behaved weed" if there ever was one. This attractive, white flowering annual performs best during our hottest weather. All plant parts are refined, the thin, wiry stems extending over a 4-foot-square area, densely covered with small, pointed, light green foliage. Individually small, the five-sided satiny white blossoms crown the plant in profusion.

PICKLEBUSH (*Allenrolfea occidentalis*) is a mid-sized shrub related to the Saltbush (*Atriplex*) that occurs in extremely saline soils. Response to cultivation is unknown. Picklebush is an unusual looking plant that may be of limited use as an ornamental.

PIÑON (*Pinus edulis*) needs no introduction, as it can be found in almost every "Southwestern" landscape installed in the last fifteen years. The contorted trunks of some specimens make the Piñon an excellent focal point, and it is the most drought-tolerant native species of Pine. The only survival problems are borers, best controlled systemically by licensed applicators, and inexperienced tree diggers, which are simply best avoided. Native-dug pines, both Piñons and Ponderosas, should have a root base proportionate to the top growth, burlapped and wire wrapped to prevent damage during shipping and transplanting.

PONDEROSA PINE (*Pinus ponderosa*), a stately, long-needled evergreen, is one of the most widely distributed Western conifers. Adapted to many soils, and available as mature specimens, Ponderosa Pines have long been a popular landscape ornamental. Widespread use on urban sites over the past twenty years yields a clear picture of cultural tolerances for this plant. At altitudes below 7,000 feet, Ponderosas are best adapted to park-like settings where surrounding sod or ground cover increases humidity and moderates air temperatures. Trees subjected to reflected glare off pavements or south- and west-facing walls often suffer needle-tip burn and overall declining vigor. As do all evergreens, Ponderosa Pines transpire moisture throughout the year and so require regular winter waterings. Aphids can be a problem in early spring, but can often be controlled by a thorough washing with a high-pressure hose nozzle. Bark beetles and borers are less obvious but more harmful pests and are best controlled with a systemic insecticide. Maintaining general plant vigor is the best preventative.

SCORPIONFLOWER (*Phacelia integrifolia*), an interesting biennial or annual, provides a mass of early blue flowers along roadsides. The curved fiddlehead shape of the flowers is the source of the common name. Often found growing with Gaillardias, the russet and blue are an effective color combination. The foliage matures to a bronzy brown in early summer heat, and a mass planting is best mowed at this point, leaving the litter to reseed.

SIBERIAN ELM (*Ulmus pumila*) is one of the best local examples of the well-intentioned introduction of an adaptable exotic that has become a noxious weed. The Elm would be an exceptional street and shade tree if not for its prolific seed and seedling production and its host of defoliating beetles.

SNAKEWEED (*Gutierrezia sarothrae*) is a small mounding shrub (2' × 2') with fine, bright green foliage and small yellow flowers in September. It is very drought tolerant and can be a useful ground cover where natural precipitation is 8 to 10 inches annually and no additional moisture is available. Snakeweed is an *extremely* aggressive competitor in mixed borders and meadows, reseeds *too* well, and can be invasive. Since it causes spontaneous abortion when it is grazed, it should not be used near livestock. In the wild, a predominance of Snakeweed indicates an overgrazed or otherwise abused range.

WILLOW (*Salix* species). In the Southwest, habitat for these water-loving shrubs and trees is limited to stream beds, lakeshores, and irrigation canals. The attractive silver-leafed, red-twigged Basket Willow, *S. exigua*, is valued for basketry, as the common name indicates.

# 🌿 FURTHER READING

## THE PROCESS

### LIVING WELL ON LESS—THE GROUND RULES:

*Desert Plants.* A quarterly journal published by the University of Arizona for Boyce Thompson Southwest Arboretum.

Kozlowski, T.T. *Physiology of Water Stress* and related papers. Madison: University of Wisconsin, n.d.

————. *Water Deficits and Plant Growth.* Vols. 1–5. New York: Academic Press, 1978.

McKenzie, K., and Green, J.L. "Selecting Plants for Adaptability Increases Survival Rates." *American Nurseryman* 153, no. 4 (1981): 94.

Miller, J.D. *Design and the Desert Environment: Landscape Architecture and the American Southwest.* Arid Lands Information Paper no. 13. Tucson: University of Arizona Office of Arid Land Studies, 1978.

Rahn, James J. *Making the Weather Work for You.* Charlotte, Vermont: Garden Way Publishing, 1979.

Rickett, H.W. *Botany for Gardeners.* New York: Macmillan Co., 1957.

Tuan, Yi-Fu et al. *The Climate of New Mexico.* Santa Fe: State Planning Office, 1969.

### DESIGNING FOR LOW MAINTENANCE:

*Site Development and Plant Selection/Microclimates*·

Miller, J.D. *Design & the Desert Environment: Landscape Architecture and the American Southwest.* Arid Lands Information Paper no. 13. Tucson: University of Arizona Office of Arid Land Studies, 1978.

Moffat, Anne Simon, and Schiler, Marc. *Landscape Design That Saves Energy.* New York: William Morrow and Co., 1981.

Simonds, John Ormsbee. *Landscape Architecture: A Manual of Site Planning and Design.* New York: McGraw Hill Book Co., 1983.

*Sunset* Magazine Editors. *Landscaping Illustrated.* Menlo Park: Lane Magazine and Book Co., 1979.

————. *Sunset New Western Garden Book.* Menlo Park: Lane Magazine and Book Co., 1979.

Wasowski, Sally, and Ryan, Julie. *Landscaping with Native Texas Plants.* Austin: Texas Monthly Press, Inc., 1984.

·*Mechanics of Design and Construction*·

Crockett, James U. *Landscape Gardening.* New York: Time Life Books, 1971.

*Landscaping.* Illustrated Encyclopedia of Gardening. Mt. Vernon: American Horticultural Society, 1982.

Smyser, Carol A. et al., eds. *Nature's Design: A Practical Guide to Natural Landscaping.* Emmaus, Pa.: Rodale Press Books, 1982.

### GETTING IT GOING:

Feucht, J. "Knowledge of Root Functions Aids Transplanting," *American Nurseryman* (February 1, 1982): 77–81.

Fuller, Wallace. *Management of Southwestern Desert Soils.* Tucson: University of Arizona Press, 1975.

————. *Soils of the Desert Southwest.* Tucson: University of Arizona Press, 1975.

Johnson, R., and Menge, J.A. "Mycorrhizae May Save Fertilizer Dollars." *American Nurseryman* (January 15, 1982): 79–87.

Martin, Laura C. *The Wildflower Meadow Book.* Charlotte, North Carolina: East Woods Press, 1986.

Parker, M., and Root, R. "Insect Herbivores Limit Habitat Distribution of a Native Composite." *Ecology* 62 (October 1981): 1390–92.

Pinyuh, G. "Nitrogen Fixing Plants—A Valuable Resource in the Landscape." *American Nurseryman* (January 1, 1981): 90–91.

"Soil Mixes for Greenhouse and Nursery Growth of Desert Plants. A Mini-Symposium." *Desert Plants* 1 (November 1979): 82–89.

Thompson, A.R. "Transplanting Trees and Other Woody Plants." Rev. ed. *Tree Preservation Bulletin* no. 1, National Park Service. Washington, D.C.: Superintendent of Documents, U.S. Government Printing Office, 1954.

Wittrock, G. *The Pruning Book.* Emmaus, Penna.: Rodale Press, Inc., n.d.

*The World of Trees.* Ortho Book Series. San Francisco: Chevron Chemical Co., 1977.

### PROPAGATION:

*Collecting, Processing and Germinating Seeds of Western Wildland Plants.* AQM-W-3, rev. ed. USDA Science and Education Administration. Reno: Renewable Resource Center, 1981.

Hamilton, David F. "Woody Ornamental Propagation: Learn to Increase Rooting of Cuttings." *Greenhouse Manager* (June 1983): 161–63.

*Handbook on Propagation.* Brooklyn Botanic Garden Record, Plants and Gardens no. 24. New York: Brooklyn Botanic Garden, 1980.

Hartman, Hudson, and Kester, Dale. *Plant Propagation, Principles and Practices.* 4th ed. Englewood Cliffs,

New Jersey: Prentice-Hall, 1983.

Institute for Land Rehabilitation. *Selection, Propagation, and Field Establishment of Native Plant Species on Disturbed Arid Lands.* Utah Agricultural Experiment Station Bulletin 500. Logan, 1979.

Missouri Botanical Garden. *Directory to Resources on Wildflower Propagation.* St. Louis: National Council of State Garden Clubs, Inc., 1981.

"Propagation Techniques for Desert Plants—A Mini Symposium." *Desert Plants* 2 (Winter 1980–81): 205–19.

Sabo, D., Johnson, G. et al. *Germination Requirements of 19 Species of Arid Land Plants.* Research Paper RM-210. Albuquerque: U.S. Forest Service Rocky Mountain Forest and Range Experiment Station, 1979.

*Seeds of Woody Plants in the United States.* USDA Yearbook of Agriculture. Washington, D.C.: U.S. Government Printing Office, Superintendent of Documents, 1961.

Whitcomb, C.E. *Propagating Woody Plants from Cuttings.* Agricultural Experiment Station Bulletin. Stillwater: Oklahoma State University, April 1978.

## PLANT PROFILES

*Audubon Society Field Guide to North American Trees.* New York: Alfred A. Knopf, Inc., 1980.

*Audubon Society Field Guide to North American Wildflowers.* New York: Alfred A. Knopf, Inc., 1979.

Benson, Lyman. *Cactaceae of the United States and Canada.* Stanford: Stanford University Press, 1982.

Benson, Lyman, and Darrow, Robert A. *Trees and Shrubs of the Southwestern Deserts.* Tucson: University of Arizona Press, 1981.

Brown, David E., ed. *Biotic Communities of the American Southwest—United States and Mexico.* Superior, Ariz.: Boyce Thompson Southwestern Arboretum, 1982.

Earle, W. Hubert. *Cacti of the Southwest.* Science Bulletin no. 4. Phoenix: Desert Botanical Garden, 1963.

Elmore, Francis, and Janish, Jeanne. *Shrubs and Trees of the Southwest Uplands.* Southwest Parks and Monuments Series no. 19. Globe, Ariz.: Southwest Parks and Monuments Assoc., 1976.

Fox, Eugene, and Sublette, Mary. *Roadside Wildflowers of New Mexico.* Natural Science Research Institute. Portales: Eastern New Mexico University, 1978.

Harrington, H.D. *Edible Native Plants of the Rocky Mountains.* Albuquerque: University of New Mexico Press, 1976.

Ivey, Robert D. *Flowering Plants of New Mexico: A Sketchbook.* Albuquerque: Robert D. Ivey, 1983.

Martin, W.C., and Hutchins, C.R. *A Flora of New Mexico.* 2 vols. Hirschberg, Germany: J. Cramer, 1980.

*New Mexico Range Plants.* Rev. ed. Cooperative Extension Service Circular 374. Las Cruces: New Mexico State University, 1980.

*Pasture and Range Plants.* Bartlesville, Okla.: Phillips Petroleum Co., 1963.

Patraw, Pauline; Arnberger, Leslie; Dodge, Natt; and Janish, Jeanne. *Flowers of the Southwest Mesas, Mountains, and Desert.* 3 vols. Globe, Ariz.: Southwest Monument Series Popular Publications, 1951–53.

Rickett, Harold W. *Wildflowers of the United States.* Vol. 4, The Southwestern States. New York Botanical Garden. New York: McGraw Hill Book Co., 1970.

Sacamano, C.M., and Jones, W.D. *Native Trees and Shrubs for Landscape Use in the Desert Southwest.* Cooperative Extension Service, College of Agriculture, University of Arizona. Tucson: University of Arizona, 1976.

*Sunset* Magazine Editors. *Sunset Western Garden Book.* Menlo Park: Lane Magazine and Book Co., 1979.

Vines, Robert A. *Trees, Shrubs and Woody Vines of the Southwest.* Austin: University of Texas Press, 1976.

Wasser, Clinton H. *Ecology and Culture of Selected Species Useful in Revegetating Disturbed Lands in the West.* U.S. Department of the Interior, Fish and Wildlife Service, Superintendent of Documents. Washington, D.C.: U.S. Government Printing Office, 1982.

# INDEX

## Index of Key Terms and Concepts
*Major entries are in bold face.*

acclimation/hardening off **47**,56
afterripening **69**, 73, profiles: 102, 112, 121, 125
alkalinity 3, 52-53

Browning, Iben, 3

caliche/hardpan 26, **48**, 49
chelated iron **53**, 55, 86
climate, arid-land, effects of, **3**
cold-moist stratification 35, 56, **69**, chart 72-73, profiles: 86-88, 100-101, 103, 105-6, 117-18, 123-24, 129-30
competitive adaptations **6-9**
container growing **49**, 54-55, profiles: 88, 93, 117
cost-effective planning **15**, 35
crassulacean acid metabolism **7**
cuttings, hardwood, **71**, 74-76, profiles: 88-89, 91-92, 94, 99, 103, 106, 112, 123; softwood, **71**, 74-76, profiles: 89, 95, 97, 102-3, 117-18, 120, 124-25, 130; root, **76-77**, 92; chart **78**

damping off **67**, 94
design **11-45**; cost-effective planning **15**, 35; practical hints 14-15; principles of **12**, sample designs 11, 13, 16-19, 20-23, 44-45; seasonal changes **14**; seasonal color chart 32-33; sense of place 10, **16**, 65; steps in designing 15; texture 6, 11, 16, 18; use areas 12-14; worksheet 43
division, propagation by, 36, **77**, profiles: 92-93, 95, 101, 103, 108-9, 112, 118, 120, 122-23, 128-29, 131
dormancies **65**
drainage **47**
drought deciduous **7**, 88
drought-tolerance mechanisms **6-9**

ecosystems ix, 2, 11, **12**, 37
erosion, control of, 9, 52, 66, profiles: 87-89, 93-95, 97-99, 102-4, 106-7, 109, 111, 118, 120, 122, 124, 126, 130
evapotranspiration rate **50**

fertilizers **54-56**; application rates, 55
form, defined, **11**, 16, profiles: 86-132
foundation plantings **14**

germination inhibitors 5, 65-66, 70
glyphosate 36, 42, 50
grading 15, 26, 30-31, 44-45
gypsum **53-54**

hardening off/acclimation **47**, 56
herbicide 36, 42, 50
hot water soak xii, **67**, 73, profiles: 93, 111
hydrogen peroxide soak **67**, 104

IBA talc/rooting hormone **74**, profiles: 86, 88-89, 91, 94, 95-97,

100, 106, 108, 117, 120, 123-24, 130
iron/FE **53**
irrigation methods **51-52** (*see* water)

landscape layouts: channeling runoff (mission-style townhouse) 27-28; color, form, and texture 11; lawn and meadow (farmhouse) 44-45; grading 30-31; large spaces 29; renovation (1920s bungalow) 26; site development, three-step, 20-23; small spaces 24-25; use areas 13
lawns, used in layouts, 13, 22-23, 28; steps in establishing, **41-42**; watering, 51; maintenance, 56
layering, propagation by, 76, **77**, profiles: 95, 118, 130
leaching 3, 52-53, **69-70**, 102

manure **48-49** (*see* soil amendments)
maintenance calendar **56**
meadows, wildflower, 22-23, **35-36**, 38, **40-45**, 51, 56, profiles: 109, 111, 118-19, 122, 126-28, 133
moisture requirements, plants listed by, 81-82; sample layouts by, 16-19
mulching 41, 49, **50-51**
mycorrhizac **54**, 55, 63

National Wildflower Research Center xi
native plants, defined, **xii**, 9; collecting from wild, xi, 47; native plant societies xii, 15
naturalized 7, **54**, 57, profiles: 90, 93-94
nitrogen/N **53-54**, profiles: 87, 102, 109-10, 121-22, 130
nutrition **52-56**

paving **14-15**, in designs, 13, 21-22, 24-31, 44-45
phosphorus/P **53-54**
photosynthesis 7, 50, 74
potassium/K **53**
propagation, by cutting, **71**, 74-78 (*see* cuttings, hardwood; softwood; root; cuttings chart **78**;) by division (*see* division, propagation by); layering (*see* layering, propagation by); by seeds, 56, **70-73**; seeds chart **72-73**
pruning 56, **61-62**

rare and endangered plants xii, 7
Robinson, William, 3, 9
rooting hormones 74; (*see* IBA talc)
root-to-shoot ratio 6, 50
root systems, types of, **5-6**, 47
rosette, "funnel form," **7**, 8

salinity 3, 52, **53-54**
scarification 35, **67**, 68-70, 73, profiles: 91-92, 100, 102-3, 106, 108, 118, 124, 128, 132
seeds, cleaning, 56, 66-67; collecting, **66** and profiles: 86, 87, 89, 93, 95, 97-99, 102, 128, 131; dormancy 3, 35, 65; mix formula for, **35-36**; pretreatments 5, **67-70**; propagation chart **72-73**; sowing, 56, **70-71**.

**137**

## Index of Plants

*Major entries are in bold face.*

# WORKSHEET

*Landscaping is problem solving. Prepare a fact base—the site analysis. Then set objectives: site modifications and a working materials list.*

## SITE ANALYSIS

### I  Site Limitations

Style of architecture _____

Placement of structures on site _____

    Solar orientation _____
        Exposures _____

Grade _____

Soil type _____

Traffic patterns _____
    Access (Driveway & paths) _____
    Patios _____

Surrounding landscapes _____
    Complement/incorporate _____
    Frame views _____
    Screen eyesores _____
    Provide privacy _____

### II  Human Considerations

Lifestyle of inhabitants _____
Visitors _____
Pets _____
Budget _____
Level of maintenance desired _____

### II  Aesthetic Considerations

Symmetrical/formal vs. asymmetrical/casual _____
Focal points _____
Seasonal interest _____
Color preferences (intensity; hue) _____
Fragrance _____

## SITE MODIFICATIONS

### IV  Organize Space

Expand or enclose _____

Create outdoor "rooms"/ecosystems _____
    Shade _____
    Windbreaks, screens, barriers _____
    Paving _____
    Groundcovers _____
    Lawns _____
    Meadows _____

### V  Develop a Plant List

Function (Shade, screen, carpet) _____

Appearance (Shape, color, texture) _____

Adaptability (Soil, exposure, scale & size at maturity) _____

# NOTES

# NOTES

# NOTES